Notre Dame's Grid Men at Pasadena, Calif. J.

LOYAL SONS

The Story of
The Four Horsemen
and
Notre Dame Football's
1924 Champions

Jim Lefebvre

Great Day Press
Minneapolis

LOYAL SONS
THE STORY OF THE FOUR HORSEMEN AND
NOTRE DAME FOOTBALL'S 1924 CHAMPIONS

SPECIAL CENTENNIAL COMMEMORATIVE EDITION

FOR MORE INFORMATION, CONTACT:
JIM@NDFOOTBALLHISTORY.COM

PRINTED AND BOUND IN THE UNITED STATES
USING SOY BASED INKS AND RECYCLED PAPER (10% PCW)
BY VERSA PRESS, INC.
WWW.VERSAPRESS.COM

SOFTCOVER PRINTING – AUGUST 2024

ISBN: 978-0-9818841-5-8

Library of Congress Cataloging-in-Publication Data
Control Number: 2008907089
Notre Dame Fighting Irish (Football team)—History—20th century
University of Notre Dame—Football—History—20th century
Football—Indiana—History—20th century
Football players—Indiana—Biography

LOYAL SONS IS DISTRIBUTED BY:
CARDINAL PUBLISHERS GROUP
2402 N. SHADELAND AVE., SUITE A
INDIANAPOLIS, IN 46219
317-352-8200
WWW.CARDINALPUB.COM

COVER DESIGN BY: PETE FAECKE

CONTENTS

Foreword

For two amazing Domers

Kerry Anne Lefebvre (B.A., 2007)

and

Elizabeth C. Lefebvre (B.A., 2009)

Thanks for letting me come along for the ride

Author's Note

Since the original publishing of *Loyal Sons: The Story of The Four Horsemen and Notre Dame Football's 1924 Champions* in 2008, it has been my great pleasure to connect with members of the Notre Dame family—alumni, fans, players and coaches— from coast to coast. It has been especially gratifying to befriend families of the majority of players from the 1924 national championship team.

One such family was that of Edgar "Rip" Miller, right tackle. On Nov. 14, 2008, the day before Notre Dame and Navy met in Baltimore, we were part of a luncheon announcing the Rip Miller Trophy, which honors the traditions of Fighting Irish and Midshipmen football. That day, we celebrated the 102nd birthday of Rip's widow, Mrs. Esther Miller. Until her death at age 109, Es would proudly show visitors the pages in *Loyal Sons* that describe how she and Rip had met and eventually married.

In May of 2009, *Loyal Sons* was honored with the Bronze Medal in the Sports/Recreation/Fitness category of the *Independent Publisher* Book Awards (the IPPYs), the highest honor in small-press publishing.

Years of further research led to the 2013 publication of *Coach For A Nation: The Life and Times of Knute Rockne* on the 100th anniversary of Rockne's senior year as captain of the Fighting Irish. *Coach For A Nation* was also honored with the same *Independent*

Publisher Book Award for overall excellence.

Along the way, I have spoken on the life and legacy of Coach Rockne, and on Notre Dame football history in general, at numerous places on campus—the press box of Notre Dame Stadium, Purcell Pavilion, the Morris Inn and others—as well as to Notre Dame Clubs and other groups from coast to coast. Uniformly, they have shown rapt attention, asked great questions and demonstrated spirited enthusiasm for the subject.

In 2017, a small group of Rockne enthusiasts and I founded the Knute Rockne Memorial Society, of which I am proud to serve as executive director. Its mission is to "perpetuate and advance the name and legacy of Coach Knute Rockne and all that he stood for, honoring his life and all the lives he touched, by teaching, recognizing and supporting coaches and athletes in their pursuit of outstanding leadership, achievement and sportsmanship."

Our signature annual event is the Knute Rockne *Spirit of Sports* Awards Celebration. The Rockne Awards have honored individuals for their achievements in both sports and society, with standouts including Rocky Bleier, Mike Oriard, Luther Bradley, Haley Scott DiMaria, Johnny Lujack, Coach Muffet McGraw, Alan Page, Mike McCoy, Barry Alvarez, Darius Fleming, John Huarte, Kory Minor, Joey Getherall, John Carney, Coach Kevin Corrigan, Thom Gatewood, and departed luminaries Coach Ara Parseghian, Elmer Layden, Charlie Bachman, Moose Krause and Tom Lieb, among many other deserving winners.

As part of our celebration of the 100th anniversary of the remarkable 1924 Notre Dame team and season, we are honored to introduce this Special Centennial Commemorative Edition of *Loyal Sons*. It includes expanded content, especially an in-depth epilogue that describes the impressive careers of so many of the players.

We are proud to tell the stories of the 1924 Irish, and the century of achievement that has followed.

For more information, please visit: www.RockneSociety.org.

J.L.
August 2024

Notre Dame Victory March

Rally sons of Notre Dame:
Sing her glory and sound her fame,
Raise her Gold and Blue
And cheer with voices true:
Rah, rah, for Notre Dame
We will fight in ev-ry game,
Strong of heart and true to her name
We will ne'er forget her
And will cheer her ever
Loyal to Notre Dame

Cheer, cheer for old Notre Dame,
Wake up the echoes cheering her name,
Send a volley cheer on high,
Shake down the thunder from the sky.
What though the odds be great or small
Old Notre Dame will win over all,
While her loyal sons and daughters
March on to victory!

1

Under the Summer Sun

THE INDIANA SUN shone brightly on the campus of the University of Notre Dame in early September 1924. In ones and twos, students at the all-male Catholic institution were starting to gather, ultimately setting an enrollment record of nearly two thousand young men.

Striding across campus under the statue of Our Lady atop the recently re-gilded Golden Dome, 22-year-old Adam Walsh felt very much at home. Ruggedly built, at 6 feet tall and 190 pounds, the handsome, sandy-haired Walsh had already experienced quite a ride. Now, as captain of the 1924 Notre Dame football team, the anticipation for his senior year and the fall football season was almost unbearable.

A nearby car backfired, and Walsh's thoughts were jolted back to his early-summer cross-country journey with younger brother Charles, known to all as Chile. The pair had driven a Ford Model T from their home in Hollywood, California some 2,400 miles to the Notre Dame campus in time to enroll for the summer term. Across the deserts of California and Arizona, up through the Rockies, past Denver and out onto the plains, to the great crossroads of Chicago, the Walsh brothers traversed one series of rutted dirt and gravel roads after another. By their estimation, they had encountered barely 100 miles of paved highway on the entire route. The car, after numerous dings, flat tires and other maladies, now resided in an off-campus garage.

Chile Walsh had always looked up to his big brother and now relished the opportunity to spend one football season with him at Notre Dame. Though freshmen were ineligible for varsity play, and Chile would spend his time with the squad of first-years, it was good knowing that Ad was nearby.

A lot of folks looked up to Ad Walsh. He had come to campus three years earlier, not knowing a soul, anxious about being so far from home and unsure whether he had made the right college choice. He battled through injuries, illness and other challenges, and now, poised to lead the "Fighting Irish" into their challenging 1924 schedule, he truly was a "big man on campus."

IT WAS A campus brimming with energy, growth and possibility. Since the Great War, the country's educational boundaries had expanded. Thousands of young men flocked to campuses looking for an education, and applicants stormed admissions offices, including Notre Dame's. Since the spring, 17 classrooms and seven labs were added to Science Hall. A plan to build three new permanent residence halls was taking shape to the west of Badin Hall and south of the Lemmonier library. What had been a ballfield was now a construction site as the crush for more campus housing fed the building boom.

The university president, the Rev. Matthew Walsh, CSC, was intent on reinvigorating the school with "la vie intime," the way it had been when he was a student at Notre Dame at the turn of the century. Back then, with virtually all students living on campus in just a handful of buildings, faith and fellowship provided camaraderie between students and faculty.

The enrollment wave overwhelmed the small school's facilities, especially housing. As a result, hundreds of students scrambled to find lodging in South Bend homes. These "day dogs," try as they might, would find it difficult to be part of the intimate campus life. By 1923, two hastily constructed wood-and-plasterboard dorms, Freshman Hall and Sophomore Hall, were built to the east of the Main Building. The "cardboard palaces" allowed 360 more students to stay on campus, a number outstripped by the continued expansion of the university community.

As president, Father Walsh had a vision for modern dining facilities. But in 1924, he had to settle for the dual kitchens behind Brownson and Carroll halls, which were housed in the east and west wings of the Main Building. The cooking facilities were separate from the refectories, and servers maneuvered carts to trundle vats of food to the students. Through sleet, snow and dust from construction, the food came: home-baked bread, vast platters of meats, square "pies." Many swore by the cooking of the Notre Dame Sisters. But the facilities and the cooks simply could not accommodate everyone. So, increasingly, students took their meals at O. A. Clark's, a commercial cafeteria in the basement of Badin Hall.

ADAM WALSH REFLECTED on how fast his time at Notre Dame had gone as he showed his younger brother the ins and outs of campus. Enjoy every minute, he advised Chile. For Adam, the inevitable challenges and pressures of the adult world were still a few months off. Adam's task at hand in the fall of 1924 was to enjoy the last vestiges of college life, the friendship of his teammates, especially the close group of seniors on the football squad. Anxious to see his mates, he started to wonder: What kind of shape will Crowley be in? Would Stuhldreher have grown at all? Who was Layden's latest love interest? What about Miller and the fellows working at Cedar Point?

Work. That had been part of Ad Walsh's life for as long as he could remember.

ADAM WALSH III was born on December 4, 1901 at the country crossroad town of Churchville, Iowa, located about 15 miles south of Des Moines. His father, Adam Jr., was a first-generation American whose parents emigrated from Ireland – his father from County Cork, his mother from County Mayo – during the potato famine of the late 1840s. In Churchville, Adam Walsh, Jr. operated a general store.

In 1906, the family struck out for southern California, leaving behind Churchville and numerous Walsh relatives. Adam Jr., his wife

Stella, Adam III, Chile and their sisters Maud, Mary and Irene would not be totally alone in their new environs. Stella's parents, Nancy and Charles Koehler, had earlier moved west.

The Koehlers had a comfortable home on Carlton Way in Hollywood, a block south of Prospect Avenue. The booming city of Los Angeles was a short carriage ride away. Adam Jr. and Stella built a home about a mile to the northeast, on Forest Avenue, in an area with few other houses. The Walsh children played in a large fenced yard where they would occasionally see deer and mountain lions wandering down from the nearby hills.

YOUNG ADAM'S FATHER began working as a clerk in a grocery store, and before long, he had become co-owner of "Walsh & Mackie Groceries," located on Prospect Avenue, just east of Vine Street. The area was becoming famous for the budding motion picture business. When he was in high school, young Adam Walsh spent his Saturdays delivering groceries to the "movie stars" – Will Rogers, Mary Pickford, Charlie Chaplin – using a horse and buggy. In summers, it became a full-time job, paying 75 cents a week.

Business prospered and a second Walsh & Mackie store opened farther west on Prospect near the Hollywood Hotel. Another son, Paul, was born. Adam Jr. raised his sons to be rugged young men; he lavished attention on his daughters, presenting them with a baby grand piano in 1910. Maud and Mary would be among the first students at Immaculate Heart High School for girls, located a short distance from their home.

Young Adam showed a sharp mind and finished grammar school when he was only 11. Rather then enter high school so young, he spent some time back in Iowa visiting relatives. When he returned to Hollywood 18 months later, he came down with the flu and fell behind in his academic progress at Hollywood High.

His mother Stella, as she so often would for her children, helped to chart what needed to be done. She and Adam met with the school superintendent, Dr. William H. Snyder, a serious academician educated at Amherst and Harvard. Dr Snyder spelled out the curriculum: Adam would be readmitted to Hollywood High and would take college algebra,

4

advanced physics, chemistry, English and Spanish. He performed so well he even instructed an algebra class when the teacher became ill.

In between delivering groceries and attending to his studies, young Adam developed an interest in sports. He started out playing football as a 132-pound "runt" but developed into one of the stars at Hollywood High, leading his team to a regional championship. Adam sometimes paid the price in injuries; one season ended when he was clipped from behind, suffering a spiral leg break above the ankle.

When the Great War broke out, Adam desired to join the armed services, but he was turned down by the Army, the Air Corps and the Marines, all due to his age. When the Armistice was signed, Adam was still shy of his 17th birthday.

Upon leaving high school, he worked to earn money for college, driving a 10-ton truck, working 10 ½ hours a day, seven days a week, for $15. The work included hoisting pigs of lead weighing 105 pounds each. It didn't take long for him to develop tremendous strength.

For a time, he worked as a cowboy rounding up cattle on a nearby ranch. Later, he joined the crew of famed automobile racer Barney Oldfield, who was developing and testing designs for new race cars that would better protect drivers while achieving high speeds.

As Adam passed his 19th birthday in December 1920, he began to think more seriously about going to college. Several of Ad's classmates at Hollywood High had gone on to Leland Stanford at Palo Alto near San Francisco, and Ad saw himself there as well. Stella Walsh had other thoughts. Though she was raised a Presbyterian in the Koehler family, she had converted to Catholicism when she married Adam Jr. She desperately wanted her son to attend a Catholic college – but not just any Catholic college. The search became more refined when Leo Ward entered the picture.

A red-headed Irish-Catholic, Ward had graduated from Notre Dame in 1920 and was just beginning a career in law in southern California. He was dating Adam's sister Maud and would always sing the praises of his alma mater when around the Walsh family.

But Adam still had his sights set on Stanford. Stanford had become an even more attractive choice when an alumnus wrote Walsh that if he came to Palo Alto, played football and kept his grades up, he would receive an annual $3,000 loan, with 10 years after graduation to repay it. With that kind of dough, there would be no need to have a job during the school year or summer. And yet others wanted to see him at the University of Southern California and its up-and-coming football program under Coach Elmer Henderson. Southern Cal, after all, had scored upset shutouts of Stanford in both 1919 and 1920.

In the summer of 1921, another ND alum visiting Los Angeles joined Ward in making a pitch to Walsh. Stan Cofall, captain of the 1916 Irish, was now a high school coach in Philadelphia. He was persuasive, especially in a tag-team presentation with Ward. Together, they painted a picture of the Golden Dome and Our Lady's university. So good was the artists' drawing that Adam couldn't help but envision himself right in the middle of that incredible campus. Stella Walsh was ecstatic. Her oldest son had finally agreed to attend Notre Dame.

How much easier a trip from Hollywood to Stanford would have been, Walsh thought as he crammed his six-foot frame into an upper berth of a tourist sleeper in early September 1921. He was filled with worry and doubt as he made the long journey to northern Indiana, wondering if he had made a mistake or if he would be able to handle the academic rigors at Notre Dame.

Walsh reported to Coach Knute Rockne on September 8, 1921, and joined the other first-years on the freshman team. He chose mechanical engineering as a field of study, and his classes began as early as 8 a.m. Labs would often go until 4 p.m. He would have to leave to go to football practice at 3 p.m., and return to make up the lab in the evening.

Practicing against the varsity took its toll and in late September, Walsh suffered a broken arm and dislocated collarbone. Coupled with his homesickness and self-doubt, Adam was terribly discouraged. In these times, it was Coach Rockne's knack for seeing into the heart of his players that provided the needed remedy. Rockne saw something of himself in Adam Walsh – a determined, self-reliant sort who was not afraid of work. Rockne, after all, had worked as a postal clerk for four years after graduation from Chicago's Northwest Division

High School before deciding to enroll at Notre Dame in 1910. He felt awkward being so much older than his classmates and worked to overcome his shyness and to improve his public speaking.

Rockne assured Walsh that this injury was only a temporary setback, that Walsh would come back stronger than ever, and that there was much good in his future, both in football and in life. As he would often tell his players, it was a matter of attitude.

"You don't have to be a millionaire to be a good man," Rock would say. "But you do have to be sincere, you do have to be honest, you do have to set your sights high. In other words, you have to want something bad enough – really want it – to be a winner. When that motivating power is instilled in you, then there is no limit as to how far you can go over your head. The limits are boundless if you believe in yourself and are willing to pay the price."

In Adam Walsh, Rockne had a young man willing to pay the price. It wasn't the first – or last – time he developed a father-son relationship with one of his players. It was Rockne who helped Walsh get a job the second semester of his freshman year working at the Northern Indiana Gas and Electric Co garage. From 6 p.m. until 11:20 p.m. daily, Walsh worked on the fleet of the company's Ford pickup trucks – washing them, filling tires and checking oil, then keeping the building's coal furnace fired. All for $65 a month. A second job with the Liggett & Myers Tobacco Co. netted another $60 a month during Walsh's sophomore year.

For someone who started at Notre Dame with $30 in his pocket and, as he said later, "for months had only pennies," the sum of $125 a month felt like a king's ransom. The jobs allowed Walsh to stick around South Bend for the summers – he was unlikely to do as well financially back in southern California, and the trips back and forth would have eaten up plenty of funds.

YET, THERE ALWAYS seemed to be another unexpected challenge. Coming off the 1923 football season, life was sailing along smoothly for Walsh. Then, as the first semester was ending in January 1924, he came down with a debilitating case of strep throat. The sisters at the

Notre Dame infirmary could do little for him. He lost 33 pounds in nine days.

Rockne saw a young man teetering on the edge of exhaustion. He strongly suggested that the best course of action was rest and advised Walsh to take the second semester to go home and get well. So, for the first time since arriving on campus as a hesitant freshman, Walsh headed back to Hollywood. He regained his health and came back for summer school in June with brother Chile in tow.

By the start of the 1924 season, the young, unsure lad of 1921 had become a grown man with a strong body, a well-honed work ethic and a tremendous sense of self-reliance. His engaging personality made Ad Walsh a magnet for other students on the team and the campus. All of which made him a logical choice as 1924 Irish football captain.

SITTING IN HIS cramped office in the rear of the Main Building's ground floor, the affable 36-year-old head coach of the Fighting Irish was busy firing off correspondence to fellow coaches, Notre Dame alums and newspapermen from coast to coast. Knute Rockne was nearing the end of another successful summer of coaching clinics, in which he liberally shared the "Notre Dame system" with coaches of high school and college teams.

Knute Kenneth Rockne, a native of Voss, Norway, was the most recognizable figure at Notre Dame. Football coach, track coach, director of athletics, ticket manager – Rockne wore many hats at Notre Dame. With a roll of tape and a bottle of iodine in his pocket, he was athletic trainer as well.

Heading into his seventh season as head coach of the Fighting Irish, he had established a record that was a source of immense pride on the campus and far beyond – 48 victories, 4 defeats, 3 ties. The record boasted two unbeaten seasons in 1919 and 1920 and just one defeat in each of the previous three seasons.

Ever since his days as an immigrant lad in Chicago's Logan Square neighborhood, Rockne had been enamored with the game of football, this testing of wits and warriors. What other competition, Rockne figured, offers such a chance to test oneself, to prove one's manhood, to work with like-minded fellows for a common goal? At a young age, he marveled at the heroics of Walter Eckersall, the quarterback for the nearby Hyde Park High School eleven who went on to star for the great Amos Alonzo Stagg at the University of Chicago. Rockne admired Eckersall's command of football situations, his leadership, and his flair.

Rockne worked at the Chicago post office for four years after high school and came to Notre Dame in 1910 as a 22-year-old to study chemistry and play football. As captain of the 1913 Irish, he teamed with quarterback Charles "Gus" Dorais to form a passing game used to upset heavily-favored Army, 35-13, which put Notre Dame football on the map.

As an assistant coach to Jesse Harper for four seasons, and as head coach since 1918, Rockne was known for his keen football mind. For years, he had tinkered with "the Notre Dame shift," a series of movements prior to the snap of the ball that confused opponents and all but set the Irish players into motion, opening up a myriad of possibilities for each play. In the passing game, Rockne remained ahead of the coaching pack by using the pass as an unexpected weapon, not as a desperation move like many other teams would.

While most of his coaching brethren continued to take their eleven strongest men and play them nearly the entire game, Rockne had come up with another innovation – his system of "Shock Troops." An entire second string unit started most games, keeping the Notre Dame regulars on the sideline for most or all of the first quarter. There, the first team and Rockne studied the opponents' plays and strategies. When the regulars entered the game, they were fresh, while the other team had lost some of its steam going up against the "shock absorbers" – the Irish subs.

Rockne, not one to dwell on past accomplishments, was always looking ahead to the next challenge. Sitting at his desk, swinging back on a rolling chair, he studied the sheet of paper in his hands. It was his team's 1924 schedule:

October 4	Lombard
October 11	Wabash
October 18	Army (at Polo Grounds)
October 25	at Princeton
November 1	Georgia Tech
November 8	at Wisconsin
November 15	Nebraska
November 22	at Northwestern
November 29	at Carnegie Tech

He was pleased with the slate he had assembled. It would be a sufficient challenge for any team, and a stiff test even for his group of returning veterans. The first two games were against strong regional elevens who would like nothing better than to knock off Notre Dame. Then a pair of long trips to play Eastern powers; all the big newspaper fellows would likely be watching those games. A battle with one of the best units in the South. Games against Wisconsin and Northwestern – Western Conference foes – were always a challenge and a big draw.

And then there was Nebraska.

Nebraska!

He shuddered as he thought back to the past two seasons. In both 1922 and 1923, the Irish took an unbeaten record into Lincoln to play the Cornhuskers. There, they were greeted by the ugliness of anti-Catholic sentiment that still simmered in many parts of the United States. "Beat the Papists!" was the fans' refrain. The Notre Dame players had avoided retaliating against the taunts, but they were distracted enough to play something less than their best game. The result: a pair of painful defeats. The final home game of 1924 provided a chance for redemption.

Playing the Georgia Tech and Nebraska games at home would tax the capacity of Cartier Field, the school's less-than-spectacular football home. Even adding more wooden bleachers probably wouldn't be enough to meet the need. Perhaps, Rockne thought, it would stimulate talk of a new, modern stadium, similar to what other schools had recently built.

Rockne knew his schedule demanded a healthy Adam Walsh.

The backfield featured abundant talent and experience, and even the second-line players would be regulars at other schools. But questions remained about the front seven, which needed several replacements for graduated players. Another concern weighed on his mind – quality backups in the line. Walsh would have to play a major role in stabilizing that group and in leading the Fighting Irish, and Walsh relished the challenge.

2
Finding A Home

THE START OF Notre Dame's fall term was now only days away. More and more upperclassmen were moving into their residence halls, rejoining their clubs and renewing acquaintances. Much like Adam Walsh in 1921, anxious freshmen who were far away from home for the first time, stepped off the New York Central or Pennsylvania stations in downtown South Bend, their grip in hand, hoping someone would be there to meet them. Making one's way through uncharted territory had been a part of Notre Dame life since its very founding.

The University of Notre Dame was established in northern Indiana in 1842 by the Congregation of the Holy Cross (Congregiazione di Santa Croce, CSC), a Catholic religious order based in France. The Rev. Basil Moreau, CSC, founder of the Congregation, envisioned a religious order whose primary task was to convert people to the Catholic faith, preach the gospel to them and provide Christian education to youth.

European Catholic missionary priests had been a part of United States history since the discovery of the "new world." By the mid 1800s, the Northwest Territories was swelling with immigration from the eastern states. Catholic churches were few and priests were even scarcer. Vincennes, Indiana Bishop Celestin Guynemer de la Hailandiere, whose diocese included the entire state of Indiana, wrote to Moreau for help. In response, Moreau sent six brothers, including Rev. Edward Sorin, CSC. The group stayed in Vincennes for a year before Sorin accepted an invitation to establish a school in St. Joseph County in the northern reaches of the Indiana diocese. The land had been purchased by Rev. Stephen Badin, the first Catholic priest ordained in the United States, and the land had been left in trust to the Bishop of Vincennes for anyone who would found a school on the site.

The school was named in Sorin's native tongue L'Universite de Notre Dame du Lac. In 1924, the University had expansion plans underway to build dormitories, additional classrooms and athletic and recreational facilities. Our Lady's University, which traced its roots to humble beginnings in a log cabin and two students in the winter of 1842, had clearly embraced Father Sorin's vision, which he described in a letter to Father Moreau shortly after arriving:

"Will you permit me, dear Father, to share with you a preoccupation which gives me no rest? Briefly, it is this: Notre Dame du Lac was given to us by the bishop only on condition that we establish here a college at the earliest opportunity. As there is no other school within more than a hundred miles, this college cannot fail to succeed... Before long, it will develop on a large scale... It will be one of the most powerful means for good in this country. Finally, dear Father, you cannot help see that this new branch of your family is destined to grow under the protection of Our Lady of the Lake and of St. Joseph. At least, that is my deep conviction. Time will tell if I am wrong."

By March 1924, a study of hometowns showed that Notre Dame students hailed from all 48 states, as well as 40 foreign countries. Some students were steered to the school by their parish priest or by another trusted adult. Increasingly, Notre Dame alumni throughout the country were active in identifying bright, talented young Catholic men in their area and in promoting the university.

For some, attending Notre Dame had simply become a family tradition.

THE MILLERS OF Defiance, Ohio, were one such family, sending five brothers to the school. For nearly two decades, at least one Miller boy had been attending Notre Dame and playing football. They were scholars, gentlemen and excellent ambassadors for the university as they went out into the world. Their mother Anne, back in Defiance, thanked God for the blessing of sending her boys to South Bend. The oldest brother, Harry "Red" Miller, enrolled at Notre Dame in 1906. He had starred on several of the first football teams at Defiance High School, including the undefeated 1904 squad, named the "Northwestern Ohio and Northern Indiana" champions. Harry went on to lead the 1905 DHS football team. He also played right field on the baseball team and set a school track record with a 5-foot, 3-inch high jump.

Harry's Notre Dame varsity career lasted from 1906 through 1909 as freshmen were eligible at that time. He started at left half all four years and served as captain of the 1908 squad. His teams produced an overall record of 27-2-2, losing only to Indiana, 12-0, in 1906, and to Michigan, 12-6, in 1908.

Harry played a major role in the one of the most historic events in Notre Dame football history. On November 6, 1909, at Ferry Field in Ann Arbor, Michigan, Harry helped Notre Dame score its first victory over mighty Michigan, 11-3. In eight previous meetings dating back to Notre Dame's first game in 1887, Michigan had prevailed. The Wolverines shut out Notre Dame five times in that stretch and outscored the Irish by a total of 121-16. On this day, Harry broke the hex. Such was his prominence that one Detroit paper simply declared "Miller Defeats Michigan." For his season-long exploits, Miller was named to Walter Camp's All-America team, just the second Notre Dame gridder to be so honored, after another "Red," fullback Louis Salmon in 1903.

Harry was also at Notre Dame for the introduction of the "Notre Dame Victory March," composed by two recent graduates, brothers Michael J. Shea (ND '05) and John F. Shea (ND '06). The Victory March was first performed at Notre Dame on Easter Sunday, 1909, in the rotunda of the Main Building, under the Golden Dome.

Harry left nothing to chance in making sure his younger brothers would continue the family tradition of heading to Notre Dame. When possible, he would show up at Defiance High practices to show the high schoolers some of what he learned on Cartier Field. The prep players were in awe not only of having a college star in their midst, but also of some of the "real" equipment he showed them, such as hard shin guards and a helmet reinforced with stiff leather straps.

Next in line was Ray, among the most accomplished students in the Miller clan. He was a champion orator at Defiance High School. Ray enrolled at Notre Dame in 1910 alongside a young Knute Rockne. After a year on the freshman squad and another as a reserve end, Ray backed up Rockne at left end on the undefeated 1912 team.

Ray earned his law degree, but he had little time to establish his career before another mission took precedent. Starting in 1917, Ray served in the Ohio National Guard, the Ohio Infantry Machine Gun Company, and finally the 135th Machine Gun Battalion, 37th Division, with whom he shipped to France during the Great War. His unit was involved in the battles of Meuse-Argonne, Ypres, and St. Michiel, and was crossing the Escault River when the Armistice was signed.

The unbroken string of years with a Miller brother at ND continued in 1914, when Walter enrolled shortly after Ray's graduation. Walter became a contemporary of the great George Gipp, starting at fullback in 1917 alongside the legendary star. He sat out the war-and-flu-shortened 1918 season and played more fullback in 1919, Gipp's next-to-last year. The Irish went 9-0-0 for the first unbeaten season under Rockne.

In the fall of 1921, the fourth and fifth brothers – Gerry and Don – arrived on campus together. Gerry was older than Don, but he had missed some school due to illness. They carried the hopes of their family – and hometown of Defiance – to continue the Miller tradition of excellence at Notre Dame.

IN MANY WAYS, the story of Defiance, Ohio was the story of America. From Indian gathering spot, to United States frontier garrison, to a regional trading and manufacturing center, it was a center of activity. At the turn of the century, the city was anchored by the Defiance Machine Works, maker of the woodworking machinery which produced wagon wheels for the great migration west, rifle stocks, and even Hillerich & Bradsby baseball bats.

Martin Miller, the patriarch of the family, was a top machinist and manager at the plant and an excellent semi-pro baseball player. At a time when most ballplayers caught the ball barehanded, Miller fashioned an early catcher's mitt and tinkered with a chest protector. He didn't patent either – he simply wanted to protect himself and play a few more years.

As Martin and Anne raised their eight children, sports and recreation were always part of their lives. At vacant lots on Washington Avenue, the schoolyard at St. Mary's Parish, or Roberts' swimming hole on the Auglaize River, Millers could be found running, playing ball, or swimming.

It was an idyllic world, comprised of just a few blocks. From the sweeping front porch of the Miller home at 814 Washington Ave., the youngsters would dart barely the length of a football field, just past the Baltimore & Ohio railroad trestle, to St. Mary's, where they all attended grade school, taught by Adrian Dominican Sisters. A fire in 1899 at St. Mary's broke that tranquility and the students were sent to nearby public schools until the parish school could be rebuilt. From St. Mary's, it was only several quick blocks to the football field next to Defiance High School, where the Miller brothers would take turns starring for the Blue and White.

From the comfort and stability of their world, the Miller kids prospered. The girls, Helen and Hazel, would join in many activities. Helen, something of a tomboy, was a lively participant in the sandlot games, and she actively participated in what became known in the Miller home as "football in the living room." Hazel would serve as referee.

The Miller's neighborhood was typically filled with youngsters playing outdoors, in games or informally, coming and going, playing and calling for one another. Children of all ages felt comfortable in the whirlwind of activities.

So it was on the afternoon of Thursday, May 23, 1912. After

the schoolday at St. Mary's ended, neighborhood kids ran about Washington Avenue as usual, playing games of tag, hide-and-seek and cops-and-robbers. About four o'clock, Mrs. Miller came out on the front porch and asked Don, then age 10, and Gerry, 13, if they had seen their brother Richard, who was just shy of six. Don and Gerry responded that they hadn't seen him in a while. Within minutes, the horrifying answer was revealed as a small woodshed in the back of the Miller property suddenly went up in flames.

"The blaze was a very peculiar one inasmuch as at first there was only a puff of smoke, and in an instant the entire shed was in flames," recorded the *Defiance Crescent News*. "It would have been almost impossible to have rescued him because of the sudden manner in which the flames enveloped the shed.

"Upon the arrival of the (fire) department the blaze was extinguished in a short time and the body of the boy found...Death must have come instantly as no outcry from the shed was heard...Evidently the flame came so suddenly that the boy was immediately suffocated before he could attempt an escape... The parents were frantic for a time."

Young Richard Miller was remembered as being "especially bright for his age, and...a family favorite as well as a favorite in the neighborhood."

As the usually joyous month dedicated to Mary was winding down, St. Mary's Church became the site of a somber goodbye to a young boy. Harry and Ray, the latter at Notre Dame, made the trip home to mourn the death of their youngest brother. On the morning of Saturday, May 25, the funeral of Richard Miller occurred at nine o'clock, "the children of St. Mary's School attending in a body." It was said that so deep was Anne Miller's grief that her hair turned white in short order. Nevertheless she continued to nurture and guide her family as well as she could.

Richard's death would not be the only catastrophe to befall the Millers. In 1917, as Don was about to enter Defiance High School, his father suffered a devastating stroke, the resulting paralysis kept him an invalid for his remaining years. With Harry building his career, Raymond in the military, Walter away at Notre Dame and their father homebound, Don would find a smaller high school family cheering section than his brothers found.

He would also be sharing the spotlight with brother Gerry. Though three years older than Don, Gerry's school had been interrupted over the years by illness, including a bout with typhoid fever. He had also left high school for a year to work. But in the fall of 1920, both Don and Gerry were raring to go one last time for Defiance High. With Don starting at left half and Gerry opposite at right half, Defiance opened its campaign after four weeks of practice, and destroyed Delphos, 85-0. In a tougher test against Findlay, "the terrific plunging of D. Miller, supplemented by the clever broken field running of G. Miller, netted two touchdowns" in a 26-0 victory.

Two weeks later, Don scored five touchdowns and Gerry two in a 75-0 dismantling of Bowling Green High, with Gerry "displaying a world of skill at skirting Bowling Green ends. When this clever half got away he wriggled thru the broken field time and again, throwing off tacklers and dazzling the opposing defense."

Such a description of Gerry's running style helped brand him as the Miller most exciting to watch. Don's contributions were considerable and consistent, but it was Gerry who more often brought the crowd to its feet. Gerry's flamboyance – and Don's seriousness – would find other outlets. When the students at the high school organized the school's first newspaper, "The Optimist" that fall, Gerry's assignment was joke editor. Don was named business manager.

Their days of playing high school football together would come to an abrupt end in mid-season of 1920. Gerry's age (21) drew an inquiry, and he was disqualified from further competition. Don and his teammates carried on without him, finishing the season with a 6-2-1 record, and outscoring the opposition 328-64. Don Miller was far and away the team leader in rushing, scoring, conversions and punting.

Yet, after the pair graduated from Defiance High School among a class of 56 students, it was Gerry who was expected to carry the Miller banner at Notre Dame. Growing up, Don was in awe of his older brothers' achievements. He was barely school age when Harry became captain of the Irish. Don fell in love with Notre Dame, although he would not set eyes on the campus until enrolling in the fall of 1921.

In September 1921, Don was disheartened when the football togs were distributed and he received mere scraps. He spent the next three weeks offering up his daily communion to help him deal with the disappointment. Gerry, meanwhile, became the star of the freshmen team. His dizzying moves resulted in three touchdowns in victories over Culver Academy and Great Lakes. Despite his 145-pound frame, he was set to take his place as the next great Miller when he opened the 1922 season as a varsity halfback.

Don simply went to work to become the best football player he possibly could be. Gathering his resolve, he worked tirelessly, often alone. Even from the sidelines, he mimicked the moves made by those in the fray, tossing aside any self-consciousness in an effort to build his skills.

In a few weeks time, the brothers' football fortunes would undergo another stark reversal. In the second game of the season, a 26-0 win over St. Louis, Gerry suffered a season-ending leg injury. Don, meanwhile, got increasing playing time, and became the first of the 1922 sophomores to start regularly, supplanting another speedster, Red Maher, at right half. Years of steady, constant effort had paid off. Don Miller, like Harry, Ray and Walter before him, was starting for the Irish.

Don had established himself as a leader on campus and was elected senior class president for the 1924-25 school year. His determination, rock-steady persona and conscientious nature made him a natural choice. On the football field, he was the definition of a Notre Dame man – playing hard, always according to the rules, never complaining or making excuses, and accepting the result with grace and dignity.

He was at ease anywhere on campus. And, as was typical for each fall at Notre Dame, Don was coming off a summer experience that was a family tradition as well. Cedar Point, a seven-mile spit of rock and sand jutting into Lake Erie near Sandusky, Ohio, had become a "summer home" for Irish football players for two decades. Since around 1905, Cedar Point had developed a tradition of hiring Notre Dame students for summer work. These students worked as lifeguards, as dishwashers, as waiters, as bathhouse attendants.

Each summer, Cedar Point dazzled hundreds of thousands of visitors with firework displays, vaudeville shows, flying exhibitions and the natural beauty of its long sandy beach. It provided a venue for one of the nation's most popular sporting events – world championship boxing. One summer, the Eastland steamer transported 200,000 visitors from Cleveland, Toledo, Detroit and points east and west to Cedar Point in a season that lasted less than 100 days. Steamers featured loud calliopes and hardwood dance floors as they transported folks to their summer vacation destination.

The massive dancing and entertainment complex at Cedar Point was two stories high, and the upper level was billed as "The Largest Dancing Pavilion on the Great Lakes." The Leap Frog Scenic Railway roller coaster, built in 1918, highlighted a number of rides and attractions. The new grand bath house, opened in 1920, was acclaimed as one of the finest in the world.

Harry Miller started the tradition of bringing his Notre Dame teammates to Cedar Point. Sam "Rosey" Dolan, Ralph Dimmick and Glen Smith all joined him there while playing for ND. In the summer of 1913, Knute Rockne and Gus Dorais spent endless hours at Cedar Point practicing the pass routes they would use in ND's improbable 35-13 upset of Army. Rockne later married a girl he met at Cedar Point – Bonnie Skiles of Kenton, Ohio, who worked as a waitress at Cedar Point's Grill Room in the summer of 1913. The two were married on July 15, 1914 at Saints Peter and Paul Church in Sandusky.

Brother Walter Miller continued the family practice of summer work at Cedar Point, and Don Miller started tagging along when he was a junior in high school, the first of his six summers spent working and playing at Cedar Point. After Don became a Notre Dame regular, he and brother Gerry brought Vince "Tubby" Harrington, Russ Arndt and Harry Stuhldreher, among others, to Cedar Point. Every afternoon, the group would run, wrestle and toss a football around on the beach. As linemen, Harrington and Arndt had fierce workouts on the sand. They knelt on the sand opposite one another and would ram heads, trying to force the other back. They found these battles would greatly increase their leg strength, and consequently their charge on the football field.

On July 21, Don Miller added another title to his resume – "life saver." While standing on the beach about 50 feet from the Breakers Hotel, he heard the cries of Mrs. M. H. Wise of Detroit, who was drowning in 10 feet of water, about 300 feet out. She was swimming in a part of the lake not typically covered by lifeguards. Miller and a bystander plunged into the lake, swam the 100 yards and reached the woman just before she started down for a third time. They carried her to shore, where she was revived with a lung motor.

Miller's teammates – Tubby, Arndt, Stuhly and brother Gerry – all praised Don for his courage and decisive action, which sprang from a sense of responsibility that was as natural to him as breathing.

Coming "home" to campus for his senior year, Don Miller was ready to lead once more.

As COMFORTABLE AS the Millers were on the Notre Dame campus, another 1921 arrival had a much tougher time shaking the bonds to his Iowa home. Elmer Layden looked the part of an athlete. Well-proportioned, with a square jaw and coal-black hair parted in the middle, he struck a handsome pose. He was confident on the playing field but was forever longing for his family and friends back home. He had a strong family bond with his father Tom, mother Rosemary, older brother Clarence, better known as Irish, sisters Elizabeth and Catherine, and younger brother Francis Louis, called Mike, just 8 years old when Elmer went off to Notre Dame. Elmer missed them all.

The Layden home, a comfortable frame house on Kirkwood Boulevard in Davenport, Iowa was the center of all sorts of activity as young Elmer grew up. The boulevard was split by a length of grass that alternately became the site of football, baseball and other games for the neighborhood youth. Elmer recalled those carefree days – one afternoon after another, running and playing. He would chuckle over the time he and Clarence and their friends were rounded up in a paddy wagon after their Sunday ball-playing drew the ire of the neighborhood's resident "nosy old lady"…and how they were "sprung" from jail by the boys' uncle, a detective on the police force.

The Layden children were all educated at nearby Sacred Heart School. Elmer's sisters went on to attend a Catholic girls' high school, while he and Clarence went to the public Davenport High School, just blocks from the Mississippi River.

At Davenport High, Elmer starred as a darting fullback, a track sprinter and a basketball sharpshooter. At the famous Drake Relays in Des Moines, Elmer and Clarence teamed with two classmates, Ike Sears and Davenport Day, to set the high school record for the half-mile relay. Everyone figured Elmer for an all-around athlete at the University of Iowa, his father's alma mater; however, a knee injury during Layden's senior basketball season caused the Hawkeyes to lose some interest.

Meanwhile, Layden's high school coach, Walter Halas, had joined Rockne's coaching staff, assisting in football as well as serving as Irish head basketball coach. Walter, whose older brother George was an excellent football player now involved in organizing and coaching professional teams such as the Decatur (Ill.) Staleys, was considered quite a find for Rockne. Walter told Rock about the lad he had coached in Davenport, and Rockne, through Halas, told Layden to come on over.

Layden's first days on the Notre Dame campus in 1921 were challenging. He was assigned to room with upperclassmen football players Joe Bergman and Tom Lieb in a basement dorm room in Corby Hall. The room contained one double-decker bunk and a cot. To permit slightly more freedom of movement, the two upper-class roommates had perched the cot on top of the double-decker bunk. "This is your bed," Layden was told. When climbing up to try it out, Layden immediately discovered if he rolled one way he would fall about 12 feet; if he rolled the other way, the steam pipes running along the ceiling were sure to scorch him. Layden picked up his suitcase and marched over to Badin Hall, where his cousin, Herman Centlivre from Fort Wayne, Indiana, was staying. The two had never met, but they had pictures of one another. Herman let Elmer sleep on his floor for the first two weeks of the school year.

It wasn't long before Layden was urging Herman to accompany him downtown. "Let's go down to the train station and look up timetables," Elmer said. Herman accompanied Elmer to the station, mostly to ensure Elmer didn't board a train for Davenport. At the station, they ran into Danny Coughlin, starting left halfback from Waseca, Minnesota, who was waiting for his younger brother Bernie to arrive. Coughlin encouraged Layden to come and watch the next varsity football practice. The freshmen had yet to "hear the call" to come for practice.

Layden followed the suggestion and was reunited with Walter Halas. "Elmer, why don't you come over to the house for dinner tonight?" Halas invited.

"Sure," came the reply, "if I can bring my cousin Herm along."

"Yes, he's invited, too."

The two freshmen enjoyed a scrumptious home-made meal. Then Elmer asked to use the phone, called his father collect, and said he was thinking of coming home and calling it quits on the idea of college. "Well, sleep on it first," Tom Layden advised his son. "Call me again in the morning and tell me your decision. Give the school a chance."

Almost on cue, there was a knock on the door, and Coach Rockne appeared. Layden and Rockne started talking and the subject of Layden's homesickness came up.

"Son, we've never lost a freshman from our team yet," the coach boasted.

Layden thought: "Mr. Rockne, your record is about to be broken."

Rockne went on to talk about his own path in life, suggesting how lucky Layden was to be able to start college at 18 and not 22. The coach gave his philosophy on the different types of personalities and made it clear he preferred the "up-and-at-'em, the go-get-'em type."

Layden, intrigued by the talk, asked Rockne what made the Notre Dame team special.

"I'd rather have 11 men," Rockne said, "who are willing to follow orders than the most brilliant collection of individual stars on earth."

And what, Elmer also wanted to know, was the outstanding characteristic of a Notre Dame player?

"Courage," came the reply. "At Notre Dame there are no quitters."

Young Elmer managed to find his way home to Davenport on several occasions that first year. He would mope around the house for a few days and listen to his dad reiterate: "You don't have to go back to college." Finally, young Elmer would muster up enough nerve and go back, only to keep making collect calls homeward for more encouragement to stay.

As often as not, Layden was heartsick as well. He'd put a photo of his current girl on his desk. And how he would "brood and pine" over that one, noted one roommate. Between his freshman and sophomore year back home in Davenport, Layden was taken with a lass headed to the University of Wisconsin. That fall, Rockne made Layden a halfback, but as the team was loaded with halfbacks, his prospects for playing time appeared slim. He researched transferring to Wisconsin.

During the '22 season, Layden worked up the courage to approach Rockne and ask about his playing time, figuring that the path to Wisconsin was always open. Rockne was surprisingly accommodating. "All right, Layden, I'll let you start the next game." The next game was the annual battle with Army, on Armistice Day, November 11, 1922 – the final time Notre Dame met Army on the plains of West Point, New York. The teams battled to a ferocious scoreless tie before 15,000 spectators. From his spot at left half, Layden had a strong game, gaining on several rushes and also passing for significant yardage.

Late in the 1922 campaign, teammates Harry Stuhldreher, Jim Crowley and Don Miller had settled into major roles as quarterback, left half and right half, respectively. Layden figured he would play out the season with spot duty behind the starting backs.

But on November 18, in a 31-3 victory over Butler at Indianapolis, senior fullback Paul Castner, the captain and star of the Irish team, suffered a broken hip. After the game, Rockne came to Layden and told him to get ready to play fullback the next week against Carnegie Tech.

"But Rock," Layden pointed out, "I only weigh 162 pounds. And we already have two other fullbacks [Bill Cerney and Bernie Livergood]." Rockne convinced Layden he was a new type of fullback – sleek and swift, able to gain yardage on quick opening plays.

The Shock Troops opened the Carnegie Tech game and drove the ball down to the 5-yard line. Then Stuhldreher and Layden entered the game, joining Miller and Crowley. Rockne, thinking it was fourth down, sent in Stuhldreher with a pass play. Once he realized it was only third down, Harry switched the play to a fullback buck into the line.

Stuhldreher called the signal, the backfield shifted, and the center snap from Bob Reagan caught Layden unprepared. The ball bounced off his knee and landed near the goal line, where Irish end George Vergara pounced on it for a touchdown. The backfield foursome's first play was successful, if in a roundabout way.

Their timing would only improve.

3
Football Towns

THE FELLOWS WERE now almost all back on campus. Walsh spent the summer catching up on his studies, showing his brother Chile around campus and heading up the sales of advertising for the football program. Miller continued his duties as the president of the Class of 1925 and Layden was now as comfortable as anyone on campus.

Joining this group were quarterback Harry Stuhldreher, the diminutive signal-caller, and Sleepy Jim Crowley, whose quick wit and ready smile always kept his teammates loose. Summer was fast disappearing. Father John O'Hara, pressed by a hectic schedule and rapidly approaching cooler weather, would be taking his last few leisurely dips in St. Mary's Lake. Harvest time on the university's farm had workers busy. Soon footballs would be flying above Cartier Field.

IN THE FIRST TWO decades of the new century, football grew exponentially in popularity on college campuses, especially in the East and Midwest. The South, Midlands and the West were starting to catch on as well. At the same time, and especially as players exhausted their college eligibility, another phenomenon was taking place – the emergence of hundreds of town teams in pockets of the country. The teams usually fought for funds from local sponsors, which included town merchants, taverns, and neighborhood and civic clubs. They would cobble together a lineup and schedule of games and battle nearby towns and teams for regional supremacy. Out of this great, loosely-organized environment came the occasional successful team, able to stay in business for more than a flash. They formed the foundation of the nascent professional and semi-pro leagues, such as the American Professional Football Association.

Two hotbeds of this growing football culture also contributed star players to the Notre Dame gathering in the fall of 1924: the Massillon-Canton area of eastern Ohio, and Green Bay in northeastern Wisconsin.

Few areas had the football bug as deeply as these two did. In the earliest years of the century, the rivalry between the town teams of Massillon and Canton was unmatched in its intensity. The great sportswriter Grantland Rice wrote:

> "In days of old when knights were bold,
> and barons held their sway—
> The atmosphere was rife, I hear,
> With war cries day by day.
> From morn to night they'd scrap and fight
> With battle axes and mace –
> While seas of blood poured like a flood
> About the market place.
> But no fight ever fought before
> Beneath the shining sun
> Will be like that when Canton's team
> Lines up with Massillon."

THE RIVALRY REACHED a fevered pitch in 1906, when the teams played a pair of games, the first won by Canton, 10-5, in a game called by darkness. On November 24 of that year, the teams had a rematch on Massillon's gridiron, at the state hospital grounds. Fans poured in from Canton and even Akron, and numerous wagers were placed on the outcome – some people even mortgaged their homes to bet on the game. With Canton clinging to a 6-5 lead in the closing minutes, Massillon blocked a punt, and the ball soared over a wire fence at the end of the field which was holding back the crowd. "Players jumped the fence pell mell into the crowd and Referee Whiting was called upon for a decision as to who had the ball. He gave the ball to Massillon for a safety...Score Massillon 7, Canton 6."

Massillon's Tigers got the ball on the ensuing kick and marched down the field for a clinching touchdown in a 13-6 victory. Later, there were allegations that Canton coach-manager Blondy Wallace had tried to fix the game with Massillon players but failed. It was also supposed that he had persuaded a Canton player to fix the game.

"When his own teammates turned on him, the Canton player involved departed the area in such a hurry he was still wearing his uniform," one report noted.

The scandal, the out-of-control betting and the constant turmoil over the scheduling of the Massillon-Canton games put a nearly decade-long halt to the rivalry, and in fact, to pro ball in Massillon. It returned strong in 1915, when former Harvard great Charles Brickley agreed to coach Massillon. Brickley signed a pair of college stars just a year out of Notre Dame – end Knute Rockne and quarterback Gus Dorais. At the time, Rockne was a Notre Dame assistant coach to Jesse Harper and would make the trip to wherever Massillon was playing on Sunday, returning in time to fulfill his duties on campus on Monday. Canton, for its part, made huge headlines in 1915 by signing Jim Thorpe, the fabled Carlisle Indian star. For two games in 1915, and another pair in 1916, Rockne and Dorais lined up against the great Thorpe in Massillon-Canton games. Rabid crowds clung to the fences circling the field, wildly cheering their hometown eleven.

It was said that at this time Rockne struck up an acquaintance with an adoring young local football player – Harry Augustus Stuhldreher. Harry, a slight lad of about 14, would occasionally help carry Rockne's football gear to and from the field. This experience planted the youngster's dream of his own football glory.

In the fall of 1915, Stuhldreher witnessed one of the most memorable Massillon-Canton tussles of all time. The teams played a pair of games two weeks apart, with Rockne, Dorais and Massillon taking a 16-0 victory on November 15 at Massillon. The return match November 29 at Canton stands as one of the strangest, most controversial games in football history. The local paper gave this description:

> "There was a large amount of money up on the game as was normal for Massillon-Canton games. There were at least 8,000 people jammed into the park at Canton on that Sunday, yet there was not one policeman or deputy sheriff on the field to keep order. The crowd surged out on the field early in the game and hindered the playing of both teams. It was the crowd that kept Massillon from making at least two touchdowns on forward passes. It was probably the largest crowd that had ever witnessed a football game in Canton, and the Canton management should have made adequate arrangements to take care of the spectators but it was not done.
>
> Massillon was trailing Canton in the fourth quarter, 6-0, and they were on Canton's 11-yard-line. Dorais executed a perfect pass to the Left Halfback Briggs who sprinted for the Canton goal line. As he approached the goal line, the crowd surged onto the field and Briggs dove into the crowd, across the goal line with the ball securely tucked under his arm, for a touchdown.
>
> While he was in the crowd of people, someone kicked the ball out of his arms, and a Canton player emerged with the ball. Briggs insisted that a uniformed policeman had kicked the ball out of his hands. The fans stormed onto the field while the argument went on.
>
> Both Umpire Cosgrove and Head Linesman Jones said that the last time they saw the ball it was in the possession of Massillon and that the Tigers had scored a legal touchdown. The Referee, Conners, failed to

keep control of the situation, and allowed the extended argument to go on and on until it became too dark to play. He finally called the game with eight minutes remaining, and said he would make a decision later on when alone with the officials.

That Sunday evening, at the Courtland Hotel in Canton, Referee Conners gave the game to Canton 6 to 0 in a sealed envelope, overruling the other two officials even though he did not see the end of the touchdown play. Conners had left his ruling in a sealed envelope, not to be opened until 12:30 the next day when he had left Canton.

Massillon outplayed and outclassed Canton in all departments of the game. The east enders (Canton), loaded to the gunwhales for the big game, could do little against the fierce playing of the Tigers who were in to win. Statistics of the game clearly show that Canton was outclassed."

Years later, the conductor on a Canton trolley car admitted to Canton's manager, Jack Cusack, that he had kicked the ball from Briggs' hands. Briggs had mistaken the conductor's uniform for that of a policeman. The conductor said he had $30 bet on the game and couldn't afford to lose it.

YOUNG HARRY STUHLDREHER developed a great love for the game while growing up near the center of Massillon, just around the corner from the imposing double spires of St. Mary's Catholic Church, where he began playing ball. Harry's dad ran a small grocery store, and his older brother Walter, not gifted athletically, was a strong student. Walter, to his mother's great joy, went off to attend Notre Dame. He served in Notre Dame's Naval Unit until the Armistice was signed in November 1918.

Harry played football for local sandlot teams, but he would be regularly teased for his slight stature. That only made Harry more focused on developing his speed, quickness and deception.

At Massillon Washington High School, "Hezzy" Stuhldreher was an undersized, scrappy ballplayer who took advantage of opportunity when it appeared. As a junior in 1918, he was a backup at the halfback and quarterback positions during a season shortened by the influenza epidemic. In the season opener, an 82-0 shellacking of outmanned Uhrichsville, Stuhldreher came off the bench to score three touchdowns.

In the season's second game, at New Philadelphia, Massillon trailed 7-6 in the third quarter when a dispute arose over a New Philadelphia gain via the pass, and "Coach Snavely ordered his players off the field in the final period of play, claiming the umpire, a New Philadelphia man, had made a biased ruling." The result was a forfeit. The season continued in a chaotic fashion, as several games – including the usual battle with Canton Central – were cancelled due to the flu epidemic. Stuhldreher played little in the remaining games, and the Black and Orange finished with a 2-2-2 record.

Prospects were much brighter when the high school team gathered for the 1919 season. A full slate of nine high school games was scheduled, plus a "practice game" against Wooster College to kick off the season. For the first time, Stuhldreher won a starting spot, at right halfback, alongside Greenfelder and behind the veteran quarterback Graybill. The Orange and Black put up a strong fight against the collegians, falling just 9-7 despite a size disadvantage of 20 or more pounds per man.

In the high school opener against Akron Central, Massillon lost its veteran quarterback Graybill for the season just six minutes into the game. Graybill was carrying the ball around left end, when he was stopped by a clean tackle "but in falling, Graybill's leg snapped." That put more pressure on backs Greenfelder and Stuhldreher, and they responded, Harry contributing touchdowns in a pair of shutout wins. He showed speed and savvy on the defensive side of the ball, and Massillon won some close battles, such as the 2-0 triumph over Youngstown South on a punt blocked into South's end zone.

In the ensuing weeks, Stuhldreher's first go-round at quarterback netted mixed results. Against Rayen High, he "played a good game, although he was not able to elude Elliott, Rayen's star, as successfully as (starting QB) Hess did." On Tuesday, November 11, the first anniversary of the Armistice ending the Great War, Stuhldreher returned at quarterback and had a number of strong gains to lead his team to a 14-7 victory. Coach Snavely's team was praised by the local paper, which noted that "in these days of turbulence and unrest, there is nothing like sports for relaxation and recreation."

Among the "turbulence and unrest" was a coal shortage due to a miners' strike, which, the paper's main headline warned, "may bring heatless days and lightless nights." Another shortage affected the Stuhldrehers, as "Sugar Famine Hits City." It was reported: "Massillon wholesale and retail grocery dealers today were without sugar and with no assurances that any supply would be received within...10 days, the city faced a complete sugar famine." The same week in Akron, the arrest of "15 alleged anarchist propagandists" foiled "red attempts to disrupt Akron factories, including rubber plants."

But unlike war and influenza in 1918, strikes and shortages were not able to stop the high school football season. On November 15, Massillon kept its winning streak alive by hammering Wooster High, 56-7, behind "a flashy attack which was featured by the open field work of Stuhldreher and Greenfelder, star performers of the local team."

Now there remained only the season-ending clash with archrival Canton McKinley. But Stuhldreher had an abscess on his left arm; he carried his arm in a sling all during the week leading up to the big game. Along with Graybill, he had to watch from the sidelines as Massillon downed McKinley, 21-0. It was a bittersweet ending to Harry's one season as a high school starter. He had had some moments, but he felt there was more out there for him somewhere. His dreams had not been met.

His size being a factor, it was decided that he could use a year of seasoning before facing the rigors of college, both athletically and academically. For the 1920-21 year, he enrolled at The Kiskiminetas Springs School, on the edge of Saltsburg, Pennsylvania, about 50 miles east of Pittsburgh. The Kiski School, as it was known, provided a quality education for boys on its picturesque, 200-acre campus. While not a military school, Kiski did devote time to "special military exercises" and "rigid inspections." The school boasted that "there is no large town within sixteen miles of the school and the temptations of larger towns and cities are entirely absent."

Under Coach John L. Marks, Kiski had developed a strong reputation for quality football, and the highlights of its season were games against the University of Pittsburgh freshmen at Forbes Field, and the University of Pennsylvania frosh at Franklin Field. Marks sent numerous Kiski players on to respectable college programs. In fact, Stuhldreher was following in the footsteps of another Massillon quarterback. Ray McLaughlin was the captain-elect of the 1917 Massillon team and chose to go to Kiski. There he starred and later went on to Washington & Jefferson.

In 1920, the archrivals from Pitt were the only opponent to defeat Kiski, as the plebes from Carnegie Tech, Washington & Jefferson and Penn all fell, as did the Punxsutawney Athletic Club. Stuhldreher played both quarter and halfback, and in his one year at Kiski, made enough of an impression to rate this goodbye in the school annual: "Now we come to our little bow-legged athlete. Here we have the rarest of combinations, namely, a whiz of an athlete and a scholar. Stuly came to us as long ago as the fall term. He immediately established his reputation as a quarterback, then played varsity basketball and made the track team. Not content with all this, he decided to graduate, and we're going to lose him. We wish you'd stay a while, Stuly."

Elsewhere, he was called "a man of soul and body, born for deeds."

Clearly, he was ready for college. Notre Dame became a natural choice given his connections with Rockne and older brother Walter's tenure in South Bend.

HUNDREDS OF MILES from the fervor of eastern Ohio football, town ball was also thriving in northeastern Wisconsin's Fox River Valley and environs. Nearly every town had a team, and from the 1890s through 1920, a rich mix of organized – and often disorganized – football elevens dotted the landscape.

A major hub was the city by the bay – Green Bay. In this era, there were dozens of teams, representing neighborhoods, athletic clubs, companies and taverns. Among the more colorfully named were the

Doo Wah Jack Football Club, the Jolly Eleven, the Nitchee Cheemans and Sorensen's Skiddoos. At one time or another there existed the Cherry Street Stars, the Hillside Boys, the South Side Maroons and the West Side Midgets.

Players and teams came and went, and schedules were uncertain, with games often planned on a haphazard basis as a result of public challenges made by one squad to another in the pages of the local sporting press. High school, college, and semi-pro players played alongside one another on a "team," and would then appear with another outfit a week or two later. Rules were minimal. It was a wild, unpredictable scene.

One rivalry that did acquire a sense of order was that between East and West High Schools. Beginning in 1907, the two set a tradition of meeting every Thanksgiving Day, and for many years it was the athletic highlight of the year in Green Bay, with crowds of several thousand. A star of these games in the mid-teens was Earl "Curly" Lambeau, who emerged from the dusty streets of the North Side, hard by the paper mills and packing houses lining the East River. Lambeau, son of itinerant carpenter Marcel Lambeau, was always looking for a game. Even as a high schooler, he organized numerous ad hoc elevens

Lambeau, a star halfback for East High, highlighted the annual Turkey Day battle with West High in 1916 gaining 165 of East's 200 yards in a 7-6 triumph over West, "and he headed off to college with a whole locker full of accolades." His first stop was in Madison, where he hoped to show his stuff on the University of Wisconsin's freshman team. He attended some classes, hung around the football workouts, but the team never got going, due to a lack of numbers, and before the fall was out, he was back in Green Bay, playing for the town team Green Bay All-Stars in a charity game against Marinette.

The next fall, Lambeau began as a key player on town teams in Green Bay. On September 15, he led the Green Bay Skiddoos against a team from nearby De Pere in a game described as "a fistic encounter and a verbal battle." Green Bay came out on top, 13-0, and Lambeau led the way. In a few days, he was on the road again, this time stopping in South Bend to take a look at Notre Dame under new head coach Knute Rockne. No longer considered a freshman, he was eligible to play varsity, and was the starter at fullback on a team that played an abbreviated six-game schedule due to the nationwide influenza epidemic and wartime restrictions on travel.

Lambeau scored a touchdown in the September 28 opener, a 26-6 romp over Case Tech, after which Notre Dame didn't play another game until November 2, a 67-7 pasting of Wabash. Four games followed. Notre Dame finished 3-1-2, with one of the ties coming in their only game at Cartier Field, a 7-7 deadlock with military power Great Lakes. At the end of November, Lambeau's Notre Dame career was history. He developed tonsillitis, went home for the holidays and didn't return. The idea of college life held little appeal to him, but organizing and leading football contingents in his hometown did. By the next fall, he had talked his employer, the Indian Packing Company, into providing $500 to buy uniforms for the dominant town team, which he renamed the Green Bay Packers.

IN ADDITION TO his role as player-coach of the Packers, Lambeau took over as head football coach at East High in 1919. There, he got a good look at a young player he had seen on a few occasions around town: Jim Crowley.

Jeremiah Crowley and Agnes Sweeney had grown up on farms amid an Irish-American enclave in the towns of Rockland and Morrison, surrounded by rich farmland a short distance south of Green Bay. They were married in 1900 at St. Patrick's Church in Green Bay and had their first son, James Harold Crowley, on September 10, 1902, while living in Chicago. Jeremiah worked a succession of jobs in the Windy City, where one of his brothers had become a doctor and another a pharmacist. Jeremiah faced a larger struggle when he came down with consumption.

Across the United States, doctors advised their patients with consumption to seek treatment in Colorado, where the fresh, dry, evergreen-scented air was considered therapeutic. Treatment locations ranged from luxurious resorts in Colorado Springs to facilities for the indigent in Denver. Dozens of sanatoriums sprang up to accommodate the many health-seekers who migrated to the area. Jeremiah Crowley, with his wife Agnes and their two young sons, Morris and James, headed to Denver. The family was hopeful that the move would reverse the effects of the debilitating disease which claimed thousands of victims each year. But the illness was too severe to overcome, and Jeremiah Crowley died in Denver.

Grief-stricken, Agnes took her two young sons back to Green Bay, where she moved in with her 70-year-old mother, Gaelic-speaking Mary Ann Sweeney. Mrs. Sweeney had 12 children, five of whom were living at the time. One of them, Agnes' brother Jack, was 36, unmarried and also part of the household. They also took in a boarder, 54-year-old Mary Hills. Agnes found work as a milliner at a shop downtown and registered the boys at nearby St. John the Evangelist school. Green Bay was a heavily Catholic town, and from the Sweeney residence, one could see the spires of three parishes – St. Francis Xavier, which was primarily German; St. Willebrord, which served a largely Dutch population, and St. John's, which had a significant membership of French or Belgian descent.

Uncle Jack, an employee of the city's fire department since it was organized in 1891, steadily advanced up the ranks until he was named Green Bay's fire chief in 1906. He was once called "Wisconsin's strongest man" after he freed a motorist trapped under a crashed auto by lifting the car himself. He never married, but delighted in watching his nephews' accomplishments. At St. John's, young Jim distinguished himself early on the playfield across the street. He was most proud of making the eighth-grade baseball team when only in third grade. In football, he played for the school team, the Green Bay Catholic Boys Club, and several less organized elevens.

After years of hard work by Agnes and Jack, the household was able to purchase a home on East Walnut Street, just a few blocks from East High School. Jim contributed to the effort by working summers at nearby paper mills and as a ditch-digger. At 16, he was able to take on "man's work" because of the labor shortage created by the 1918 flu epidemic.

As a sophomore at East, young Jim was anxious to get on the football field and show his stuff. During the first game, he was on the sidelines when he heard his coach bark, "Get in there, Crowley." So excited to be playing, Crowley grabbed a helmet and dashed onto the field. After faking a block, he raced for the end zone and waited all alone for a perfect pass. A roar from East rooters expecting a certain touchdown turned to a groan as they watched what unfolded. Crowley had put the helmet on backwards, and it slipped and covered his eyes. The ball bounded off his helmet and rolled away.

That ignominious start belied the feats to come. As a junior, he captained the East Hilltoppers and established himself as a multi-talented back, capable of dazzling runs and well-timed passes. He also excelled at place-kicking, doing all of East's booting. On defense, it was said, he had no equal. A standout of this type, Coach Lambeau realized early, had a future in the game. Rockne would love him.

But football wasn't his only athletic skill. On April 15, 1920, Crowley had a tryout with a traveling scout from baseball's Cincinnati Reds, who offered Jim a contract on the spot. He imagined what the money would mean for his family. Perhaps his mother could stop working. He turned the idea over in his mind, weighed his options, but finally turned down the offer. Football and enjoying high school were too much a part of his life. He enjoyed playing a game that included childhood friends. Two of his St. John's buddies, Oswald Geniesse and John O'Connor, were also on the East High football squad in 1918 and 1919. Expectations were high for the 1920 squad. Crowley, the star back, and O'Connor, the standout lineman, were named captains.

But just a week before the first game, O'Connor complained of feeling ill after practice and less than three days later, on September 21, 1920, O'Connor died of pneumonia. Crowley and his mates were stunned. How could someone so strong and healthy be gone seemingly overnight?

"He longed and waited for this year, the time when he would lead the East High football forces in battle against the enemy," one account said of O'Connor. "Coach Curly Lambeau declared that he was one of the best linemen who ever donned the colors of East High and that his death was a hard blow to the entire team." Much beloved by his classmates, O'Connor was remembered fondly:

> "He was first in the hearts of his classmates;
> He led East High's team thru the fight;

He toiled for the fame of his high school;
He strove for the red and white
And now he is gone, and his classmates
Unite this hero to honor
This leader, student, athlete
'Bonny' John O'Connor."

A skilled artist and cartoonist, O'Connor's work livened the school's annual. He drew caricatures of his teammates in action; one showed a series of dazed opponents left behind by "Cyclone" Crowley. A three-day period of mourning was declared at East High. Scores of students attended the funeral at St. John's. Despite their pain, the East gridders vowed to go on. "The entire squad," one newspaper account said, "from coaches Lambeau and Schneider down to the greenest substitute are determined to offset the loss of their star line man and gridiron leader."

The opener was a tough challenge against a college squad, Oshkosh Normal, and East fell. But from that point, Crowley and his fellows demolished six prep opponents, outscoring them, 220-20. In the pivotal battle with West High on a frozen Green Bay field, Crowley and the Toppers romped, 43-6, the "largest score ever recorded in the annals of the yearly clash." Crowley, it was reported, "was hurling the ball with deadly accuracy all over the gridiron." He flung two touchdown passes to Len Dorschel, one each to Paul VanLaanen and Ed Skogg, and added a 36-yard drop kick field goal.

With Crowley flinging passes, East's quarterback was mainly a running threat and a stalwart defender. Tom "Red" Hearden, only a sophomore, would continue to excel the next two years, and follow Lambeau, Crowley and Geniesse to Notre Dame.

At season's end, a challenge was issued to the only other team in the state of Wisconsin with a possible claim as the best, the Superior Central High School eleven led by the already well-known Ernie Nevers. The Superior team never accepted, and the game was never played. The East annual lamented the playoff that never occurred. An ode to the "Champions" started:

"Why East High won state's championship,
I'll try you folks to tell,
How they went unbeaten through the year,
And made Superior yell.

"Reason 1 was Crowley, of course—
The head and brains was he;
As "cap" and star, he led the team
To certain victory."

And, after lauding all the star players, the poem concluded:

"Well, there's the gang, and you now know why
They never met defeat;
And doubtless now you understand
Why Superior got 'cold feet.'

"In years to come this Old East High
Though crowned again with fame,
Will remember with pride these Champions,
For they surely deserve that name."

For all his athletic achievement, Crowley was equally known for his demeanor characterized by a razor-sharp wit, clever comebacks and living in the moment. One classmate described him this way: "He never works, and never worries, seldom flunks and never hurries." One classmate described Crowley at a St. Patrick's Day parade, when he exhibited his Irish pride by declaring, "Hurrah for Ireland!" A nearby man of English descent responded, "Oh! Hurrah for hell!" Crowley's answer: "That's right; every man for his country."

He took roles on the stage for East theatrical performances, and volunteered to give a series of four-minute speeches as part of an anti-tuberculosis campaign sponsored by nearby Lawrence College to stimulate the sale of Red Cross seals.

In the wintertime, Crowley took to the ice of the municipal rink on the frozen Fox River as goaltender for the hockey team sponsored by the Green Bay Press-Gazette in the City League. Hockey was new to Green Bay, but the Press-Gazette reported that "the class of play improved remarkably fast and during the closing league contests, a fairly good caliber of puck chasing was being displayed." Both Crowley and Tom Hearden won second-team all-city honors.

Crowley was also a skilled billiards player and a frequent visitor to the combination pool hall/bowling alley/sporting goods store operated by one Robert "Bobby" Lynch on Washington Street. Lynch was a former Notre Dame baseball standout and captain of 1902 team. He had bounced around minor-league baseball for a decade before landing in Green Bay as player-manager of the local Bays in 1913. He led a succession of Green Bay ballclubs, operated his business, and was in demand around town as a talented baritone singer. He eventually parlayed his popularity into a long career representing the area in the Wisconsin Legislature.

Lambeau, Lynch, and other Notre Dame men around Green Bay made it clear to Crowley—the only place for him to take his talent was South Bend, Indiana.

Once on campus, Crowley found in Rockne the perfect mentor for his development, both as a football player and as a man. Rockne's skill in understanding personalities, and finding the right way to communicate with each player, was never more evident than in his relationship with Crowley. The two were a match for each other's rapid-fire humor, and Rockne granted Crowley great freedom to banter with the coach. Crowley developed an excellent impersonation of Rockne's staccato delivery.

On the practice field, one was likely to hear Rockne bark: "What's dumber than a dumb Irishman?" and Crowley retort, "A smart Swede." The alliteration worked, even though the players knew Rockne was, of course, Norwegian.

4

A Cautionary Tale

DURING HIS FOUR years as assistant coach to Jesse Harper in the football seasons of 1914-17, Knute Rockne moonlighted as a player and coach in the slowly developing game of pro and semi-pro football. Rockne played for the Massillon team when he could make it. A couple of evenings a week during football season, Rockne would go from coaching at Notre Dame to running practice for the Muessel Brewing Company team.

Rockne's good look at the type of athletes who continued to hang on to playing the game in these venues had convinced him this type of player was not what he wanted for any Notre Dame team. Pro or semi-pro ball, he felt, kept men from their appointed professions, turned them into "football tramps." How could they be considered for respectable jobs if they were forever slipping off to knock heads on a potato patch for a few bucks a match?

Throughout the 1910s and early 1920s, college football was plagued by a trend in which players would head out on Sundays, usually under an assumed name, and be paid a few dollars to play for a pro or semi-pro team. The movement of players also included those who showed up for one college after another.

Even at Notre Dame, Rockne had some experience with "here today, gone tomorrow" athletes. Green Bay's Lambeau, for one. Another vastly talented but erratic star, Johnny McNally, made a brief cameo in South Bend en route to football fame elsewhere. And the most talented player he would ever coach, the inimitable George Gipp, kept Rockne constantly on edge with his lackadaisical approach to school, rules, schedules, training and the like.

Rockne believed in the educated man, the well-rounded man. He had been one himself at Notre Dame, serious about school, involved in the arts. After Gipp's death, he confided to friends that he would much prefer coaching a team of dedicated students than having a singular, insolent talent like Gipp. In short, he was looking for young men loyal to their school and to their teammates. Those, as he had said to Layden, willing to follow the rules.

When Layden, Miller, Stuhldreher, Crowley, Walsh and their fellow '24 seniors were impressionable freshmen in the fall of 1921, they saw firsthand what happens when one strays from that path.

IN TWO COAL-MINING towns in central Illinois – Carlinville and Taylorville – football fever was raging. On Thanksgiving Day 1920, Carlinville defeated their archrivals 10-7 in a game that, typical of the time, made numerous Taylorville supporters a few greenbacks poorer than when the day began.

As the 1921 season unfolded, the teams' annual battle neared. This time, it was set for November 27, the Sunday after Thanksgiving. There were whispers around town in Carlinville that the team would be sporting something of a "new look" this time around and that it might be advisable to go a little deeper into one's savings to put money down on the local eleven.

Before long, it became common knowledge on the streets that "the Notre Dame team" was going to show up and play for Carlinville. A lad who had grown up and played high school ball in Carlinville, Si Seyfrit, was now a backup to All-American end Eddie Anderson for the Irish. It didn't take much convincing for the local folks to believe that Notre Dame's stars were going to show up in Taylorville and bring it home for Carlinville. And what a strong bunch it was at Notre Dame. True, they had stumbled in their third game of the year, a 10-7 loss at Iowa, but since then the Irish racked up eight straight wins to finish 10-1. Among the wins was a 33-0 thrashing of Purdue, a 7-0 triumph over mighty Nebraska, and a pair of impressive shutouts in the span of four days in the New York area – a 28-0 pounding of Army at West Point on Saturday, November 5, followed by a 48-0 thumping of Rutgers in a rare Tuesday game on November 8. Notre Dame had closed out the season with two more strong victories, first going to Milwaukee to defeat Marquette, 21-7. They returned home to rout the Michigan Aggies, 48-0, before a record Cartier Field crowd of 15,000 on Thanksgiving Day, just three days before the Carlinville-Taylorville clash.

The Irish featured a solid unit of veteran players. Johnny Mohardt at left half and Paul Castner at right half were the backfield stars, behind a line that included Anderson and Roger Kiley, guard Heartley "Hunk" Anderson and tackle Lawrence "Buck" Shaw. As the excitement in Carlinville grew, more and more folks found the dollars to put money on the game. Eventually, word spread to Taylorville about Carlinville's planned imports, and before long, a representative of Taylorville had made contact with several University of Illinois players to counter.

Two of them – Roy "Dope" Simpson and Vern Mullen – were Taylorville products. In almost no time, seven others agreed to join them. They included star halfback Laurie Walquist and quarterback Joe Sternaman.

So, residents of Taylorville also began emptying their wallets to place bets on the local squad. Folks in both towns "went to the bank, the family stocking and the cupboard to bring forth, in some cases, the savings of years." By game day, an estimated $100,000 was in play. Carlinville fans, many on a special train, flooded into Taylorville, accompanied by a band. Farmers from the region joined the parade of fans. The attendance at the game was an estimated 10,000 – nearly equal to the combined population of the two towns.

On a chilly Sunday afternoon in Taylorville, the two faux squads took to the field. Taylorville coach Grover Hoover decided to keep most of the Illini players on the bench for the first half and to use them as needed to take over the game in the second half.

Carlinville came out with four regulars from the Notre Dame line – ends Eddie Anderson and Kiley, tackle Shaw and center Mehre. There was less Irish firepower in the backfield, as fullback Chet Wynne was the only Notre Dame starter on hand. So Anderson switched to quarterback and tried to run the "Notre Dame" offense, to little success. The remaining three imports were Notre Dame subs – backs Bob Phelan and Earl Walsh, and hometown end Si Seyfrit.

Carlinville was able to move the ball with some success in the first half and tried a drop-kick for a field goal that went wide. Taylorville made the game's biggest play, smashing through the Carlinville line and blocking a punt, then returning it 50 yards to inside the Carlinville one-yard line. On third down, regular Taylorville quarterback Charlie Dressen – also a star baseball player in the region – went around right end for a score. At the half, it was Taylorville 7, Carlinville 0.

After the rest of the Illinois players poured into the Taylorville lineup in the third quarter, Carlinville's offense had an even harder time of it, only crossing midfield once in the second half. Taylorville, meanwhile, launched three long drives, each setting up a field goal by Sternaman. The final: Taylorville 16, Carlinville 0, and there were a lot of celebrating, instantly-richer fans from Taylorville.

Word of the game quickly spread among certain athletic circles in the Midwest. Back at Notre Dame, there were a few snickers and sideways glances at the men who "lost to Illinois." The Illini, after all, had only posted a record of 3-4 that season.

The following Sunday, December 3, another game was played involving current Notre Dame athletes, this one on a slightly larger stage. Curly Lambeau's Green Bay Packers, completing their third season in the American Professional Football Association, had a season-ending battle with the Racine (Wis.) Legion "to settle the professional championship of the state." The game was to be played at the home of the Milwaukee Brewers baseball park, known locally as "Otto Borchert's baseball orchard."

The game ended in a 3-3 tie, and was called "as good an exhibition of football as could be wished for." But it wasn't so good for Notre Dame. Almost immediately, it was discovered that three Irish linemen

– guard Heartley "Hunk" Anderson, tackle Art "Hec" Garvey and center Fred "Ojay" Larson – had been recruited by Lambeau to play for the Packers that day. The school acted swiftly, disqualifying the three from further athletic competition and withdrawing their athletic letters.

Father William Carey, CSC, head of the Faculty Athletic Board, wanted to take as strong a stand as possible against the growing allurement of pro ball. Notre Dame was in the midst of an effort to increase its academic standards and dispel charges that it was becoming a "football factory." On December 16, Father Carey sent a letter to 70 Midwest colleges with major athletic programs, calling attention to the threat of professionalism entering the college ranks.

He asked cooperation in a concerted movement to clean it out: "In conducting this investigation (of the game in Milwaukee), the members of the Faculty Board have been confronted with a situation that merits the serious attention of the Faculty of every college and university in the Middle West. We have reason to believe that a number of other players from leading colleges and universities of the Middle West have participated in similar games. Indeed, we have almost conclusive evidence that professionalism is making serious inroads into our great college sport, and that it will require close supervision and very watchful care to prevent our college football players from competing as members of professional teams on Sundays during the football season."

The letter went on to add, "It is hoped that this communication will rouse the Middle West colleges and universities to concerted action against the promoters of professional football. Our cooperation with any such effort may be relied upon."

Father Carey issued a statement saying "there seems to be an insidious propaganda to keep alive the old superstition that Notre Dame does not observe eligibility (rules). As a matter of fact, since 1913 Notre Dame has observed the same rules as the Western Conference. Freshmen are not permitted to play, every athlete must be up in his classes – and most of our athletes make a very high grade – and every hint of violation of any rule is carefully investigated…we are untiring in our efforts to combat this evil and that we act without leniency."

A FEW WEEKS LATER, Notre Dame would again be put to the test. The story of the Taylorville game finally bubbled to the surface in the Chicago papers, accompanied by a flurry of publicity over similar transgressions. In mid-January, four Indiana University athletes lost one year of athletic eligibility after rival Purdue protested that the four had participated in "extra-legal games", in particular a football game between Indiana's ROTC unit and Culver Military Academy. Days later, Purdue decided against renewing the contract of football coach William Dietz after he confessed that he offered $100 a month to eight Pacific coast football players if they would attend Purdue.

Then, on January 28, news arrived that Illinois had investigated the Taylorville game and decided to suspend its nine athletes from further athletic competition. That included Sternaman, the quarterback who was supposed to be the nucleus of Coach Zuppke's 1922 team.

"$100,000 FOOTBALL SCANDAL" screamed the massive main headline of the Chicago Herald Examiner on Sunday, January 29.

In subsequent coverage, Taylorville coach Hoover described the situation: "This time they were down hook, line and sinker to defend the name of Taylorville. They had mortgaged their restaurants, poolrooms and barber shops to raise money to bet, and I had to protect them. Fifty thousand dollars is a low estimate for what was pooled here. I never saw so much money in a bank as was bet on that game."

AT NOTRE DAME, confusion reigned. Initial reports placed Irish stars Johnny Mohardt and Gus Desch playing in the Taylorville game under assumed names. Father Carey said that the university had been conducting a thorough investigation since the rumors that Notre Dame men played in the game first began to spread. All players suspected of participating would be brought before the Athletic Board, and representatives of the University were sent to the Illinois towns to gather facts.

On January 30, Father Carey said that "their report now is not needed," as eight Notre Dame athletes confessed to playing in the game. They were immediately disqualified from further athletic competition at Notre Dame. While most of these players had exhausted their football eligibility, several were stars of the Irish basketball and track squads.

Kiley was captain of the basketball team and a track star. Shaw was the defending champion Western shot putter. Wynne, a star hurdler, was track captain. Mehre had been a basketball captain as center and was a regular on the baseball team. Eddie Anderson was also a basketball starter.

The athletes maintained that they received no money for their play, and that they agreed to play merely as a lark, going to Taylorville with the idea of "just having a little fun during the Thanksgiving holidays." Four of the players were from Iowa, in addition to the two Illinois natives, Seyfrit from Carlinville and Kiley from Chicago.

Mohardt and Desch were exonerated from the scandal, described as "innocent victims of a case of false identity." The game's umpire, Wilfrid Asa, substantiated the eight suspended players' claims that Mohardt and Desch were not present.

In announcing the discipline, Father Carey said that "we will stand for no taint or hint of professionalism here. Not even if it wrecks our teams forever. We don't permit a man to play on any team unless he is well up in his studies, and we won't permit any other rule to be broken."

BUCK SHAW SPOKE for the Notre Dame players and gave a detailed account of the whole affair:

> "We are the goats and will take our medicine. It was our first time out but we might have known we would be caught. We played our last game of college football (Nov. 24) and thought the game would be a small town affair, which would attract no attention. Only two of the fellows were going at first, but later eight of us went. The thing was not arranged until the day before we left.
>
> We didn't know Illinois was to play, and when we got to the town and found how big the affair really was, we were going to back out. We had a meeting, but decided to play when we were told the people of Carlinville had bet considerable money, which they would lose if we did not play. We were sick of the entire business before we went

into the game, but thought the Illinois men were taking the same chance and the matter would never get publicity as the town was buried in the lower part of Illinois.

We didn't use the shift and ran most of our plays from kick formation. We played to win, but didn't have a quarterback and the man who did our passing had never passed in a game. If Mohardt and Desch had been playing with us, as reported, there would have been nothing to it (beating Taylorville). The circles Sterneman ran around the ends, were made around a second string end.

I suppose the papers will make a big thing of it and people will never forget it. We didn't think we were doing anything wrong; we never stopped to think how the affair would reflect on the university. I don't think people should let our actions harm the name of the school. When the affair began to attract so much attention, we went to Father Carey and admitted everything to save the athletic board further embarrassment.

It will do us good in the end. We thought we were taking one chance in a thousand. We have learned our lesson, and when in future life the temptation comes to depart ever so slightly from the straight and narrow, we will remember our plight today."

A few days after the Taylorville scandal broke, Notre Dame suffered another black eye when a story headlined, "Johnny Mohardt Admits Playing in 'Pro' Football Game" appeared. After being cleared of playing at Taylorville, Mohardt had come before Father Carey and admitted that he, too, had played in the Dec. 4 game in Milwaukee – not for the Packers, but for the Racine Legion.

However, "no action has been taken in the case, as Mohardt has finished his college course and will leave school shortly."

Mohardt, captain of the 1921 Notre Dame baseball team, had received offers from several major league teams, and in early February he signed with the Detroit Tigers. He maintained that his participation in the Milwaukee game was above-board, as he was scheduled to graduate at the semester and had "no athletics left from which to be barred." Mohardt played under his own name for Racine, and an article about him appeared in the local paper the week of the game.

Throughout the next weeks, several prominent Western Conference and other Middle West college athletes faced charges of professionalism. John Pucelik and Clarence Swanson, stars of the Nebraska football team, were found to have played in a pro game at Sioux City, Iowa, on November 27, the same day as the Taylorville game. Some launched charges that fullback Gordon Locke and quarterback Aubrey Devine, stars of the championship Iowa team, had extensive records as pro baseball players.

One observer noted that if eligibility rules were to be enforced, especially as related to summer baseball, "most Western Conference schools wouldn't be able to field a football team."

Notre Dame leaders were quick to call for a "clean up" of college athletics. The school's investigation of the football scandal discovered that "emissaries from promoters of professional football frequently visit universities to tempt their athletic stars." Father Carey said that "the only salvation for the colleges is to meet the threat of professional football fairly and squarely." In early February, he presented a six-point plan to his fellow college administrators:

1) Organize alumni and letter men to combat professionalism.
2) Solicit pledges from every graduating athlete not to play in pro games in which men still in college are used.
3) Solicit a pledge from each man in college eligible for athletics not to play pro games while still in college. Expel violators.
4) Publish each fall the name, home town and high school of each high school athletic prospect entering college.
5) Disqualify men playing contests after leaving high school and before entering college.
6) Remove the belief that it is unfriendly for one college to notify another concerning its players.

In making the recommendations, Father Carey advised high school and college athletes to "stop, look and listen" when faced with the lure of professionalism. "I have never known a young man who chose wrongly to whom the inevitable regret did not come," he said. "The disappointment which he knows he must have caused his faculty, the resentment he is aware his fellow students feel, should be examples. When the temptation comes he will do well to hesitate and ask himself: 'Is it worth while?' "

Among those paying close attention to the entire affair were the freshmen football players at Notre Dame. Crowley, Layden, Miller, Stuhldreher, Walsh and all the others were given a precise lesson in the temptations of "outside games" and the likely repercussions. It was a cautionary tale they were not apt to soon forget.

In the three succeeding years, the new institutional guidelines helped to tamp down the likelihood of players wandering off-campus for extra football games. Just as important, the group of Notre Dame players that were now seniors in the fall of 1924 had developed such a bond and sense of loyalty that such an idea was not even thinkable. It had become clear what Rockne looked for in building his Notre Dame teams – nothing short of "loyal sons."

5
Building A Line

WITH THE FALL semester underway, the call for football practice went out, and on the afternoon of Monday, September 15 some 130 candidates assembled on Cartier Field under Rockne's watchful eye. In the coming days their ranks would swell to more than 250, when the freshmen were counted. Football was never more popular at Notre Dame.

Not everyone on the field had a realistic chance of making either the varsity or freshman squads. Yet, the dream of chasing the pigskin remained alive. Teams representing the residence halls, often coached by varsity regulars, would undertake full schedules, both against one another, and often venturing off-campus to take on town teams, small colleges and other elevens in the region. All told, nearly one-quarter of the student body would be involved in organized football this fall.

Over the years, the Notre Dame campus had developed a healthy sports atmosphere in which everyone was encouraged to participate. From the earliest days, the Holy Cross priests and brothers recognized that physical activity and competition was an important part of a young man's education. Numerous playing fields ringed the developed portions of campus.

BUILDING A COMPETITIVE team to face the 1924 schedule was more than a matter of numbers. Rockne's challenge was to identify his eleven best players, then develop depth behind them. Rockne spent the last few days prior to the start of practice much the way he had during the summer, sharing his knowledge with aspiring coaches from coast to coast. His final clinic was at the College of William and Mary in Williamsburg, Virginia, ending on Saturday, September 13. On the train ride back to South Bend, he busied himself with a vital task: "studying the prospects for his guards and tackles."

The headline as practice began laid out the challenge: "Line is Chief Worry of Notre Dame." The returning backs – Stuhldreher, Don Miller, Crowley, Layden and their backups – were proven, experienced and ready for their final year. On the line, meanwhile, graduation had left some significant holes. Gone was left guard Warren Brown, who had captained the '23 squad to its 9-1 record. George Vergara, the primary right guard from last year was on the field, but his role had switched from player to assistant coach. And at right tackle, Rockne searched for someone to take over for giant Gene Oberst, 6-foot-4 and 200-plus pounds, who made his mark both on the football field and as a track star. Besides Walsh at center, the main returnee was Joe Bach at left tackle. Short of injury, it would be unlikely for anyone to wrest the spot from Bach.

BACH'S JOURNEY TO South Bend was unique and circuitous. Born and raised on the rugged Mesabi Iron Range of northern Minnesota, Bach came from a family and a town steeped in iron ore mining. His parents, Josef Bach Sr. and Marija Pecnik Bach, had been born, raised and married near Ljubljana in the Austro-Hungarian empire. They were among thousands who immigrated to the Iron Range in the late 19th century, creating the most varied ethnic stew outside of the major United States cities. The couple settled in the Shenango location, one of the myriad mining camps outside of Chisholm. Joe Sr. began working in the mines, and later the family operated a boarding house for miners, before moving into the town of Chisholm.

It was a hard life at Shenango for the Bachs and their four children. Houses built by the mining company and rented to the miners had no indoor plumbing aside from a cold water tap in the kitchen. Despite the austere conditions at home, Chisholm's schools were a different story. Heavily funded by the tax base of the mining companies, they were far advanced, with well-furnished classrooms, excellent instructors, a "college prep" curriculum and extensive activities. The goal of getting an education – and preferably a college education – was something the Chisholm kids heard early and often. Community education was offered, with adults, mostly immigrants, attending night school to attain citizenship and take classes to learn English.

Improving the public's health was also a high priority. Chisholm schools not only had a school nurse, but starting in the fall of 1917 – as Joe Bach entered Chisholm High – a school doctor as well, which was a rarity. A young Dr. Archibald Graham saw an ad for the Chisholm schools' doctor position and traveled from his home in North Carolina for an interview. Upon arrival, he announced himself as the doctor the town sought. The authorities agreed, and he began his tenure, dedicated to raising the awareness of community health starting with the school kids. Doc Graham had a background that included a stint in organized baseball. A farmhand of the New York Giants, he was called up to the big team in the 1905 season. Graham saw action in one game, playing one half inning in right field in a June 29, 1905 game against the Brooklyn Superbas. Instead of returning for another year, he left the game and began his march toward a degree in medicine.

For Joe Bach, sports were an outlet for an active, sometimes rambunctious youth. Joe was just six when his father died, and in Joe's teenage years, his exuberance once got the better of him, resulting in a brief visit to the Minnesota Training School in Red Wing. But he rebounded from that episode, focusing his considerable energy into sports of all kinds. Bach named himself captain of the school's newly-formed swimming team, and once challenged Duluth Central, 1919 state champions, to a meet. He was also a splendid running back in football and a major force in basketball. Young Joe's first love was football, but it was basketball that garnered him attention outside the

Iron Range. In his sophomore year, 1918-19, he poured in 15 field goals in a 60-5 win over Biwabik.

The basketball team, much like the area, was an ethnic melting pot —Walter "Baldy" Rahja, Gene Sullivan, Omar Johnson, and the three Franks – Fabro, Babnick and Kochevar. The coach was the esteemed Ferdinand Drotning, known affectionately to CHS students as "Streets," after the phonetic Slovenian word for "Uncle." The basketball squad lost only once in the regular season, to Eveleth, and avenged that loss in the District final, after which "a delighted band and student body went out and paraded through the principal streets of the village."

The state basketball tournament was held not in Minneapolis or St. Paul, but the small town of Northfield, at Carleton College. Although Chisholm fell short of the state title, it was awarded a special honor as the team that "showed the most gentlemanly and sportsmanlike conduct during its stay in Carleton." Bach was named second-team all-state and caught the eye of Carleton football coach Cub Buck. Two years later, he was invited to attend Carleton – the "Harvard of the Midwest." Freshmen were allowed to play on Carleton's varsity, so in the 1921 football season, Bach started at right half. He was a bruising, powerful runner, and helped Carleton to a successful campaign, including a 42-0 whipping of Beloit, which had beaten Northwestern earlier in the year.

Bach's play in a hard-fought battle with rival St. Thomas College in St. Paul caught the eye of the St. Thomas coach, former Notre Dame quarterback Joe Brandy. He and others convinced Bach he could excel on a larger stage, and after one semester at Carleton, Bach – the son of an immigrant miner – reached a pinnacle few back in Chisholm could have imagined, when he transferred to Notre Dame.

Due to transfer rules, the time spent at Carleton cost him the '22 season in South Bend, but Bach's willingness to contribute led him to a role as a trainer/manager, and he endeared himself to Rockne for his intense curiosity and studying of the game. By the fall of 1923, Bach was ready to go. When regular Gus Stange broke his leg in the Army game, Bach took over and excelled. Bach was raring to see the '24 season start. He had spent the summer back in Chisholm, mowing lawns and trimming hedges around the school grounds, and helping out in the greenhouse, proudly wearing his green and gold Notre Dame baseball cap. In the final days of summer, Bach helped organize an outing for Notre Dame students from the surrounding area at Lake Vermillion. Now, it was time for school – and football.

ON THE SECOND DAY of practice, September 16, Rockne turned his attention to the tackles and guards. He spent an hour explaining his system of blocking to "about 43 men evenly divided for both positions." Once drills began, several linemen from the '23 freshman squad made their presence known. John McManmon, a big farmboy from Dracut, Massachusetts, was already 190 pounds as a sophomore and showed well at tackle. Dick Hanousek, from Antigo in northern Wisconsin, did the same at guard.

But the man making the strongest bid to play tackle opposite Bach was senior Edgar "Rip" Miller, the fellow from Canton, Ohio who had gone up against Stuhldreher when Miller played at McKinley High School. The handsome Miller cut a dashing figure wearing the latest from Hart, Schaffner & Marx at the latest school dance. He bore a striking resemblance to the young lad featured in the Canton newspaper advertisements for the Homer-Miller Co., his dad's clothing firm. A ferocious tackle, Rip captained the undefeated 1920 McKinley team. In Canton, he was a delivery boy for his father's store and earned extra money as a "soda jerk" and laying cement. He spent two summers in the plains states working on the wheat harvest.

In his three years in South Bend, Rip Miller had made an impression as a sharp student and a strong competitor on the field. He was also a valued teammate whose optimism and attitude could lift up the entire team. He sported a ready smile of bright white, even teeth undamaged by football and his other sporting interest, boxing. With a shock of blond hair, he had a boyish look that belied his toughness. Toughness would be needed as Rip was five inches shorter and 25 pounds lighter than Oberst, the man he was trying to replace.

Rip originally planned to attend Grove City College in Pennsylvania when his uncle, Leo Stock, suggested Miller chat with a local Notre Dame alumnus. The talk was a convincing one as Miller decided to head for South Bend, a town he had never visited. Rip's means of transportation to Notre Dame was "riding the blinds," which meant occupying the snug cramped place behind the coal car. It wasn't much for comfort, but it was free – for as far as the train went, which turned out to be Elkhart – 15 miles east of South Bend. In Elkhart the train yard police picked him up and asked Miller his plans. "I'm going to Notre Dame to try out for the football team." The officer replied, "Get in the car and I'll drive you the rest of the way."

Elkhart would play another part in Miller's Notre Dame years. As a junior, Rip's teammate Russ Arndt was dating Phyllis Templin of Elkhart. On one planned visit to Elkhart, Arndt asked Rip to come along for a "double date," with Phyllis' sister, Esther. Before the pair hopped the interurban, Rip warned Arndt: "If I don't like the girl, I'm holding up one finger, and I'm out of here. Two fingers means I'll stick around."

Neither realized that Esther was only 16, but Rip was smitten with her and before long, Rip was making return trips to Elkhart – with or without Arndt. As the 1924 football season was starting in South Bend, the two young sweethearts said their good-byes as the 17-year-old Esther headed to Simmons College in Boston.

AT THE GUARD POSITIONS, the early favorites were a pair of monogram men, seniors John Weibel and Noble Kizer. Neither was exceptionally big for the position, both about 5-9, 165 pounds. Weibel, a studious, serious son of a physician from Erie, Pennsylvania, took the lead to replace Harry Brown at left guard. In 1924, Weibel balanced football with a rigorous academic schedule set to prepare him for entrance to medical school. Kizer, who came to Notre Dame primarily as a basketball player from nearby Plymouth, Indiana, had split time with Vergara at right guard. Kizer seemed a natural to take over that spot. Vergara was originally scheduled to be part of the 1924 team until it was learned that he played one half of one game for Fordham three years earlier before coming out from the Bronx to Notre Dame. The school declared him ineligible when the news was discovered. Vergara then joined Rockne's coaching staff and completed his course work at Notre Dame.

Kizer, who was active playing and coaching basketball at the South

Bend YMCA, had never played football because Plymouth High School did not have a team at the time. At Plymouth, Kizer had already shown leadership and initiative. He coached the track team and helped coach the basketball team. He dropped out in 1918 to join the Marines and was sent to Quantico, Virginia. After the Armistice was signed in November 1918, Kizer came back to Plymouth and graduated high school in 1919. He began working at the South Bend YMCA to earn money for college. Rockne saw him working out at the Notre Dame gym and was impressed enough to ask Kizer to come out for football.

A key backup at guard was another senior, Charlie Glueckert, better known as Glick. Glueckert was a former star at South Bend High. Glueckert, similar to Rockne, worked after high school rather than going directly to college. He was making deliveries for a local beverage company when Rockne spotted him and, remembering Glick as a local star, asked him to consider joining the Irish.

The potential depth in the line suffered a blow just three days into practice, on Wednesday, September 17, when Glick seriously injured his ankle. He was expected to be unavailable for several weeks. Another setback followed the same evening. Walsh was taken to St. Joseph Hospital for what was called "a minor operation" which would knock him out of the season opener October 4 against Lombard College.

"Rockne's Worries Are Increased By Injuries," read the Tribune headline. But Notre Dame's line woes aside, there was no disputing the fact that Rockne's squad was being touted as among the nation's best. In The Sportlight, Grantland Rice's syndicated column, of September 15, the *New York Herald Tribune* writer looked ahead to Saturday, October 18, when Notre Dame would meet Army, Dartmouth would take on Yale, and Michigan would meet Illinois in "three of the best games of the year. We have an earnest desire to look upon all three contests, and yet so far have discovered no answer to the complication."

Rice went on to note that "Rockne rarely leaves the east without his annual supply of scalps. But the odds are he will have a better Army team to overthrow this fall than he has faced for some time. Wilson alone is half a team."

Rockne was anxious to see how much of a team he had, particularly at the backup spots. He had to wait a day, though, when rain washed out the much anticipated first scrimmage on Friday, September 19. The weather cleared the next day, setting up a brilliant Saturday afternoon at Cartier Field.

In the Tribune, George Strickler, a Notre Dame student reporter, used expansive prose to describe the scene:

"Sun rays, clear white from sheer intensity, beat down on Cartier Field yesterday afternoon like a driving rain of molten lava. In the stands a cluster of curious onlookers gazed in wonder at some 250 athletes, playing and sweating on the long stretch of green before them.

A man, bareheaded and clothed in a uniform symbolic of no particular profession, but strangely different from that worn by other persons in the enclosure, was shouting commands and inspiring these athletes, while other elements seemed to be undermining their morale and ordering a halt.

In the scale with which he was measuring the ability of the individuals at their every turn, time had no specific value for him, just as his goal was neither far nor near. Now he was on his knee studying some particular chap, who had solicited his plaudits a moment before with a startling achievement, not uncommon throughout the afternoon. Now he was racing toward a group of men who had failed in their attempt to execute his commands. Spectators shifted their eyes from him only when some extraordinary event was being enacted in another section of the field. There was something picturesque about him, and worth remembering.

He was, without shouting or advertising the fact, Coach K. K. Rockne, Czar of football at Notre Dame and premier grid specialist of the day. His assignment for the afternoon, as selected by himself, was the directing of the first scrimmage in the Irish camp. Unmoved by the weather or other conditions embarrassing to his charges, he drilled them hard and long. Long after the large stands had been clothed in the blood of the dying sun and the last enthusiastic bleacherite had forsaken his post along the sideline for a more popular position in the university dining room, Rockne was picking flaws in a substitute offensive unit.

At the close of the afternoon's activities, the famous mentor voiced satisfaction over the outcome of the mix-up, declaring his primary objective had been accomplished."

In the scrimmage, sophomores McManmon and Hanousek again impressed among lineman. Another man new to the varsity, Joe Boland, was "also among the better tackle aspirants."
Boland, a huge lad of 6-0, 215, was one of three sophomores who came to Notre Dame from Philadelphia's Roman Catholic High, where they had played for former Irish back Stan Cofall.

With Walsh out, the center position was a battle among a group of lettermen and newcomers. Joe Harmon, a senior of slight stature from Indianapolis, and Joe Maxwell, one of Boland's Philly sidekicks, were among the better candidates.

At the end positions, Rockne only had to replace right end Gene Mayl. Senior Chuck Collins returned on the left side, while Clem Crowe and Ed Hunsinger were backups with experience. Crowe also came from a strong Indiana basketball family from Lafayette. Hunsinger, from St. Mary's High School in Chillicothe, Ohio shared a similar football experience with Kizer in that St. Mary's did not play high school football. Hunsinger's football experience came through playing in Notre Dame's inter-hall league. Rockne counted on Collins, from St. Ignatius High School in Chicago, for the grit needed to play through the tough '24 schedule. Collins showed his mettle when his younger brother fell through the ice of the Des Plaines River, and Chuck led a daring rescue to save him.

In building a line, Rockne would stress to his players that blocking, far from being routine, should be a source of great satisfaction. He felt it was a special man who worked to become an excellent blocker.

"Love to block, and let them know that you like it. If all teams could do just that thing, they would always be winning."

Rockne had two former Irish standouts – Hunk Anderson and Tom Lieb – helping coach the linemen. George Keogan was in charge of the freshman. The athletic director had more help in running the business aspects of the athletic department. And Rockne, who had previously been known to carry a roll of tape and bottle of iodine in his coat pocket, made a bold hire in arranging for a team trainer. At a moment when college football was a virtually all-white enterprise, he enlisted a Black man named Verly Smith to care for the injuries of the Four Horsemen and their teammates. A native of southern Indiana and son of a Baptist minister, Smith became a student of athletic performance and physical fitness. When he lived in Benton Harbor, Mich., he found his way into area boxing camps and served in the corner of heavyweight champion Jack Dempsey for some of his fights in the region.

Rockne consistently praised Smith's work in treating the bumps and breaks, cuts, and contusions of the Fighting Irish. His methods were considered on the cutting edge in the field of athletic training. Smith is thought to be the first Black employee of the university. It is likely, though, that he did all his work on or near campus. There is no record of him accompanying the team to road games, as accommodations would have been an extreme challenge in that Jim Crow era.

Smith was also active as a boxing impresario, staging fights on Friday nights before big Notre Dame home football games. They were a precursor to the campus Bengal Bouts that became a Notre Dame tradition.

Rockne thought back to his summer nights and early fall days when he pondered the lineup. He knew life never allowed the luxury of setting anything in stone. Yet he sensed this 1924 group had extraordinary potential. He had gathered a group that typified what he cherished most: loyalty, respect for the game, spirit and unselfish service. He could see it in all of them starting with his anchor and captain Adam Walsh, whom Rockne felt would solidify the line. Rockne reflected on his four senior backs: Miller, Layden, Stuhldreher and Crowley. Their athletic talent was unquestionable, and their unbridled enthusiasm was waiting to be unleashed.

Everything was ready as the season was about to start. Rockne was pleased, as he had instilled in this group his most trusted idea: "Work, work hard, prepare, and then go."

6
Fighting Back

THE RISE OF Notre Dame football prominence in the early decades of the 20th century coincided with the ascent of anti-Catholic fervor taking hold in the United States. The words 'Catholic' and 'immigration' were almost interchangeable. Notre Dame football did not exist in a vacuum. In 1924, the Ku Klux Klan, the city of South Bend, and the University were destined to cross paths.

The immigration boom of the late 19th and early 20th centuries had left its mark on a changing American landscape by the early 1920s. Between 1900 and 1920 more than 14 million immigrants entered the United States, their origin being Irish, Italian, Polish, Hungarian, Czech, Slovak, and Croatian. The predominant religious background of most of these was Roman Catholic. Along with rich cultural traditions, this wave of immigration also brought with it a backlash from many who feared the loss of "American values." Anti-Catholicism was fueled by the belief that Catholic doctrine and practices pledged an allegiance to a foreign power – the pope.

The United States enacted several laws in the early 1920s to limit the number of immigrants from southern and eastern Europe as well as Asia. The fervor to "close America's doors" culminated in the Immigration Bill of 1924, which was strongly supported by the Ku Klux Klan, who proudly took credit for its passing.

The Klan, as it grew from its southern origins to the Midwest and West, structured itself as a fraternal organization and made huge membership inroads on the local and state political levels, primarily within the states' Republican parties. Indiana proved to be one of the Klan's most fertile growing areas, due in large part to the efforts of David Curtis Stephenson, a transplanted Hoosier who became one of the Klan's top leaders. A man with a flair for the spoken word and who possessed the skills of a successful salesman, Stephenson dazzled crowds from Kokomo to Valparaiso, frequently warning his audiences about "foreign influences in the country."

Stephenson employed innovative communication techniques and used the dissemination of misinformation of American Catholic doctrine to spread the Klan's messages and play on the fears of the population. The telephone became a new marketing tool and when Stephenson took control of the *Fiery Cross*, the weekly Klan newspaper based in Indianapolis in late 1923, he had a built-in audience of 500,000 in Indiana and neighboring states in which to urge his audience to work for "pure Americanism to triumph in America." Klan membership in Indiana reached 400,000 by 1923, and in 1924 it was reported that 30 percent of Indiana's white native-born male population had joined the Klan and that local chapters had been established in all of the state's 92 counties.

NORTHERN INDIANA, AND in particular St. Joseph County with the cities of South Bend and Mishawaka, proved to be major exceptions to the Klan's swelling ranks. Three critical factors that stemmed the Klan's tide there included: the presence of Notre Dame, the large Catholic immigrant populations of the two cities, and the strong anti-Klan position taken by the South Bend Tribune.

The 1924 state political scene offered Stephenson what he viewed as an opportunity to make inroads in an area in which Klan organization was weak. Stephenson and other Klan leaders decided something needed to be done in order to persuade state Republican convention delegates to accept the anticipated primary election victories of Klan-endorsed candidates as politically correct and irrevocable. Stephenson pushed for staging an incident during the two week interval in May between Indiana's primary election day (May 6) and the opening of the Indiana Republican Convention in Indianapolis on May 21. It was hoped that such an event would provide evidence of Catholic aggression and would solidify the hold of Klan-endorsed candidates for state office. The message from the Klan was clear: Proudly show the hooded robes of the Klan, but do nothing to incite the local populace. South Bend proved to be the likely setting for such a confrontation, and when St. Joseph County local Klansmen agreed to host a tri-state meeting in South Bend for Klan members and their families on Saturday May 17, 1924, the stage was set.

It was an uneasy spring weekend for all involved – Notre Dame administration, staff and students, the local South Bend police force, and the Klansmen who arrived via the interurban, car, bus, and street car. Although Father Walsh and Father J. Hugh O'Donnell, CSC, prefect of discipline at the university, had worked with local officials and promised to do what they could to keep students on campus, the large number of students living off-campus at the time proved to be a force that the university could not easily control.

Trouble began early on the morning of Saturday May 17 in the South Bend business district. The Klan would claim 25,000 visiting members in South Bend that day, although police estimates were lower. No matter the number, hooded Klansmen began appearing on downtown South Bend streets and soon afterward, "young men, identified by reporters for the South Bend Tribune as Notre Dame students, traversed the main thoroughfares of the business district. At the same time, bands of young men showing intense hostility to the Klansmen showed up on foot and began surrounding the masked men wherever they could find them. Some of those bands were identified as being composed of Notre Dame students. Others were made up of West Side Polish and Hungarian ethnics. Within an hour, robes and masks had been torn from about a half a dozen Klansmen and several of them had been very roughly handled."

By early afternoon, a large crowd of anti-Klan demonstrators had congregated in front of the local Klan headquarters at Michigan and Wayne Streets and once again a riotous atmosphere prevailed. Mounted policemen broke up the crowd into smaller groups, but the confrontation continued, including one small group who hurled potatoes at the local Klan headquarters.

A mid-afternoon meeting between Notre Dame student leaders and Klan officials at the Klan's headquarters resulted in a truce of sorts. Local officials had denied Klansmen a parade permit, meaning that any Klan march would be breaking the law. By 3:30 p.m. the crowd had dispersed to a large pool room at the corner of Washington Avenue and Michigan Street, where about 500 students heard one student leader plead for vigilance and restraint. The crowd was asked to disperse and return to the Jefferson Blvd. bridge at 6:30 p.m. to prevent Klansmen from coming into the city center from the east to participate in an illegal parade – an event that never occurred.

Stephenson, who had come by car from Indianapolis to South Bend that morning, decided not to push for any more Klan activity or a parade without a permit. In Stephenson's eye, his goal had been accomplished: Peaceful Klansmen had been attacked by Catholic students from Notre Dame and by ethnic ruffians. The Klansmen had been denied their constitutional right to peacefully assemble. No Protestant voter in Indiana need know more than that.

Sunday morning accounts in the South Bend Tribune proved embarrassing for Fathers Walsh and O'Donnell. They had been unable to control the student body, and Notre Dame students had failed to respect authority or behave as Notre Dame men were expected to behave. Even worse, the fathers were helpless to prevent another occurrence. Walsh and O'Donnell's fears were validated within 48 hours. Local Klansmen had reinstalled the fiery electrical cross that had been damaged earlier outside of Klan headquarters. By 7 p.m. on Monday May 19, the Klan was holding a meeting and reports filtered out that a payback to Notre Dame students was being planned. Word spread via phone to the Notre Dame dormitories of a Klan meeting in progress and of Notre Dame students under attack at Michigan and Wayne.

As night fell, nearly 500 students raced onto Michigan Street where they began marching toward the intersection of Michigan and Wayne and right into the Klan "ambush." The South Bend Tribune reported that the Klansmen had dispersed to nearby strategic locations to await the arrival of the students. Also awaiting the students were local police who were on the scene in force. Together they surprised the anti-Klan forces as they neared the intersection of Wayne and Michigan streets. Bottles, stones, clubs, and many other objects were thrown about at random. Police charged the scene and injuries resulted among the demonstrators, Klan participants, police and bystanders. Some were even taken to local hospitals.

By 10 p.m. Fathers Walsh and O'Donnell arrived on the scene and were both appalled and frightened by what they saw. Walsh, who climbed atop a ledge on the Civil War Memorial outside the courthouse, addressed the students within earshot. By midnight most students were back on campus. Relations between the University and city officials were now strained. Campus security was beefed up to include volunteer night patrols by faculty and priests for the rest of May and most of June. Walsh met with Rockne and implored the coach to speak to the student body in Washington Hall the next day on the importance of law-abiding conduct. Following the Washington Hall talk, a pledge to abstain from Klan confrontations in South Bend was administered to the students.

An uneasy calm engulfed the campus and the city from that point. The Klan moved on to the State Republican convention and focused its work on securing the nomination of its members for state offices. Summer months offered students, administration and city leaders a time of respite. After Labor Day would come the state and national election campaigns, the start of a new school year at Notre Dame with record enrollment and the excitement of a promising football season scheduled to begin in early October.

As THE FALL semester began, Father John O'Hara, Notre Dame's prefect of religion, was entertaining ideas on how to counteract the hooligan image of Notre Dame students held by many throughout the country. The Klan had done an excellent promotional campaign since May portraying the picture of privileged Irish Catholic students assaulting innocent American Protestant patriots, and O'Hara knew something needed to be done.

O'Hara had not forgotten the editorial that had appeared in the *New York Times* in December 1923, months before the May incident. The Times tried to inject "humor" into a less than humorous situation: "There is in Indiana a militant Catholic organization…engaged in secret drills. They make long cross country raiding expeditions…worst of all, they lately fought and defeated a detachment of the United States Army. Yet we have not heard of the Indiana Klansmen rising up to exterminate the Notre Dame football team."

Even earlier in October 1923, one New York writer penned the following after Notre Dame's convincing 25-2 win over Princeton: "In every branch of the sport Knute Rockne's pupils gave the easterners a lesson in how this game is played and tonight with the Orange buried deep under the Green, it looks as if it is up to the klan to do something about these happenings."

Father O'Hara and other university officials were keenly aware of the enormous public relations value the University could garner if Rockne's men had another outstanding football season. Winning – and winning in the style of Notre Dame men – could show the American public and anyone who professed to be a reader of the Klan's *Fiery Cross* what Catholics and Catholic education was all about. For O'Hara, the 1924 season became a "spiritual crusade."

Father O'Hara was born in Ann Arbor, Michigan May 1, 1888 and became prefect of religion at Notre Dame in October 1917. O'Hara was the driving force behind the establishment of required religious courses and the inspiration for establishing a department of religion in 1924. He viewed difficulties as challenges – and problems were meant to be solved. He worked tirelessly to promote the Catholic tradition of daily communion as an integral part of the students' lives.

Students embraced the practice of daily communion for many reasons, with higher attendance noted during exam week and lower attendance noted after St. Patrick's Day celebrations. It was said that Father O'Hara could keep a daily birds-eye view of students walking into Sacred Heart Church from his residence window in the tower of nearby Sorin Hall. The nation learned more of the daily communion ritual when the Notre Dame football team prepared for its trip to West Point in November 1921. Paul Castner and Roger Kiley, after taking a look at the calendar, pointed out the obvious, "We'll be on the train First Friday. How are we going to get to Communion?" Castner and Kiley checked the train schedule and noticed a 20-minute stop-over at Albany, N. Y. Father O'Hara dispatched a telegram to a priest in Albany, who made all the necessary preparations. When the team arrived Friday morning, a fleet of limousines was waiting to whisk them away to the Farrell Institute, where they received Communion at the Grotto of Lourdes. Papers across the country carried the story. Notre Dame went on to beat Army, 28-0, with Kiley scoring two touchdowns.

In addition to his unrelenting push for daily communion, in 1921 Father O'Hara founded the *Religious Bulletin*, a daily one page paper packed with messages and statistics to keep Notre Dame men focused on "clean living." The same year he launched the *Religious Survey*, which tapped into his deep respect for scientific research, statistical analysis and data. The Survey consisted of a number of student-directed questions to be answered anonymously. Typical questions on the survey were whether frequent and daily communion had lessened their reverence for the Blessed Sacrament, whether it had helped them to be better Catholics, or whether daily communion had helped the students in their studies. Father O'Hara spent the summer collating the replies.

As prefect of religion, he personally knew many students who regarded him as father-confessor, someone to whom they could confide anything and everything without fearing retribution from the University. His door in Sorin Hall was always open, and the students would bring to O'Hara their problems of the heart, their problems of the pocketbooks and their problems with their studies. He never failed to provide an answer.

But now, O'Hara, the "answer man," looked to Rockne and the Notre Dame squad to provide a piece of the response to the Klan dilemma. This year's football team and season could provide the opportunity to restore pride and dignity to Our Lady's University.

7
The Greatest Curtain Raiser Ever

FOOTBALL WAS A source of great pride on the Notre Dame campus. The winning course of the last several seasons had turned the sports world's attention to the small university in northern Indiana, and the team's fortunes were celebrated by virtually every student. But win or lose, the spirit and effort of the men representing Our Lady's University were attributes to which every Notre Dame man could claim a share. After all, the football men lived among the "regular" students in the residence halls. They ate at the dining halls and attended classes and masses along with the rest of the students.

In the days leading up to the season opener on October 4 vs. Lombard College, the air of anticipation on campus grew to even greater heights. A week before the game, students gave a grand welcome to the newest "keeper of Irish fortunes" – Tipperary Terrence II. The terrier was put under the watch of "Rockne's righthand men, keepers of the gymnasium and custodians of the first mascot, who came to his death under the wheels of an automobile." Terry, as he would be known, was from the same kennel as his predecessor, and, similar to the Tipperary Terrence I, was a gift of the Notre

Dame Club of Toledo, and "from a long line of registered stock."

Everything was ready for the football opener. Walsh, Miller and their mates had done a bang-up job with the game program, which was now headed to the printer. Orders for tickets were flowing into the ticket committee. Reserved ticket prices were announced: $1.50 for the Lombard and Wabash games, $2.50 for the Homecoming game with Georgia Tech on November 1, and $3 for the big clash with Nebraska on November 15. Available box seats would sell for $3 for Georgia Tech, and $4 for Nebraska.

Fans traveling to the games at Princeton, Wisconsin and Carnegie Tech would find a $2.50 reserved admission, while $3 was expected to be the price for the games against Army and Northwestern. "The popularity of Rockne and his cohorts is steadily increasing in all sectors and applications for admissions certificates are being received from all parts of the country," South Bend Tribune writer George Strickler reported.

ON THE FOOTBALL field, Rockne's task remained to develop a strong line. Hunk Anderson, former star lineman and now a pro with the Chicago Bears, arrived on campus September 22. Rockne immediately put Hunk to work with the guards in one corner of the field, while Tom Lieb handled the tackles, and Rockne drilled all the other positions.

Lieb had played tackle on the 1921 and 1922 teams and had become one of Rockne's greatest track stars. Lieb grew up in Faribault, Minnesota, pitching rocks in his family's quarry. The strength he developed there would help him become one of the world's best discus throwers. Lieb held the world record for a time and earned the bronze medal in the 1924 Paris Olympics before returning to campus to help coach the Irish.

Rockne made something of a surprise announcement September 25: there would be no official cut of the roster. He would let attrition take its course and work with everyone who remained.

"The boys who feel themselves outclassed withdraw after an honest try, and retire to the sidelines where they become more intelligent observers and sympathetic critics," the Tribune explained. "Rockne always allows every man to judge his own courage and capabilities."

One reason the coach didn't mind carrying a larger than usual squad was the quantity and quality of the senior class – 22 members of the Class of 1925 were among the top 50 or so prospects, and Rockne wanted as good a look as possible at their potential replacements. In order to handle the size of the squad, Rockne also announced a different approach. Rather than simply having varsity units scrimmage repeatedly against the freshman team, he divided the varsity, putting about 30 players directly under Lieb's supervision. Lieb was instructed to develop an offensive scheme for his unit which would differ from the main varsity. The two groups would be pitted against each other in daily scrimmages.

A week before the opener, Rockne had the varsity squad scrimmage the Mishawaka Athletic Club, a collection of mostly former high school and college players. Rockne used the session to point out errors, particularly mental ones, coupling "each mistake with a statement that generally stimulated the desired action. Every error in line play was cited as it presented itself and even the slips of the famous backfield were not passed by without a half mordant, half pedagogic comment."

The reserve unit traveled to Bourbonnais, Ill., and defeated St. Viator College, 21-0. Livergood, a senior backup to Layden at fullback, led the Irish rushers, while O'Boyle dazzled onlookers with his display of passes. Back with the entire squad, O'Boyle continued to impress with his kicking, "tying Layden and Cerney in many of his boots." Captain Walsh was released from the hospital and returned to his room on campus, but prospects for Walsh playing in the opening games remained uncertain.

IN LOMBARD, NOTRE Dame would face one of the top smaller college units in the Midwest. In the teams' first meeting a year earlier, the Irish had managed only a 14-0 win, handing Lombard its only defeat of the past three seasons. Getting a return crack at Notre Dame was huge for the Lombard seniors, and the game was causing a buzz on the campus in Galesburg, Illinois. Lombard belonged to the Illinois Intercollegiate Athletic Conference, nicknamed the Little 19 Conference though membership surpassed 20 schools when Knox, Lombard's cross-town rival, and Wheaton College joined in 1920.

Coach Harry Bell's team had won the conference three years running, and from 1921 through 1923 amassed a stunning scoring margin of 987 to 103. In addition to Illinois rivals, Lombard had beaten teams as notable as the University of Detroit's Titans. So it was not mere hyperbole when the Tribune's October 1 headline read: "Lombard Regarded as Mighty Foe in Notre Dame Camp."

Lombard's senior quarterback and captain, Roy Lamb, had made an impression with the game he played against ND a year earlier. He led his team in an "open style of football" featuring an "aerial attack worthy of no little consideration" and an "assortment of intricate plays." Nearly all of his '23 teammates were back and eager to spring the upset.

Lombard certainly had Notre Dame beat in one area. Lombard had drilled for six full weeks of workouts prior to the opener, and on September 27 took on Marquette University, itself on a three-year undefeated roll, in a heated scrimmage. Irish assistant coach George Keogan took in the game and reported that "the Lombard's ran wild through the Marquette defense, scoring five times to Marquette's once." Lombard may not have had the cache of later rivals, but the game was being billed as "the greatest curtain raiser ever staged at Notre Dame."

If nothing else, Lombard was certainly a step up from the opening game opponent of the previous five seasons. Kalamazoo College had trudged to Cartier Field five straight times and left with five shutout defeats, to the cumulative score of 229-0, including a 74-0 pasting to start the 1923 campaign.

As the Irish football team toiled under the daily routine of drills, and looked forward to actually playing a game, the signs of readiness abounded on campus. The strains of the Victory March filled the campus, as students loudly sang... "while her loyal sons are marching onward to victory." The tune was now fully established as the school fight song a dozen years after first being performed on campus. The Notre Dame Band, which traced its roots to the 1845 commencement, had suffered through some lean times in the early 1920s, but was bouncing back under the dynamic leadership of a young music department graduate student, Joseph Casasanta. It now numbered 75 strong.

On the Sunday prior to the opener, the Student Activities Council re-elected senior Eddie Luther to be varsity cheer leader, a singular position of prestige and responsibility, central to guiding the school spirit of the student body.

The Luther family had strong South Bend and Notre Dame roots. A number of Luthers, all carpenters, were involved in the building of Sacred Heart Church. Eddie's father, James N. Luther, was part of the crew that drove the eight-horse hitch team that pulled the Golden Dome into place in 1879. James also operated a dairy distributorship and served as superintendent of the city's water works. Eddie was the third oldest of seven children and had spent two years of high school at Holy Cross Seminary before switching to the prep school program at Notre Dame. As a collegian, he was studying law.

Despite living in town, Eddie had no problem being involved in campus activities, and his enthusiasm and spirit made him a perfect choice. He was active in the Blue Circle, the Glee Club, the Knights of Columbus, the Law Club, the Indiana Club, and he served as president of the Off Campus Club.

ON THE EVENING of Thursday, October 2, the campus came alive for the 1924 season. There was a huge gathering to kick off the season, the first time in the school's history that such an event brought together nearly all the 2,000 students for such a rally. The first groups gathered in front of the Main Building at 6:30 p.m., with residents of the Brownson and Carroll Hall wings of the Main Building, along with those of Freshman and Sophomore halls, falling in behind the Marching Band. The procession began toward Walsh Hall, where another group of students joined, and then past the campus post office, where the day students had been instructed to join in.

With the Band keeping the march organized, the assembled students wound their way past Badin, Sorin and Corby halls, with great waves of upperclassmen joining the parade at each stop. With the student body fully assembled, the parade proceeded across campus to the Gymnasium. Once inside, the students first heard from George Bischoff, president of the Student Activities Council, who introduced "master of the mob" Luther. Directing the students in the traditional yells and introducing some new ones, Luther revved up the crowd before serving as master of ceremonies.

Great rounds of cheering shook the walls of the old gym as each of several speakers said a few words. Captain Walsh was first to the podium, receiving a thunderous welcome back from the sick list. Next up was Rev. Hugh O'Donnell, CSC speaking in place of president Rev. Walsh. O'Donnell, who had been at Walsh's side during the ugliness back in May, was enthusiastic about the role of athletics on campus and had just taken over as varsity golf coach. Among his duties this night was to announce the destination of the annual students' football trip. Each year, the university selected one away game, made train and ticket arrangements and accommodated any students who received their parents' permission to travel to an away game.

This year, O'Donnell told the excited crowd, the student trip would be…to Madison, Wisconsin for the Nov. 8 game with the mighty Badgers of the Western Conference.

The evening's principal speaker, Tim Galvin '18, now an attorney in Hammond, Indiana, stressed the need for enthusiasm, support and sportsmanship to make for a successful football season. After brief speeches by Noble Kizer and assistant coach Lieb, Rockne took to the podium and echoed Galvin's remarks. He "pleaded with the students for sportsmanship on behalf of the visiting teams," and cited the positive aspects of the reception Notre Dame had received at Army, Princeton and even Georgia Tech as examples of how to treat visitors. He made a special request for "nothing but the highest respect and sportsmanship" for Nebraska on its November 15 visit to South Bend.

When the pep rally ended, the Notre Dame students poured out from the Gym, anxious to see what kind of team Rockne had assembled.

As for Lombard, the weeks of strenuous workouts brought the players to a level of preparedness that Coach Bell hoped would achieve a victory. Bell was in his first year as the Lombard boss, having replaced Paul Schissler, who guided Lombard in the hard-fought 14-0 loss to ND in 1923. After the 1923 campaign, Schissler made the jump from tiny Lombard to Oregon State University in Corvallis, aided in part by a letter of recommendation from Rockne.

Notre Dame's connection to Corvallis went back to 1911-12, when Sam "Rosey" Dolan coached the Beavers. Dolan, who had come east from Albany, Oregon, to attend Notre Dame, preceded Rockne as a player in 1906-09. Rockne had kept in touch with Dolan through the years.

Rockne also had a fond spot for the Corvallis campus and selected it as the site of one of his coaching clinics in the summer of '24. There, he was able to instruct numerous west coast college and high school coaches, further widening his sphere of influence – and his array of contacts.

SATURDAY, OCTOBER 4, burst out with a hint of fall in the air. In the early afternoon, lines of automobiles snaked toward Cartier Field. Two main approaches to the campus, Notre Dame Avenue and the Dorr road, were closed for paving, leaving only Eddy Street as a means to reach the grounds. The ideal weather spurred a large number of box holders to attend the game, and the boxes in the west stand were a colorful display of finery worn by the men and women of South Bend's leading families.

All told, the stands were about half filled when the game began, and the crowd totaled about 9,000, including an estimated 300 organized Lombard rooters. Several thousand potential attendees chose to head downtown instead and stood in front of the Tribune building, gazing up at the mechanical board showing play-by-play of the first game of the World Series. The New York Giants defeated Walter Johnson and the Washington Senators, 2-1, in 12 innings.

At 10 minutes past two, seven full teams of Notre Dame players streamed onto the field to the delight of the home fans, followed in a few minutes by Lombard's squad of 22. At 2:28 p.m., the 1924 season began as O'Boyle kicked off for the Irish. Notre Dame started its "Shock Troops" with Scharer, Connell and Cerney joining O'Boyle in the backfield, along with an entire second-string line.

After the teams traded punts, Lamb led Lombard to Notre Dame's 25 yard line, and Rockne responded by sending in three of his famous backs, with Layden at fullback, and Crowley and Miller at the halfback spots. Stuhldreher was kept out of the game due to a shoulder injury. Lombard fumbled on a kick attempt, and the Irish were set to go with the ball.

A pair of runs by Crowley and one by Miller lost yardage, and Layden was forced to punt. The Irish held Lombard again, and after Scharer fielded a Lombard punt at his own 23, Rockne sent in the first team line. To nearly everyone's surprise, it included Adam Walsh, only days removed from his hospital stay. His presence lifted his teammates' spirits against the feisty opponents.

But penalties and sloppy play hurt ND, and the punting duel continued. Only when Miller broke loose a run around left end for 20 yards as the first quarter ended did the Irish look as if they were poised to dominate. As the second quarter started, Layden sliced for five yards off tackle, and Crowley added eight more through the same spot to the Lombard 24. From there, Miller dashed through left tackle and into an open field for the first score of the season.

After forcing another punt, the Irish kept up the pressure. Miller raced 21 yards to the Lombard 27. Crowley and Layden advanced the ball deeper. Even after another offside penalty moved the Irish back to the 15, Miller got free around end and again reached the end zone. Crowley's kick put ND ahead, 14-0. Miller and Layden left for subs, and after forcing another punt, ND gave it back with a fumble. Lamb missed a 30-yard place kick, but Crowley then lost a yard and left the game due an injury.

A Notre Dame punt was fumbled by Lamb, and ND's Livergood recovered. Then penalties struck again, with a 25-yard run by Coughlin wiped out. A holding call sent ND back another 15 yards. Late in the half, ND's Red Edwards lofted a 45-yard punt fielded by Lamb, who was swarmed under by the Irish and fumbled. Worse for Lombard, he couldn't get up and was carried from the field with a badly dislocated shoulder. The half ended with ND ahead 14-0 – not an impossible margin to overcome, but Lombard was deflated watching its star and leader hurt and out for the day.

The teams slogged through the third quarter, and even with most of the Notre Dame regulars in the lineup, the Irish could not add to their lead. Typical was a series in which Crowley completed a 20-yard-pass to Collins, only to watch the drive stall due to penalties. Scouts from several of Notre Dame's upcoming opponents viewed the action from the press box. Though poker-faced, they had to be wondering what the problem was with the vaunted Irish attack. But the fourth quarter brought the offensive fireworks many had expected. Lombard's troops were now nearing exhaustion, and it showed.

On the first play of the quarter, Crowley connected with fellow Wisconsinite Ward "Doc" Connell for a 25-yard pass completion, which Crowley followed by breaking through right tackle for a 13-yard touchdown. After another Lombard punt, Connell lit up the crowd by breaking through left tackle and racing 57 yards for a score. Crowley's kick put the Irish ahead, 28-0.

More Notre Dame substitutions entered the game, and the backups relished the chance to show their stuff. On the next Irish possession, O'Boyle broke loose for a 50-yard rumble before being dropped at the Lombard two-yard line. On the next play, Cerney scored on a line buck. In almost no time, Notre Dame powered its way to a 34-0 end. Again ND forced the punt, and on the first play O'Boyle again broke loose from the line and raced 55 yards for the game's final touchdown. When the final gun sounded, it was Notre Dame 40, Lombard 0. It would look better in the papers than it did on the field.

Observers who went into the game wondering about ND's reserve strength were reassured, given the performances of Connell and O'Boyle at halfback, Cerney at fullback and sub quarterbacks Edwards and Sharer. The line play received less favorable reviews, due especially to penalties and to some less than textbook blocking. But the Irish were able to overcome their errors against a squad that struggled all day with the ball and wilted after losing Lamb.

In only a couple of weeks, the Irish would have far less room for error.

8

To Radiate Football Contests

EVERY YEAR UNDER Rockne, Notre Dame had faced at least one in-state opponent. In previous years, the Irish had met Purdue, Indiana, DePauw, Valparaiso and Butler. In 1924, it was to be the Little Giants of Wabash College from Crawfordsville, 30 miles south of Lafayette. The schools' history was intertwined. Jesse Harper, the coach who launched Notre Dame into national prominence, came from Wabash. And Pete Vaughan, another Crawfordsville product, starred at Notre Dame and was now Wabash's coach.

Notre Dame had posted six straight wins in their series against Wabash, the last a 67-7 pasting in 1918, Rockne's first year as head coach. But, an earlier game held greater historical significance.

On October 21, 1905, Wabash scored the lone touchdown and defeated Notre Dame 5-0 on Cartier Field. Since then – 19 years and 75 games – the Irish had not lost on their home turf. The win over Lombard made their record 73 victories, 0 losses and 2 ties. Granted, the opposition was not always stellar. The week after the Wabash loss in '05, ND hosted "American Medical" and after a 25-minute first half, led 111-0. The parties agreed to shorten the second half to eight minutes, supposedly to allow the doctors enough time for a meal before their return train trip to Chicago. Final score: 142-0.

In the ensuing years, there were many more visits from St. Viator, Ohio Northern and Rose Poly than from the region's elite teams. Economics played a part in the situation. Teams, especially those building huge new stadiums, were not interested in a return game to cramped Cartier Field.

Once Rockne became head coach, he used his powers of persuasion to coax an occasional visit from Nebraska or Purdue in return for several Irish trips to Lincoln or West Lafayette. Because of Notre Dame's wide travels to play most of their games against major opponents, newspapers had given the team nicknames such as "Ramblers" and "Nomads."

THE FIRST ATTEMPT to create an enclosed athletic field at Notre Dame included a campaign of letters sent to alumni in 1899, asking for support. None was offered, but in June, 1899, the University decided to go ahead with the project. Warren A. Cartier, a 1887 graduate of the University, was approached with a request to help the project. His answer overwhelmed then-president Father Andrew J. Morrissey, CSC. He offered to supply the lumber needed, build a fence around the field and construct a grandstand that would seat 1,000.

Cartier was part of a successful lumber family in Ludington, Michigan. His father, Antoine, grew up on a pioneer farm near Quebec and was a descendent of the great French explorer Jacques Cartier. Young Antoine made his way to the great woods of Michigan and went into the lumber business in 1853 in Manistee, Michigan, working his way up from the bottom level to eventually become owner of several lumber-related companies based in nearby Ludington.

Warren, the third of seven children, came to Notre Dame in 1883 and graduated four years later. He then returned to Ludington and worked in the family lumber business. His younger brother George followed him to ND and played quarterback on the first team to represent the University in a game of football, against Michigan in the fall of 1887.

Warren Cartier was a respected business and community leader and was elected mayor of Ludington in 1899, with reelection in 1903. During this tenure, he saw the building of the field that bore his name. Over the years, various modifications and expansions gradually enhanced Cartier Field so that in 1924, its seating capacity was approaching 20,000. This capacity would come in handy for the two "big name" home games of the season – Homecoming November 1 vs. Georgia Tech, and the big grudge match against Nebraska two weeks later on November 15.

As the phenomenon of college football swept the nation, it seemed that everywhere one looked, another large concrete stadium with huge numbers of permanent seats was being built. During the 1924 season alone, new stadium dedications were planned at Illinois, Minnesota, Purdue, Marquette and the United States Military Academy at West Point, N.Y., where new Michie Stadium would be opened with a game against St. Louis University Oct. 4, two weeks before the Army-Notre Dame clash in New York City.

As with many such trends, the building of college football stadiums began in the East. In 1903, Harvard Stadium was built, the "first massive structure of reinforced concrete in the world," as well as the first large, permanent arena built exclusively for college athletics in the United States. And it was a multi-sport facility – the Harvard men's hockey team played its games, weather permitting, inside Harvard Stadium for three seasons. Its Roman columns and arches gave it a classical feel, and 40,000 seats provided superb viewing. It was built on the site of a small, dilapidated wood structure and served as an apt reminder of the growth of the sport.

In 1914, Yale endeavored to out-build its long-time rival with the construction of the huge 60,000-seat Yale Bowl. It was the first stadium in the country with stands completely encircling the playing field, and as such, inspired a number of other major stadia in the country, including the Rose Bowl, built in 1922. Princeton, the third member of college football's Big Three, also built Palmer Stadium in 1914. The cavernous horseshoe was constructed with more than 45,000 seats of concrete, and quickly became a famous destination to watch Princeton's fighting Tigers, such as 1922's "Team of Destiny".

The building boom headed west in the early 1920s. In addition to the Rose Bowl, the 75,000-seat Los Angeles Memorial Coliseum hosted its first game in October 1923. In the San Francisco Bay area, mammoth stadiums were built at the University of California in Berkeley (80,000-seat Memorial Stadium) and Leland Stanford University (Stanford, 60,000 seats).

Both Nebraska and Oklahoma opened their Memorial stadiums in 1923, starting with smaller seating capacities of 31,000 and 16,000, respectively, and Colorado was preparing to christen its new 26,000-seat stadium. In the South, a new stadium at Louisiana State University was set to open late in the 1924 season. In Atlanta, additional construction brought Grant Field at Georgia Tech up to 18,000 seats.

BUT IF NOTRE Dame lagged behind other schools in the size and stability of its home stadium, there were other areas in which Rockne's program clearly had the lead. One of these areas was publicity.

More than most football coaches, Rockne keenly understood the value of publicity, especially in major news centers such as Chicago and New York. With so few Notre Dame home games against "name" teams, the big-name sports writers rarely ventured to South Bend. But over the years, Rockne made it his business to get to know and be known by the major scribes, whose stories and columns made it into print in papers across the country. The giants of journalism – Grantland Rice, Damon Runyan, Westbrook Pegler – all knew that Rockne was a good source of copy. By 1924, Rockne had actually joined their ranks, in a way, as he, Pop Warner and Tad Jones of Yale were hired by the Christy Walsh Syndicate to write a series of columns.

Rockne's connections throughout the college football world – via former Notre Dame players now coaching, other coaches he worked with in developing coaching clinics, and writers of all types – put him in an excellent position to dispense the latest information. He was always interested in what others were saying and writing, especially about his teams.

As for the day-to-day news coming out of his football camp, Rockne had developed and pioneered a novel approach – each season, he would hire one Notre Dame student to serve as his publicity aide and be the "source" of news regarding his team. The student writer would have access to Rockne and the team, travel to away games, and pen articles for either or both of the South Bend newspapers, the News-Times and the Tribune, and for as many out-of-town papers as could be enticed into paying a few dimes or nickels per column inch for the dispatches.

The first of these aides was Arch "Archie" Ward, who transferred to Notre Dame after starting college in Dubuque, Iowa. The Irwin, Illinois native was recommended by none other than Rockne's backfield teammate, Gus Dorais. Ward held the job for the 1919 and 1920 football seasons, after which he graduated and went on to start his sports writing career in Chicago. Rockne had arranged for Ward to cover the team for both the News-Times, which published both morning and afternoon editions, and the Tribune, which was strictly an afternoon paper.

Ward tried a delicate balancing act, "saving" some items for the Tribune despite the News-Times' more advantageous schedule. After one season, the News-Times balked at continuing the relationship and asked Ward to write exclusively for one paper or the other. Rockne, displeased at the News-Times' move, advised Ward to stick solely with the Tribune and promised that Ward would receive the best news items, a pledge Rockne usually upheld.

During the 1920 season, with Ward writing exclusively for the Tribune, another aspiring Notre Dame journalist arrived on the scene. J. Francis "Frank" Wallace, an energetic, earnest philosophy major from Bellaire, Ohio, in coal country on the West Virginia border, was hired by the News-Times to cover campus events and inter-hall football, then basketball. He did so dutifully, noticing how much more cooperative Rockne was with Ward.

When Ward graduated, Wallace was offered the job. In addition to covering the team for, at various times, one or the other paper, he began sending out press releases to various papers, paying for the postage himself. By the time he graduated in 1923, Wallace had a wealth of writing experience – in the Scholastic, in the Dome, and for newspapers. He went directly to New York, where he began working as an editor for the Associated Press and continued as an unofficial press agent for all things Notre Dame. Part of that role was conveying information back to Rockne, especially about the two big Eastern opponents, Army and Princeton.

Wallace wrote Rockne in the summer of 1924 and lamented moving on from the fall afternoons spent in Rockne's office, soaking in the wit and wisdom of the coach. Now, in the fall of 1924, the job was the province of George Strickler, a local fellow in his second year at the university.

Strickler had been around Notre Dame all his life. His father was the butcher in the slaughterhouse on the university farm and ran their threshing crew in the summer. Brother Leo, who was in charge of the farm, would bring in cattle from Texas; these cattle were fed and cared for by the elder Strickler, who often turned them into prize-winners at the local stock show before slaughtering them.

Young George showed up at South Bend Central High School in the fall of 1918 and tried out for football. Equipment was each player's responsibility, and Strickler, who had been a batboy for Jesse Harper's ND baseball teams of 1915-16, was able to round up hand-me-downs from Notre Dame athletes. His shoulder pads had been worn by Leo DuBois and came down to his elbows; his pants, once worn by Bodie Andrews, nearly came up to his armpits. Then there was his helmet. Nearly flattened on top, it had several names scrawled onto it, among those – Knute Rockne.

Strickler was a decent football and baseball player. On October 22, 1921, as a warmup to the Notre Dame-Nebraska game on Cartier Field, Strickler did all the kicking for South Bend Central in a one-sided win. A knee injury ended Strickler's football playing days, but Rockne, a family friend, hired him to be his student publicity aide starting in September 1924. Strickler provided daily reports for the Tribune and sold stories to out-of-town papers as he could.

Neither could envision what the next few weeks would bring.

WHETHER IN SOUTH Bend, Chicago, New York or elsewhere, Notre Dame football fans couldn't wait to read the day's papers to find whatever news awaited about the "wonder team" Rockne had built. Following the actual games as they happened was a different challenge.

In just a few years since Pittsburgh's KDKA radio first went on the air in November 1920, the number of radio stations across the United States had grown significantly, along with the number of radio sets. Newspapers carried elaborate articles on building and modifying those sets and improvements were happening so fast, commercial manufacturers could not keep up.

Within its first year of hitting the airwaves, KDKA became the first station to broadcast a live voice-transmission of a college football game when it offered the Pittsburgh vs. West Virginia game of October 8, 1921. A year later, on October 14, 1922, KDKA again broadcast Pitt-West Virginia. On the same day, a game between Carthage College and Culver-Stockton in Carthage, Illinois was broadcast over WCAZ in Carthage and reportedly reached nearly 40 states.

Two weeks later, on October 28, New York station WEAF broadcast Princeton's historic victory over the University of Chicago from Stagg Field in Chicago, using telephone lines provided by the station owner, AT&T. The broadcast did not feature an announcer, but simply picked up the public address announcer at the stadium.

The next Saturday, November 4, 1922, Notre Dame entered the radio age when its homecoming game against Indiana was broadcast by new 100-watt South Bend station WGAZ. Its call letters stood for "World's Greatest Automotive Zone" in honor of the massive Studebaker plant located in South Bend. The broadcast consisted of Tribune sports editor Eugene Kessler's description of each play, phoned to the newsroom, and connected to outgoing "broadcasting apparatus." In 1923, Notre Dame's game against Army at Ebbetts Field was carried by WBAY of New York. The following week, WJZ broadcast the game at Princeton. And KDKA carried the season finale at Carnegie Tech.

In 1924, stations in the East were preparing an ambitious schedule of college football. Under the headline, "To Radiate Football Contests," the New York Times described the new technology:

"Microphones and control apparatus have been installed in all of the big football stadiums, fields and bowls. The radio observer is generally located in a small wooden house, resembling a sentry box, placed above the top row of seats. By means of field glasses he watches the plays and describes them in the microphone. Several other microphones are scattered about the cheering sections so that by throwing a switch the different microphones can be placed in the circuit by the announcer. The pick-up devices and control apparatus connect with telephone or telegraph wires which lead to the broadcasting station, in some cases several hundred miles away from the scene of the contest. Some of the big games will be broadcast by three or four stations."

WEAF, with headquarters on Broadway, set a schedule of weekly games beginning with the Columbia-Wesleyan tussle October 11 from Baker Field and running through the Army-Navy game from Baltimore November 29. Included on the schedule were both big Notre Dame trips east – vs. Army at the Polo Grounds October 18 and at Princeton a week later. Another New York City station, WJZ, and its partner station WGY of Schenectady, New York, announced a schedule which also included both big Notre Dame visits as well.

Elsewhere, WBZ of Springfield, Massachusetts arranged to broadcast all of Harvard's home games, in addition to the Boston College-Vermont match and "the struggle for the Catholic football supremacy of the East between Boston College and Holy Cross" on November 29. In Chicago, KYW began broadcasting all of the University of Chicago's home games from Stagg Field. The Chicago Tribune's station, WGN, planned five broadcasts, including Notre Dame's home game with Nebraska. And Columbus, Ohio stations WEAO and WBAV made plans to broadcast all of Ohio State's games, WEAO carrying five home games and WBAV the road games at Iowa and Illinois.

The station that started it all, KDKA, planned one of the most ambitious schedules, carrying several games involving Pittsburgh, Carnegie Tech and West Virginia. The fans' insatiable appetite to be part of the college football scene that was sweeping the nation created a ready, sizable audience for the work of the pioneering stations. Radio's emergence coincided with the country's exploding interest in following college football.

9
Slaying The Little Giants

FOOTBALL SEASON WAS now in full swing on the Notre Dame campus. The air was silly with flying pigskins. The varsity and freshman teams were now fully formed, and the inter-hall league was underway; even the grade-school boys organized teams and held afternoon practices.

An air of boundless energy and optimism swirled around the campus. These characteristics of buoyancy and confidence had been part of the Notre Dame fabric since Father Sorin founded the university. It had been said of Sorin that he was "always receptive to inspiration from great ideals. In most things, he was spontaneous, quick to decide and react, and above all supremely self-confident in all of his undertakings." One of his major undertakings was to create and sustain an all-encompassing community that eventually included "minims," preps, seminarians, collegians, lay faculty, Holy Cross priests, brothers, and sisters. All had something to contribute to the Notre Dame community.

For more than three quarters of a century, the Minims' School in St. Edward Hall educated grammar school-aged boys who hailed from all parts of the country. The nuns who taught the boys took great pride in providing the lads with a solid Catholic education. Minims typically stayed for a year or two of schooling and an active life filled with both mental and physical education activities. St. Edward Hall was a school unto itself and was best described as being "in" the University but not "of" the University, sharing in all the advantages Notre Dame had to offer.

The minims were permitted to see football and baseball games, track meets and moving picture shows in Washington Hall, when age appropriate. St. Edward Hall afforded the boys dormitory-style life with wholesome food, prayers in the chapel, and lessons in a large study hall. St. Edward Park, on one side of the building, was complemented by a great stretch of the campus, which reached to the lake on the other. The minims, bounding with energy and racing around the campus, embodied the atmosphere on campus before the kickoff for Game 2 in 1924.

The visit of Wabash College's "Little Giants" for Saturday's game at Cartier Field would bring one of the great characters in Notre Dame football history back to campus. Robert E. "Pete" Vaughan was born in Lafayette, Indiana and raised in an Irish-Catholic family in Crawfordsville, home of Wabash. He was a star football and basketball player for Crawfordsville High before enrolling at Notre Dame in the fall of 1908 as a 6-foot, 190-pound fullback.

The next season, Vaughan scored the decisive touchdown in Notre Dame's historic 11-3 upset of Michigan at Ferry Field in Ann Arbor. A legend had developed that Vaughan smashed through the Michigan line with such force that his head broke the wooden goal post. In the 15 years since, he argued that it must have been his shoulder that drove into the post. But that didn't stop the story of how Pete Vaughan broke the Michigan goal post from being repeated on countless occasions – even by president Rev. Walsh.

In 1910, Vaughan had an opportunity to attend Princeton, where he starred for the Tigers, played semi-pro football, helped coach the freshman team and even played some pro basketball. After brief stints as line coach at Purdue and California, Pete was sent to Europe during the Great War and coached football teams of Camp Shelby and the

38th Division of the 152nd Infantry. After the armistice, he continued with the Army in Europe, and on a tour of Belgium explained the game to an interested spectator, King Leopold.

Following his discharge, Vaughan returned to Crawfordsville and began coaching Wabash in both football and basketball. The Little Giants, representing a school of a few hundred students, regularly took on much larger institutions. 1924 was no exception, with games set against Purdue, Notre Dame and Indiana. The season opener was at Purdue, and the Little Giants fell, 21-7. Until then, they were considered every bit as challenging for the Irish as Lombard, with its one-sided winning record of previous years. Wabash did recover and trimmed Monmouth College, 26-7, on October 3.

Similar to Lombard, Wabash would bring to South Bend a team significantly heavier than the Irish. The Little Giants also were known for making good use of the passing game, causing Rockne to concentrate during the week on stopping the overhead attack.

Rockne loosened up the Tuesday practice with a surprise visitor. The News-Times provided this description:

"Press representatives who gained admittance to Cartier Field last night were thrilled at the sight of Rockne's new star, versatile enough to play in the line and backfield with a brand of talent far above reproach. Cameras clicked...as "Snub" Pollard, famous motion picture comedian, went through the paces as full back on the Notre Dame football team. Pollard also gave an exhibition of his ability in the line when he supplanted Captain Adam Walsh in the pivot berth.....Rockne kept Pollard on the side lines during the better part of the practice session for fear of injuries to the find of the season."

On Friday afternoon October 10, 1924, in Washington, D.C., the professional baseball season came to a close when Walter Johnson and Bucky Harris led the Senators to their first World Series championship with a 4-3, 12-inning victory over the Giants. President and Mrs. Coolidge were among the crowd of more than 30,000 that were driven into "an outburst of victory-inspired frenzy unprecedented in the history of the national game." The Wabash team arrived in South

Bend Friday night, greeted by a group from the Notre Dame Villagers Club, an organization of day students. Ed Luther and about 20 other students with cars greeted Coach Vaughan and his 34-player squad and formed a caravan to transport the visitors from the Vandalia station to the Oliver Hotel.

For the second week in a row, the Irish's vaunted backfield would not be intact. Stuhldreher was back from the shoulder injury that kept him out of the Lombard game, but Don Miller, Rockne announced Friday, would be held out of the Wabash game due to illness. Saturday October 11, dawned clear and warm in northern Indiana. By the 2:30 p.m. kickoff, it was a sweltering Indian summer day which, one observer noted, "fired its scorching rays unmercifully into the ranks of the fighting men." An estimated crowd of 10,000 came out in the heat at Cartier Field.

The Shock Troops again started for Notre Dame and completely held the Wabash attack in check, forcing three straight punts, the third from the shadow of the Scarlet goal line. Scherer fielded it and the Irish started from the Wabash 45-yard-line. After Cerney dove for seven yards, O'Boyle hit Crowe with a 20-yard pass and the Irish were in business at the Wabash 11. Three plunges later, Cerney followed Harmon's block in the middle of the line, and scored from the 1.

The Irish held Wabash again, and the Scarlet punted to start the second quarter. Rockne sent in his first unit, with Doc Connell playing in place of the injured Miller. After an offsides penalty and an exchange of punts, the Notre Dame regulars started to get untracked. From the Notre Dame 40, Crowley cut behind Joe Bach and ran for 20 yards. Layden carried twice for another first down. Crowley went wide on the right and broke free for a touchdown, only to have it called back on a penalty. Connell came right back and circled the other end for 11 yards.

Wabash stiffened, though, and a placekick attempt by Stuhldreher sailed wide. After another Wabash punt, Layden boomed one of his own, a 56-yarder that pinned the visitors down at their own 10. Wabash tried to regain the yardage with an immediate punt, but Stuhldreher fielded the ball at midfield and wound 25 yards on the return.

Crowley went wide again for another 10-yard gainer, then Connell drove behind Bach for another nine yards. A penalty on Wabash set up a short plunge by Layden for the second Irish TD and a 14-0 lead. Having secured the lead, Rockne didn't want his regulars to wilt under the unrelenting sun. He sent young Benda in for Hunsinger at end, Hanousek replaced Weibel at a guard, and Prelli gave Connell a rest.

After an exchange of punts, Wabash took to the air and made one six-yard completion. But on fourth down, Hackett was buried trying to pass, and Notre Dame took possession, with Crowley passing 17 yards to Layden as the half ended.

The third quarter became a battle of field position, with Layden consistently outkicking the opponents, and Stuhldreher gaining significant yardage on punt returns. But penalties slowed the Notre Dame attack. Stuhldreher missed another placekick, and two other drives were halted when Layden was stopped by Wabash's Logan behind the line of scrimmage, and when Layden fumbled and the Scarlet recovered on their 20.

Late in the quarter, Stuhldreher was fielding another punt by Parr when he was thrown for a five-yard loss and was injured. Edwards took over at quarterback. A game that might have been a cakewalk was becoming a real tussle. Still leading just 14-0, Notre Dame did not look as if it was ready to take on two Eastern powers the next two Saturdays.

But Stuhldreher's injury seemed to put some life into the boys. Crowley followed Rip Miller's interference for six yards. Layden plowed up the middle for another six. Connell made another eight to close the quarter, and Layden opened the fourth with a first-down run. With the Irish at the Wabash 44 and driving, the sun-baked crowd showed some life. And on the next play, Crowley took the snap and circled wide to the right. Evading a couple of Wabash defenders, he raced the distance for another Irish touchdown and a 21-0 lead.

Wabash, which had every opportunity to reprise its heroics of 15 years earlier, was now a beaten squad. Drenched in sweat and with few substitutes able to offer relief at this level of play, Coach Vaughan's regulars tried to pick themselves up and keep fighting. But after the ND kickoff, it was a minus 6 yards on two plays, then a punt that didn't reach midfield, and a 16-yard return by ND's Scherer set up a short field for the Irish. With the Shock Troops back in, Cerney, O'Boyle and Hearden took turns pounding the ball forward, setting up O'Boyle for another score.

More Irish reserves made it into the game, with Livergood making a good gain and Prelli carrying as well. Reese punted to the Wabash 3-yard line, then returned the ensuing Scarlet punt 26 yards for the game's final touchdown. Notre Dame had prevailed, 34-0. Similar to the Wabash game, ND pulled away from a very tired team in the final quarter.

SCOUTS FOR ARMY And other future opponents left South Bend with mixed reports. At times, the Irish backs worked the shift to perfection and made large gains behind the blocking of Bach, Weibel, Walsh, Kizer and Rip Miller. The punting of Layden and Cerney kept the opposition bottled up in its own end. And on defense, the Irish solved nearly everything sent their way. Yet, a lack of execution at times still remained. So too did repeated penalties, and an inability to crack the defense when it stiffened deep in Wabash territory.

The Rockmen would need a crisper display when they headed east to take on Army and Princeton, not to mention the other major challenges further down the schedule. And everyone was left wondering about injuries. Was it simply a precaution that Rockne held Stuhldreher out after he was jarred on the punt return? And were there any other injuries?

BEFORE HEADING HOME, Rockne tried to gather up as many out-of-town scores as possible. It had been an interesting day in college football. Georgia, coached by former Irish stars Frank Thomas and Harry Mehre, came within one point after touchdown from tying mighty Yale. Princeton was unable to avoid a similar fate, being tied by Lehigh in what was considered quite an upset. Another Eastern power, Gil Dobie's Cornell squad, saw a three-year, 26-game winning streak come crashing down in a 14-7 loss to tiny Williams College.

Army prepared for the Notre Dame game with a strong showing in defeating an always tough University of Detroit team, 20-0. Wood,

Wilson, Gillmore, Hewitt and Yoemans showed why "the West Point cadets seem to have one of the most promising teams in the east." Their counterparts at the Naval Academy had a much tougher result, dropping a home game to Marquette, 21-3. The huge victory extended Marquette's unbeaten streak to 20 games, stretching back to late in the 1921 season, when the Irish trimmed the Golden Avalanche, 21-7, in Milwaukee.

Some fans and scribes were proclaiming Marquette as "the next Notre Dame." In going 19-0-1 in their last 20 games, coach Frank Murray's squad had dispatched fellow Catholic foes Creighton, Detroit and Boston College. The trip to Annapolis put Marquette on the national stage. On the team's return to Milwaukee, thousands of citizens and students gathered at the train station and "every factory, fire and locomotive whistle in the city shrieked" to welcome the team home. A "riotous parade up Grand Avenue to the Marquette gymnasium" and a huge outdoor demonstration followed, with team captain Lavern Dilweg and others making speeches.

"It was declared to be the greatest demonstration (in Milwaukee) since Armistice Day in 1918." The team and the city would take the momentum of that boisterous scene into the upcoming October 18 game, which celebrated the opening of the new Marquette stadium designed to eventually seat 45,000. "In the middle west, it is believed only those of Illinois, Ohio State and Michigan will be larger," offered one report. Undefeated John Carroll of Cleveland was to be the stadium-opening opposition.

Much of the middle west's focus on Saturday, October 18, would be on the big Western Conference matchup between Michigan and Illinois at Champaign where the mammoth new Memorial Stadium would be dedicated. Built with two large decks of seating on both sides of the field, the new stadium was being hailed as the gem of the region. Seating for more than 67,000 was expected to be filled when Michigan came to town. Notre Dame, however, had its eyes on the trip east for the battle with mighty Army at the Polo Grounds.

10
The Stage Is Set

THE PRELIMINARY GAMES now in the books, the stage was set for the intersectional battle of the year – Notre Dame's trip to New York City to play Army at the Polo Grounds. With the World Series wrapped up and the Giants finished until spring training, the ballclub's front office was able to focus on selling tickets to their big college game.

The weekend heat wave in South Bend broke in time for Monday afternoon's practice, and it was a good thing since Rockne had a marathon session planned. It was clear to most anyone seeing the first two games that the Irish would need to show "a decidedly better brand of football" to defeat the Army. In blanking St. Louis University, 17-0, and Detroit, 20-0, the West Pointers had relied primarily on their superior size and strength, using "straight football." The exception came in the closing minutes of the win over Detroit, when the Cadets started "heaving passes in all directions more for practice perhaps than the need of a score."

Straight, power football was what most people expected from Army on a year-to-year basis. Army coaches would point out that they had their charges for fewer hours each week than most college teams, owing to the tightly-structured regimen of the Academy. West Point had one huge advantage over all other teams: the ability to enroll superlative football players who had completed their normal athletic eligibility at their original school. This season, the big-name "new" player was Harry Wilson, the flashy back from Penn State. In the backfield, he joined Tiny Hewitt, former star at Pitt. Wilson, of whom Walter Camp wrote in 1923, "on his good days has no peer," was known for breaking off tremendous runs. Against Navy in '23, he scored on runs of 95, 80 and 55 yards. Against Penn, he went in from 49, 45 and 25 yards.

Coach John McEwan could work Wilson and Hewitt into a backfield that included Gillmore and Wood, along with quarterback Yeomans. Up front, a veteran line was expected to clear the way. Centering the line was the most veteran player on this or any other college football squad, 24-year-old Ed Garbisch. A product of Washington, Pennsylvania, southwest of Pittsburgh, he played four years for his hometown university, Washington & Jefferson, from 1917 through 1920. He was now in his fourth and final year playing for Army, his eighth campaign overall.

This would be his fifth time facing Notre Dame. The first was November 24, 1917 in a battle between ND and Washington & Jefferson, a 3-0 Irish win that marked the end of Jesse Harper's tenure as head coach in South Bend. Garbisch, at 6-feet tall and 185 pounds, was the mainstay of the West Point line, as well as an accomplished place-kicker and drop-kicker. In 1922, he had place-kicked a 47-yard field goal to lift Army past Navy, 17-14. Garbisch was captain of the Army football team, captain of the corps of cadets, and one of the top students in his class. The previous week against Detroit, Garbisch had recorded one of his typically strong performances, "playing a stellar brand of football in line play, kicking and covering punts." With Army ahead 13-0 late in the game against Detroit, the Titans opened up their aerial attack, but Garbisch made an interception and returned it 15 yards for a touchdown. He added a drop-kick conversion to seal the victory.

Going up against Garbisch would be a challenge for an opposing center on any day. Adam Walsh would carry a handicap with him into the battle. He came out of the Wabash game with a broken bone in his right hand. Stuhldreher was fine, but Walsh's injury, which Rockne would carefully keep from becoming common knowledge, was sure to be a major hindrance. There was no question that Walsh would take his normal position against the Army. By now injuries had become part of football for him. He lived for the contact and enjoyed hearing the grunts and groans of an opponent into which he had driven with great force. With only a handful of games left in his college career, Walsh was determined to play on. There would be time to heal later.

THE IRISH PLAYERS sensed that Rockne would demand intense workouts in the three practices before the squad headed to New York on Thursday. Monday's was a three-hour drill, primarily consisting of mental calisthenics. It was a shadow scrimmage, in which the Irish freshmen simulated the Army attack, which used elements of the Notre Dame shift. Rockne drilled his squad on the proper defensive techniques, the responsibilities of each position and the mental focus needed to adapt to the game situation. The mental work, he figured, was much more important than a long, grueling scrimmage. The squad engaged in a more physical workout Tuesday and then worked through another shadow scrimmage Wednesday. This time the team concentrated on perfecting offensive skills, especially the rhythm and timing of the shift.

Wednesday evening, several of the players walked from their halls to Washington Hall, where Brother Cyprian would occasionally show second-run movies. The bill this evening featured "The Four Horseman of the Apocalypse," a drama starring Rudolph Valentino. The film was based on the novel of the same name written by Vicente Blasco Ibanez and propelled Valentino to stardom. Valentino played Julio, the hero of a story based on greed, self-indulgence, love and war set in Argentina and France before the Great War. In the movie's climactic scene, Julio encounters a prophet known as the "stranger" who foresees the end of the world and calls out the Four Horsemen of the Apocalypse from the Book of Revelation. They charge out of the clouds on horseback: the helmeted Conquest, the hideous War, then Pestilence and finally Death. Among those watching Wednesday night's showing was George Strickler, Rockne's young publicist and student newspaper writer who had become a great fan of the movie.

SOME MEMBERS OF the sporting press still expressed doubts about the level of the Irish line play, while other scribes questioned the quality of Notre Dame's reserves. In Rockne's system, developing dependable reserve players was an annual goal. It was never more important than in this matchup with the Army, a team which would outweigh the Irish by a significant margin. The Cadets would be led into battle by second-year head coach John McEwan, a 1917 graduate of the Academy. "Big Mac" was an imposing presence at 6-foot-4 and 200 pounds and had started at center from 1913 through 1916. He had unusual speed for a man of his size, and his exceptional blocking and tackling allowed him to cover large areas of the field. He had crossed paths with Notre Dame and Rockne in his playing days, which coincided with the first four Army-Notre Dame encounters.

As a starter in his first year at West Point, McEwan was at center when Dorais and Rockne made history in ND's 35-13 upset of Army in 1913. In 1914, he played as a "rover" behind the line and gained a reputation for his ability to diagnose and break up opponents' plays. He did plenty of that in Army's 20-7 win over the Irish. An incident in the 1915 game, a 7-0 Notre Dame win, highlighted the competitive nature of both head coaches in the 1924 game.

Notre Dame's starting center in 1915 was J. Hugh "Pepper" O'Donnell – the same man had accompanied Father Walsh downtown to help calm the ND student situation with the KKK. O'Donnell played the 1915 game with a broken rib. Harry Tuthill, the trainer for Army, designed a specially padded shield for O'Donnell prior to the game. As the opposing centers lined up for the first play from scrimmage, McEwan asked O'Donnell which side was injured. O'Donnell pointed, and through the game, McEwan never made contact with the injury. As if to balance this act of sportsmanship, McEwan focused his attention – and aggression – at leading Irish rusher "Dutch" Bergman. Every chance he had, McEwan gave Bergman an extra pounding. After a while, the rough play was evident to all.

Rockne, then assistant coach to Harper, was incensed by the beating

McEwan was giving Bergman. After a particularly nasty tackle near the ND bench, Rockne bolted onto the field to confront the Army center. Big Mac saw him coming and hollered: "Get the hell out of here. You're a coach now, and this is a fight among us players." Rockne retreated. The 1916 battle, McEwan's last, featured the running, passing and scoring of the Army great Elmer Oliphant, the nation's leading scorer. Army scored on a fake field goal late in the third quarter to go ahead, 13-10 and won going away, 30-10. Oliphant gave total credit to McEwan's outstanding blocking for the victory.

Building a strong tradition of athletic excellence at the Academy became the mission of newly appointed Superintendent of West Point, General Douglas MacArthur. MacArthur had served with General John Pershing and as commander of the 42nd Division in France during the Great War. He assumed his new duties in 1919 and commented: "Upon the fields of friendly strife are sown the seeds that, upon other fields, on other days, will bear the fruits of victory."

West Point Chief of Staff of the Army, Peyton C. March, who appointed MacArthur was concerned by reports of the Academy's "weaknesses," and March charged MacArthur with rebuilding the institution. MacArthur was convinced that athletes make better officers in the Army. He embarked on an ambitious plan that promoted the idea of "every cadet, an athlete." While MacArthur served as superintendent, from 1919-22, the number of Army's intercollegiate varsity teams grew from four to 19; intramural sports became compulsory for all cadets, and MacArthur led a move to lure football stars into the ranks of the Corps.

JUST AFTER NOON on Thursday, October 16, a squad of 33 Notre Dame players, along with their coaches, manager Sutliffe and cheer leader Luther, boarded a train at the South Bend's New York Central station. The cheers of several hundred fellow students and townspeople serenaded the entourage. As the train rolled through the Indiana and Ohio countryside, the thoughts of several players drifted to their two previous trips to play Army. In 1922, the Irish made their final visit to West Point's Cullum Hall Field. Included on the squad were then sophomore starters Layden, Don Miller and Ad Walsh and reserves

Stuhldreher, Collins, Weibel, Cerney and Crowley.

The Hudson River valley, in full fall color, was a stunning setting for college football. But the increasing popularity of both West Point football, and especially the Army-Notre Dame game, necessitated changes. Plans began at the Academy for a permanent football stadium, and the game with Notre Dame needed an even larger stage.

Layden recalled the 1922 trip. Notre Dame arrived at West Point on Friday morning, went through a light workout, had a meal at Washington Hall Cadet Mess, and spent the night at an old guest inn on campus. At 6 a.m. Saturday, the entire team was jolted awake by the boom of a cannon signaling reveille. The team followed its predecessors by entering Washington Hall through a rear door and reaching the dining room via the kitchen. This tradition started with the Rockne-Dorais team of 1913, and only once since had Notre Dame used the front door to enter the mess hall – 1916, the year of the 30-10 defeat.

Davenport, Iowa seemed light years away when Layden got the call for the first play of the '22 game, dashing 6 yards. Later in the first quarter, with Stuhldreher in at quarterback for Frank Thomas, Layden broke loose around the right side and sprinted 30 yards to the Army 35. But the Irish drive stalled. The game developed into a bruising battle of hard hitting and rough play. Early in the second quarter, a series of jarring hits caused four fumbles – two by each team – in just several minutes. At the half, it remained a scoreless tie.

Crowley entered the game at left half in the third quarter and had several solid gains. Miller, who caught a flip pass from Stuhldreher over his shoulder, danced his way to near midfield as the quarter ended. On the first play of the final quarter, Crowley sliced off tackle but without the ball. Stuhldreher had masterfully hidden it, and popped up to complete a pass to McNulty at the Army 25. From there, Crowley slipped through a hole created by Gene Oberst for 12 yards. Miller's run around left end and Castner's blast took the ball to the 4-yard-line. The Cadet line braced for the next charge.

Crowley, deep in formation, churned forward until stopped by the Cadet line, which forced a fumble. Army recovered but could do little against the tough Irish defense and the Cadets were forced to punt. After three Notre Dame incomplete passes, the Irish were forced to punt again. This time, Army's Storck deflected the punt straight up, and Breidster recovered for West Point on the ND 43.

Three plays netted just six yards before Army called a timeout to plot strategy. Garbisch trotted back onto the field to attempt a 44-yard placekick that sailed straight and end-over-end but fell short of the crossbar. Racing the clock, the Irish advanced into Army territory, and on fourth down, Castner attempted a drop-kick from 55 yards for the win. The Army line surged one more time and blocked the kick. Army recovered the ball as darkness enveloped the field. There was even talk of calling the game, but the Cadets had time for one final push.

Army's Wood went back to pass and was smothered for a 20-yard loss. A final desperation, fourth-down pass from Smythe to Lawrence advanced the ball to ND's 28. All that remained was time for one last game-winning field-goal attempt. Garbisch set up for a 40-yard kick from a difficult angle. The Irish defensive line, which had matched Army all day, was not about to let the Cadets score on the last play of the game. The kick was blocked, and the game ended in a scoreless tie.

WHEN THE 1923 football season started, all that was certain about the October 13 Army-Notre Dame game was that it would not be played at West Point. The actual site remained a question. The World Series between the Giants and the Yankees meant the Polo Grounds and the new Yankee Stadium would be in use. The Brooklyn Robins offered their stadium, Ebbets Field, and representatives of both schools agreed.

Unlike Notre Dame's other visits to West Point, which earned the school a guarantee that had gone from $1,000 in 1913 to $5,000 in 1922, the game in Brooklyn carried more financial risk. West Point was on the hook for the stadium rental, and Notre Dame had all of its travel expenses at stake. Any worry was a waste of time. A capacity crowd of 35,000 packed the stadium, with thousands more mobbed outside hoping to gain admission. The great crowd slowed the march of the Corps of Cadets from Prospect Park Plaza to Ebbets Field. When the Army team, which outweighed their counterparts by an average of 15 pounds per man, took the field, "they looked like giants compared with the Rockmen," said one observer. On this day, it would be the guile of Irish quarterback Harry Stuhldreher and his mates that would confuse Army and dazzle the spectators.

The teams parried via punts in the early going, including Layden launching one on first down from the shadow of the ND goal post. Army had the first scoring chance, but Garbisch misfired on a drop kick from the 15. The Cadets' next charge into Irish territory was stopped when Wood's pass was intercepted by Crowley on ND's 20. Early in the second quarter, ND was moving when Stuhldreher hit Don Miller for a long gain to the Army 20. Miller then faked a kick and ran for 10 yards to the 10. Three rushes gained four yards and on fourth-and-goal at the 6, Stuhldreher stepped back to pass, eyeing Crowley and Miller to one side. Army defenders converged on the pair, and suddenly Stuhldreher pivoted, spotted Layden alone on the other side, and hit him for a score. It was the first touchdown of the season Army had allowed, after shutting out Tennessee (41-0) and Florida (20-0).

Army threatened late in the half, but was stopped when Layden intercepted Smythe's pass at the Notre Dame 30. The half ended 7-0, Notre Dame. The crowd, buzzing at halftime, marveled over the play of the four ND backs. Their shiftiness, speed, deception and daring were all as advertised. Up in the lines, it had been a brutal matchup, with several players from each side laid out on the turf.

The game's grueling style continued in the second half, with several more stoppages for injuries, and Army was penalized 15 yards at one point for slugging. Each team looked for the field advantage with punts on any down, and the Irish ran with some success after faking kicks. Despite its strength on the line, Army was unable to break free. The Cadets needed a big play, and midway through the final quarter, Garbisch intercepted a Crowley pass on the Army 30-yard-line.

Three plays later on a long Army pass attempt, Crowley turned the tables, picking off the ball and slipping past several Cadets racing to the Army 24. Sleepy Jim added 17 yards from scrimmage on the next play, setting up the Irish at the Army 7. Don Miller took the next snap and faded into pass formation. He executed the fake perfectly, and once West Point's defense was diffused, he whirled and dodged his way into the end zone. The extra point was missed, but ND had a 13-0 lead with little time left.

Army's Wood tried some desperation passes that fell incomplete. For the game, Army was 0-for-11 on passes, compared to Notre Dame's 4-of-6 for 89 yards. All told, the Irish had outgained the Army, 254-49, and had 13 first downs to Army's 2. The team was welcomed back to South Bend with a raucous display, with five thousand folks jamming the area around the New York Central station. A parade escorted the team to the Elks club building, where an organized demonstration was held.

The seniors on the '24 ND team knew the feeling of such a triumphant return. Could the feat be repeated?

11
A City Abuzz

BACK IN SOUTH Bend, excitement for the game had been building all week. For students, Saturday began as usual, with classes until noon. An hour before game time, the entire student body would pack the dirt-floored Fieldhouse, just east of Washington Hall. They would come to "view" the game on the grid-graph, an innovation first used for major away games in 1922, provided by the Student Activities Committee.

A large rectangular glass-like screen was marked off with the lines of a football field. A student would hold a flashlight behind the screen to indicate the progress of the ball. Student runners would receive updates on the game at the Western Union telegraph office, on the ground floor of the Main Building, and race what seemed to be the length of a football field to the Fieldhouse and give the details to the "light man." The university Band would play before the game and during breaks, and the atmosphere was lively and loud. Admission was 25 cents.

A few days before the Army game, the South Bend News-Times announced, in news stories and large advertisements, that it too would offer a grid-graph covering the big game, at the Palais Royale, a downtown dance emporium. The News-Times also charged 25 cents, "to cover the cost of the special wire from fields far from this city… the direct wire to the field will enable the play to be reproduced just a few seconds after it is received." In past years, the News-Times had offered updates of away games via an announcer with a megaphone outside the newspaper's office. The paper promoted the grid-graph so fans could be out of the elements and follow the big game. At the Palais Royale, there would also be music throughout the afternoon, provided by the Miami Lucky Seven Orchestra.

ON THE TRAIN, the ND entourage could read what other folks were saying about the upcoming Army tilt as well as what was happening around the country as passengers, who boarded along the train route, shared their copies of local newspapers. Two stories caught the attention of players and staff.

In Anderson, South Carolina, the entire 1200-man student body of Clemson College "went on strike" to protest the suspension of Butch Hoolohan, football captain and senior class president. Hoolohan had been suspended after presenting the school with a petition, signed by hundreds of students, complaining about the quality of food on campus. A faculty committee claimed Hoolohan was intoxicated when he presented the petition. And in Morgantown, West Virginia, Gordon McMillan, star kicker for West Virginia University, was fighting for his life. He was taken ill Wednesday and was battling a septic sore throat, pneumonia and other complications. The Irish players, even Walsh and Stuhldreher nursing their wounds, could give thanks for their health and the relative calm that embraced their daily lives on the ND campus.

For Eddie Luther, the cheer leader and South Bend native, riding on an overnight train with meal service was both a thrill and a challenge. He had never previously ordered food on a train. When the waiter came, Luther gave Rockne a worried glance. "Get a poached egg," advised Rockne. "There's no such thing as a bad poached egg."

IN NEW YORK City, tickets for the game were disappearing fast. The Giants were selling tickets from their offices at 15 West 44th Street, the Spaulding & Bros. stores at 105 Nassau St. and 523 Fifth Avenue, and the Winchester Store at 47 East 42nd Street. In the final days leading up to the game, the ballclub had to dispel a rumor that standing-room tickets would be sold, and another that the game was already a sellout by midweek. On Friday morning, several thousand seats remained. Steady activity at the various locations throughout the city quickly reduced that number. Close to 60,000 people were expected at the event.

Despite the anticipation of being on such a huge stage, this was not Notre Dame's first visit to the Polo Grounds. In an unusual scheduling move in 1921, Rockne had agreed to face Rutgers at the famous baseball park on a Tuesday afternoon, November 8, following a game at West Point on Saturday, November 5. The Irish routed Rutgers, 48-0, in front of 12,000 spectators.

Much like the Army-Notre Dame series itself, the Polo Grounds was steeped in history. A massive edifice tucked between the Harlem River and a lofty outcropping of mica schist known as Coogan's Bluff, the stadium was built on land that was originally granted to John Gardiner in the early 1700s by the British Crown. By the late 1890s, one of Gardiner's descendants had married James J. Coogan, for whom the bluff was named. Coogan became Manhattan borough president in 1899.

The 1924 Polo Grounds was really a continuing history of four stadiums. The original stadium was built in 1876 and was the only one on which polo was actually played. It stood on the corner of 110th Street and Fifth Avenue, just north of Central Park. John B. Day, the owner of the Giants in the late 1880s, searched for a home for his team, moving them from Staten Island to their new location, just off the Harlem River in the southern half of Coogan's Hollow in Manhattan, at 155th Street and 8th Avenue. This ballpark was referred to as Manhattan Field.

In 1890, Day built the "New Polo Grounds" immediately to the north of Manhattan Field. On Friday, April 14, 1911, a fire of unknown origin consumed the wood structure, leaving only the steel uprights in place. The Giants decided to rebuild on the same site, and construction of a new concrete and steel structure began on May 10, 1911. By late June, fewer than 11 weeks after the wooden Polo Grounds had burned, the new stadium was ready for baseball.

Renovations begun in November 1922 were completed in September 1923 and gave the Polo Grounds its final familiar look. The facelift was completed in time for the Polo Grounds to host a record-setting crowd of more than 82,000 for the world heavyweight title fight in which Jack Dempsey defended his championship with a second-round knockout of Luis Firpo, who had gained fame as the "Wild Bull of the Pampas."

The train carrying Notre Dame pulled into the New York Central station about mid-morning Friday, and the team had breakfast at the Belmont Hotel before being ferried by vehicles through the Bronx and up the Boston Post Road to their headquarters at the Westchester-Biltmore Hotel at Rye, New York. The pastoral setting was to Rockne's liking since it lacked the noise and distractions of the big city. He took the squad through a signal drill on the hotel's polo field Friday afternoon.

About 30 miles to the northwest, along the Hudson, the cadet corps at West Point was going through its typical days of classes and drills. After a late afternoon football practice, the squad prepared to board a bus for the train station. The cadet corps assembled in front of the barracks and gave the team a rousing send-off. The traveling party included the players, Coach McEwan, and his unusually large staff of five assistant coaches, some of whom had played a role in two of Army's previous victories over the Irish.

Robert Neyland, a Texan who was commissioned an officer in the Corps of Engineers and served in France in the war, was the starting left end in the Cadets' 20-7 triumph in 1914. Gene Vidal, who came out of the University of South Dakota, was a fleet halfback who scored three touchdowns and drop-kicked a 45-yard field goal to lead Army to its 30-10 win in 1916. Vidal was also a star trackman, participating in the 1920 Olympics at Antwerp. He helped coach the United States' pentathlon and decathlon teams in the recently completed Paris Olympic Games.

The Irish arrived in a city bustling with activity, where monumental achievements were nearly routine. Earlier in the week, officials of the "Highway under the Hudson" announced a major milestone in building the tunnel expected to double the amount of traffic carried between New York and New Jersey. The two sections of the north tube, begun by teams of diggers and muckers four years earlier, would be joined by November 1. At 9,250 feet, the tunnel was considered "the most important work of its kind in the world." The Presbyterian Hospital and Columbia University laid out plans for the world's biggest hospital complex, with a price tag of $20 million, on a 20-acre site at 168th and Broadway. Presbyterian had been founded 52 years earlier by philanthropist James Lenox, who was "indignant because an old negro servant, who was ill, could not find admission into any hospital because of her color."

At Grand Central Palace at Lexington Avenue and 46th street, the New York Edison Company was sponsoring the Electrical and Industrial Exposition, where electric trucks, electric elevators, electric refrigerators and "a wide variety of household applications" would be on display. A highlight of the two-day show was the appearance of the great inventor, Thomas Edison, himself. The gigantic Gimbel's Department Store was celebrating Founders Day, in honor of Adam Gimbel, who opened his first Gimbel trading post in 1842 in Vincennes, Indiana – the same year Father Sorin left Vincennes to found Notre Dame. Now the "House of Gimbel" dominated downtowns from Philadelphia to Milwaukee.

The biggest buzz of all in the great city was over the arrival of the German-made dirigible ZR-3, which commanded front page headlines tracking its epic maiden voyage from Friedrichshafen, Germany to Lakehurst, New Jersey. "Z" stood for lighter than air. "R" stood for rigid construction, and the 3 indicated the model type. Captained by Dr. Hugo Eckener, the ZR-3 represented the height of technological advancements and the hope of future air travel.

Averaging 55 miles per hour, the ZR-3 captivated the nation. Citizens tracked the ZR-3's daily progress and The New York Herald Tribune screamed headlines of its nearing arrival and confirmed radio contact on October 14. Other papers carried editorials stating that if the ZR-3 landed safely, it would hail the dirigible as "making a step forward in the development of regular transoceanic air service. Not to be overlooked was the fate of the British-built ZR-2, which blew up over Hull, England with the loss of 62 lives, or the airship Roma, a dirigible acquired by the United States from Italy that crashed near Hampton Roads, Virginia with the loss of 35 lives. More than 400 sailors and marines were on hand to safely ground the ZR-3 into its New Jersey quarters as it landed on Thursday Oct. 16. The New York Times reported that when it circled Manhattan, "people dropped what they were doing, crowding to see it." Football was but one of many news items captivating city residents.

FANS UNABLE TO attend the game were making plans to listen to the game on either of the two radio stations providing live coverage. On WEAF, Graham McNamee would be announcing. On WJZ, J. Andrew White would have the call. The 36-year-old McNamee had worked as a railroad clerk and salesman for a meat-packing company while pursuing his love of music. He had sung as a baritone on several stages, but was without engagements and out of cash when he wandered into WEAF's studios in 1923. He was hired as an announcer and singer.

White had become a familiar voice on WJZ and held the distinction of calling the first live broadcast of a prize-fight. Billed as the "Battle of the Century" between Jack Dempsey and George Carpentier, it was staged from Boyle's Thirty Acres in New Jersey in 1921. Seconds after describing Dempsey's knock-out punch, radio transmission lines blew and the broadcast abruptly ended.

Many of those nestled in front of their radio sets would be families of Irish Catholic descent. Immigration and the rise of Catholicism in New York City had gone hand-in-hand during the last part of the 19th century. In 1850, 80 percent of the Irish-born Americans lived in the Northeast, and as late as 1920, approximately 90 percent of first-generation Irish-Americans resided in urban areas, chiefly in the Northeast. Their numbers helped swell the rolls of Catholics in the region. The Archdiocese of New York City now boasted more than 1.3 million Catholics, the largest ethnic groups being Irish and Italian. Close-knit Catholic communities, anchored by the local parishes and the nuns who taught in parish schools, dotted the city's landscape from lower Manhattan and East Harlem to the Bronx and Staten Island.

Being Catholic and "American" was a source of pride for the immigrant wave and their first generation American-born children.

New York's Catholics were especially proud of their Irish-Catholic governor, Al Smith, dubbed the Happy Warrior. Smith had risen to New York political prominence from a poverty-ridden childhood in the lower east side of Manhattan. When New York City hosted the 1924 Democratic National Convention at Madison Square Garden, it appeared Smith would have a legitimate shot at becoming the first Catholic candidate for president. The twice-elected governor was backed by powerful Eastern urban elements of the party.

The political role of the Ku Klux Klan remained as strong on the national stage as it was in Indiana, and the 1924 convention earned the nicknamed "the Klanbake" because of the strong influence the Klan wielded in naming the 1924 Democratic presidential nominee.

Franklin Roosevelt put Smith's name into nomination at the convention, and Smith was immediately a serious contender for the party's presidential nomination. Smith's major opponent was Klan-backed candidate William G. McAdoo. Smith's Catholic faith brought strong opposition from the Klan and western delegates who backed McAdoo. The convention, which lasted from June 24 to July 9, featured an unsuccessful attempt by the Democratic Party to pass a platform plank condemning the Klan – it failed by one vote. On July 4, 1924, thousands of Klansmen converged on a nearby field in New Jersey, where they participated in cross burnings, burned effigies of Smith and celebrated the defeat of the anti-Klan plank.

"This convention," wrote H.L. Mencken, "is almost as vain and idiotic as a golf tournament or a disarmament conference." After 15 days of stalemate, the name of former West Virginia congressman John W. Davis was put into nomination as a compromise candidate. Davis, the former ambassador to the Court of St. James, finally secured the nomination on a record-setting 103rd ballot. Al Smith left the convention to seek re-election as New York's governor.

Just weeks before the Democratic gathering, the Republicans re-nominated President Calvin Coolidge at their convention in Cleveland. Perhaps the most notable occurrence at the convention was the advent of the radio as a major communications force. Radio station schedules had to be flexible, so most booked soloists and readings so they could easily switch back and forth to Cleveland as events warranted. An AT&T publicity statement read:

"This will be the first occasion that a program will be supplied continuously to twelve cities, enabling stations at these points to broadcast such features of the Convention as they desire to make available to their respective radio audiences . . . An announcer will be in constant attendance with concise and vivid descriptions of the events taking place in the Convention Hall and explanations of the significance of what is going on. The announcer will introduce the various speakers so that the entire matter will be an interesting broadcasting program."

Radio broadcast of the convention was noted everywhere. Schools across the nation closed to allow students to listen, radio demonstration rooms in department stores were packed with people, and sales of radio sets hit record levels. For the first time, the American people were able to "look in" on a national political convention.

The Democrats, not to be outdone, rescheduled some of their major speeches for a more favorable evening broadcast on radio. Roosevelt received high praise for having a "radio voice" after his fiery speech to nominate Smith. The worst performance was given by 64-year-old William Jennings Bryan, the Democratic candidate in 1896, 1900, and 1908. A renowned orator of the old tradition, Bryan was used to wandering around the stage. He wouldn't stay inside the railings near the microphone and lost his radio audience for most of his speech.

Radio played a role in keeping the nation intrigued with convention happenings despite the drawn-out, drama-filled days in New York before Davis' nomination. The nation listened attentively to its political leaders. At Sing-Sing prison in upstate New York, loudspeakers were set up allowing the prisoners to listen in as a special treat on July 4. In New York City, one cab driver increased business by putting a radio and two headsets in his car.

In the days leading up to the big game at the Polo Grounds, the National Democratic Campaign Committee officials hired the Balloon

Advertising Co. to paint a 50-foot-long blimp with the names of Davis and Smith and to fly it above what was expected to be a huge crowd. W. G. Coogan, owner of the field, intervened and nixed the idea as unsafe. "It would be dangerous to let that fly over this crowd, and I won't permit it," Coogan said. Party and balloon company representatives insisted the craft, formerly an Army blimp, had been declared safe after inspections by the police and fire departments, but Coogan would not be moved. No blimp on game day, he ruled. He agreed to allow a test flight Sunday above an empty stadium.

On Friday evening, Notre Dame spirit was riding high at a meeting hosted by the NYC–ND club at the Inter-Fraternity building at Madison Avenue and 38th Street. Club president John Balfe presided over the gathering, at which alumni and fans rehearsed songs and cheers. The highlight came when Coach Rockne addressed the gathering, giving his assessment of both upcoming games against Army and Princeton.

12
October 18, 1924

SATURDAY, OCTOBER 18 dawned sunny and pleasant in New York City. The Irish bused into the city from Rye for Mass followed by breakfast at the Belmont Hotel. Conversation was minimal. The task was at hand. By late morning, the subway lines came alive with the bustling activity generated with the arrival of college football fans. Some fans arrived by exiting the subway station at 155th Street; others approached the stadium from atop the bluff along the Harlem River Speedway, descending a series of ramps that brought them to the ticket booths. Another set of ramps led fans down to the lower seating levels. Fans came across the Hudson River from the Bronx via the elevated trains of the Macombs Dam Bridge and the Putnam Bridge. Many entered on the Eighth Avenue side.

Fans carried pennants, lunch boxes, and jackets. Throngs arrived from a distance and appeared as columns of determined ants converging on the great stadium from several directions. The ticket booths were jammed by customers who hadn't availed themselves of the advance ticket sale. Spread below was the green grass and green grandstands of the Polo Grounds. It was almost as though the Emerald Isle was smiling on the Irish. But the crowd would be composed of a variety of people. Some, like the Irish-Americans eager to see Notre Dame, were true partisans. Others were drawn by the prospect of seeing two powerful gridiron elevens match wits, strategy and strength. And still others looked forward to the great spectacle and pageantry of the day.

The Polo Grounds sported a patriotic theme, with red, white and blue bunting decorating the façade of the upper deck left over from World Series. The Army team made the short journey from the Hotel Astor while Notre Dame entered the city from its headquarters at the Westchester Biltmore Club up in Rye. Back on both campuses, Saturday morning classes went on as usual for the non-varsity football students. After classes, the corps of cadets boarded a special train, which would take them as far as High Bridge, near the Polo Grounds, to begin their formal march. At Notre Dame, students would jam the gymnasium an hour before kickoff, enjoying the sounds of the Notre Dame Band.

AT TEN MINUTES after two, as many in the huge crowd were settling into their seats, the ceremony began. From deep in center field at the east, or "open" end of the horseshoe, the huge gate slowly opened. To the roar of the crowd, in marched the West Point Band. They played grand marches as they led the corps of cadets onto the field. Column after column of gray-clad cadets entered the stadium, and they made an immediate right flank and continued to march along the north stands. The "long gray line" marched with crisp precision, their arms swinging in seemingly-effortless unison. Toward the west end they spread and then turned and paraded along the end zone behind the goal posts. Another "left flank, march" and they continued to their destination, at the midpoint of the south grandstand. All along the route, the 1,200 cadets were greeted by loud, sustained cheering.

After the cadets took their places in the seats, forming a solid block of gray in the midst of the grandstand, their star performer arrived. Bessie the mule was led onto the field by Cadets Hopkins and Nobel and was greeted with a riotous welcome by the corps. She was bedecked in a gray blanket with gold piping and a large "A" framed by stars.

EARLIER IN THE WEEK, the Notre Dame Club of New York City had offered an invitation to President Coolidge to be their guest at the game, but his schedule didn't allow it. The highest ranking civilian in attendance was Secretary of War John W. Weeks, a graduate of the Naval Academy. Accompanying Weeks was West Point military hero, Major General Robert Lee Bullard. He graduated from West Point in 1885, saw action against Geronimo in 1886, and eventually became commander of all National Guard forces along the Mexican border. In the Great War, Bullard served as commandant of the infantry specialist schools in France, and then commander of the 1st Division, which he led in the first independent U.S. attack of the conflict at Cantigny in May 1918.

By now, Coach McEwan had led his troops onto the field for a brief warm-up, then back into the dressing room for final plans. Rockne's squad hit the field with full force, with three full elevens breaking off a series of dummy plays in perfect formation. Every ten yards, the men would set themselves, await the signal, then erupt in motion for another "first down." The crowd, which now filled the place to capacity, loved the show.

At zero hour, two-thirty, referee Ed Thorp blew his whistle and called the captains together at midfield. Adam Walsh, right hand in a cast, greeted Ed Garbisch with a left-handed handshake. The two warriors had great respect for each other. As referee, Thorp too commanded great respect. At more than six feet and 200 pounds, he was a towering presence, and his intricate knowledge of rules and sense of fair play made him among the most respected of football officials. A graduate of Manhattan College, he also took studies from Columbia and was well known to coaches and fans throughout college football.

NOTRE DAME WON the coin toss and elected to kick off. A great roar reverberated through the horseshoe as Stuhldreher drove his foot into the ball from midfield. Army's Gillmore, showing the expected nervousness in this setting, took the kick at the 15 and momentarily fumbled it before regaining possession. A minute later, Stuhldreher would do the same thing, in fielding the first of Wood's punts.

Both teams started cautiously, like a great pair of heavyweights parrying and thrusting, seeking the opponent's strategy. Depending on field position, they might run only one play from scrimmage before punting, in the hopes of pinning the opponent deep in its own end. Every play was a fierce skirmish; every yard was hard-won. On one of the first plays of the game, Walsh went to block Garbisch, but the wily cadet jumped like a rabbit to avoid the hit. When he came down, one foot landed squarely on Walsh's left hand, Garbisch's cleats carrying the weight of the 180-punder. Walsh felt a searing pain radiating from his hand. This can't be happening, he thought to himself. The game meant everything to him and his fellow seniors. The pain wasn't subsiding, but it had to be overcome. Somehow, he willed himself to continue.

Army showed the first signs of offensive life. A short, low punt by Layden was returned by Yeomans 15 yards to the West Point 25. Wood found room to run through the right side of the Notre Dame line, and Yeomans also circled right end Hunsinger for a Cadet first down at their 45. But, as he would so many times, Walsh stopped Gillmore's effort at center, and Wood ended up punting again. After another exchange of punts, Notre Dame's famous backfield started to get untracked. All four were now in the game, having replaced Shock Troops such as O'Boyle and Cerney.

Crowley tried circling left end. Then Layden followed Rip Miller at right tackle and picked up eight. Miller found the same spot and rumbled for 10 yards, putting the Irish into Army territory for the first time, at the 48. The ground game seemed to be working, but Stuhldreher wanted to mix it up and called for a delayed pass. After faking a handoff, he threw across the field to Layden, but Army wasn't fooled and the result was a big loss. The Cadets took over the ball on downs near midfield. Wilson, the Penn State All-American, was now getting his number called with regularity. He rolled off right tackle for three yards and then caught a short third-down pass and banged for a first down at the Notre Dame 36.

Army sensed it was time to strike for a score. Wood faded back and unleashed a long pass toward the Notre Dame goal. Wilson broke free and got his hands on it, but dropped the ball at the Irish five-yard line. Undeterred, Wilson ripped off a six-yard rumble through the line, only to have it wiped out by an offside call. Then Yeomans tried to take to the air again, but was thrown for a two-yard loss by backup right end Wilbur Eaton, who had come in to relieve a beleaguered Hunsinger.

On fourth down, the Cadets rechecked their blocking assignments and then set up for a placekick by Garbisch. The ball was snapped and the lines collided. But the snap had gone directly to Garbisch, who took off around left end. Picking up steam, he raced past a surprised ND defense and rolled to the Irish 25 – one yard short of the first down. The ball went over to Notre Dame. The Irish lost two yards, then gained five, before Layden launched a punt that traveled nearly 50 yards, to the Army 25. Yeomans fielded the kick, eluded Collins and ran 15 yards to the 40.

Again, West Point rode the many talents of Wilson. First, he got the ball on a delayed pass and went for eight yards around left end. Then he charged through the line for another five, into ND territory at the 48. Gillmore powered for two hard yards, then hurdled the line for five more. But the Irish stiffened, and the scoreless quarter ended with Army facing fourth down. This time, Garbisch set up for a drop kick and got it away cleanly, but the ball sailed wide of the upright. Notre Dame took over at its 20. Aware they were fortunate to still be tied, the Irish gathered with a new resolve.

Crowley took a reverse handoff from Miller, darted through an opening and broke free for 15 yards out to the 35. Layden followed Joe Bach's interference and worked his way to the 41. It was Miller's turn, and he dashed for 10 yards into Army territory. This was more like the South Bend attack that had flummoxed opponents the past three seasons. The shift, and its myriad of fakes and feints, along with cross-blocking in the line, in which Army's linemen were never sure who would be coming at them, was creating confusion through the West Point defense.

Garbisch, as was his wont, would often drop out of the line and play a yard or two back, more as a rover to get to the ball. As the lines set, one of the Irish shouted, "Hey, Ed, we're going right through the middle. Better get back where you belong." Stuhldreher, the savvy signal-caller, mixed plays brilliantly, firing a pass to Crowley for another 12 yards. Crowley then rushed for another five through the line. On another reverse, Miller skirted left end and dashed 20 yards before being driven out of bounds at the Army 11. The Notre Dame rooters were frenzied as their heroes marched downfield. And the non-partisans in the huge crowd were getting a sense of just what this team, and backfield, could do.

Crowley adroitly picked the opening off of Rip Miller's block, twisted through right tackle for eight yards down to the three. From there it was power football, with Layden smacking into the line once for a yard, then again for the game's first touchdown. Stuhldreher missed the kick, but ND led, 6-0. The Irish machine kept rolling, with a dizzying array of plays befuddling the soldiers. Layden took Army's kick and followed a phalanx of blockers for 24 yards. Then Miller broke loose around right end for 17 yards. Layden crashed through at left tackle for five more.

An out-of-bounds play involving Wilson on the tackle led to some harsh words and shoving, but the scuffle was quickly broken up. Miller went around right end again for five yards and another Irish first down at the Army 45. Stuhldreher, again finding the right spot to change the pace, hit Miller with a pass that the left half carried 27 yards to the Army 18. Layden powered six yards to the 12. After Miller was thrown for a four-yard loss, Crowley got the yardage back with a sprint around left end. On fourth down and 4 to go, the Irish again decided to switch to its air attack. Miller faded and lofted a pass near the goal line, only to watch Yeomans pick it off. He had a clear line along the sideline and sprinted nearly 40 yards before Stuhldreher and Miller knocked him out of bounds to prevent a total turnaround.

Army still had some life before the half ended. Wilson gained six yards before being stopped by Walsh. Then Collins batted down a Yeomans pass, and the Cadets punted again. The half ended with Notre Dame leading, 6-0, and with a huge measure of momentum on its side. In the second quarter, the Irish had eight first downs to none for Army. The Irish appeared as if they could march almost at will. The teams made their way to their dressing rooms. A quick examination of Walsh's battered left hand showed that it, too, had broken bones. Two broken hands and yet no one – least of all Walsh – suggested he leave the lineup.

UP IN THE WOODEN press box, newspaper men were marveling at the precision and skill shown by Notre Dame in the second quarter. One group of sportswriters included some of the biggest names in the business. Grantland Rice of the *New York Herald Tribune* and syndicated column fame was holding court. Rice was considered the dean of newspaper sports writers, and his mere presence was enough to grant significance to any event. His syndicated newspaper accounts were circulated six days a week to more than 100 newspapers nationwide with an estimated audience of 10 million readers.

It was said by Rice's peers that he was a "disciplined craftsman who turned out a prodigious amount of work." In addition to writing for the Herald Tribune in '24, Rice was dazzling readers – and collecting royalties – by writing *Sportlight,* his syndicated columns, as well as authoring numerous books and writing for several magazines. Included among them were Colliers, American Magazine, McClure's, Outing, Literary Digest and Country Life.

Behind Rice's booming Southern voice and six-foot frame there was a depth of feeling and warmth that was often noticed by others. He was known as someone who listened as well as he talked – a person to whom others naturally gravitated. Such was the case this October Saturday at the Polo Grounds. With Rice in the press box at half time were: Damon Runyan, who had gained fame covering baseball and boxing for William Randolph Hearst's *New York American* and was called by Hearst "the best reporter in the world;" Gene Fowler, serving as backup to Runyan; Jack Kofoed, who had started his newspaper career in Philadelphia as an 18-year-old in 1912 and was now with the *New York Post;* Paul Gallico of the *Daily News,* at 27 already one of the most powerful sportswriters in the city; Davis Walsh, lead football writer for the United Press and Notre Dame alum Frank Wallace, reporting for the Associated Press.

Into this conclave strolled young George Strickler, Rockne's publicist and *South Bend Tribune* correspondent. Part of his assignment from Rockne was to keep an ear open for scuttlebutt and analysis from the "big guys" in the newspaper business. The conversation revolved around the exceptional work of the Notre Dame backfield in thwarting Army at every turn.

"Yeah, just like the Four Horsemen," Strickler piped up, recalling Wednesday's movie. No reaction was noted from among the professional scribes. The confab eventually broke up as folks settled into place for the second half.

NOTRE DAME, EAGER to continue its charge, hit the field first for the second half, followed a minute later by the Army. Layden stood on the goal line on the east end, awaiting the kickoff from Garbisch. The Irish fullback took the ball near the goal, and followed the formation out to the 20. After Crowley was dropped for a two-yard loss, Miller again came up big. Charging out of the backfield, he picked his spots, changed direction and evaded Army tacklers for 40 yards before Wilson finally wrestled him to the turf. The crowd let out a huge roar as the Irish machine again looked to be cooking.

Layden picked up four yards on a smash through the line. Crowley faked an end run for one tough yard. On third down, Layden followed with another fake end run, pulling up and throwing. But Wilson leapt to make a nifty interception, and Army had the ball at its 46. A timeout was needed to attend to an injured Hunsinger, who was replaced by Eaton. Three plays later, Layden made up for his miscue, giving the Irish the ball back by intercepting a Yeomans pass intended for Wilson. First down Notre Dame at the Army 43. It was a typical big play for the senior, and it lifted his teammates. Walsh, playing with excruciating pain, continued to have an impact on nearly every play.

On first down, Crowley feigned right, then ran left again and sprinted to the Army 35 before he was forced out of bounds. Rip Miller created an opening, and Don Miller obliged for another five yards. Layden followed Kizer's block for another 10 to the Army 20. Again, the crowd was buzzing at the tremendous coordination and sophistication of the Irish attack. Notre Dame, lining up quickly, going into the shift and snapping off plays in rapid succession, seemed to be catching the Cadets flat on their feet.

After Miller lost a yard on first down, Crowley's number was called. He took off around right end behind a wedge of blockers – Miller, Layden, Stuhldreher, Kizer and Rip Miller. Crowley shot through an opening, shook off the grasp of a pair of Cadets, then stiff-armed another to break free. Racing the Army secondary, Crowley eyed the corner of the field. Striding full-tilt, he arrived ahead of a defender, made a last-second cut to avoid going out of bounds and barely sliced across the last foot of the goal line for a touchdown.

Army's defenders were scattered about the field. Some had just missed making contact with Sleepy Jim, some had him but lost their grip, others could only watch his flying cleats as they gave chase. The turf on the west end of the field, laid to cover the baseball infield, was new and caused some slips. But Army couldn't blame the field; they had been bettered by an attack that hit on all cylinders. Poor turf or not, Army had had enough of their end of the field. After Crowley kicked the extra point for a 13-0 ND lead, Garbisch chose to kick off, hoping to pin the Irish deep, hold them and gain possession on a short field.

Layden fielded the kick deep, dodged several tacklers and reached the 30, but the ball was knocked loose in a collision, and Garbisch recovered at the Notre Dame 32 – exactly the type of break the Cadets were seeking. But the West Pointers were not able to penetrate further. The Irish were using the momentum of their offensive success to play stellar defense. Before each play, Walsh barked out defensive orders, reaching out his damaged hands to point out where to concentrate the Irish effort. A pass by Gillmore was knocked to the turf, and Garbisch tried and missed a 40-yard dropkick.

Notre Dame took over on its 20 and swung back into action. Crowley circled left end for 17 yards. Layden bruised for three. Don Miller again followed Rip Miller's block, dodged would-be tacklers and rambled 25 yards to the Army 35. Layden broke through the line for 17 more. Crowley, again finding room around left end, added six.

They Irish appeared headed for a clinching score. But just as suddenly, Garbisch and his mates stiffened. Layden was stopped on a pair of plunges and was injured on the second one. At the Army 9-yard line, the 71-yard drive stalled, and the ball went over to the Cadets on downs.

On Army's first play, Wood dropped into punt formation, but instead ran seven yards to the 16. Line rushes netted a first down. Then Wilson showed his All-American form. With knees pumping high, he broke free from the Irish line, spun away from another defender and raced out to midfield before Stuhldreher tripped him up, preventing an even longer gain. As it was, the 32-yarder was his best of the day.

It was now Notre Dame's turn to stiffen. A battered Kizer had to leave the game, and Hanousek came in at right guard. Word finally reached the press box that Walsh was playing with two broken limbs. But the courageous Californian continued to make play after play. Twice he stopped Wilson in the line, and then Wood's pass on third down was incomplete as the quarter ended with Notre Dame ahead, 13-0.

WHILE PLAY CONTINUED in the third quarter, Secretary Weeks left his sideline box and accompanied a special guest on a walk that twice circled the playing field. Thousands in the crowd craned their necks and started cheering once they recognized Weeks. Most could only wonder who the blond-haired, dark-suited man was with him. Dr. Hugo Eckener, commander of the ZR-3, was taking in his first game of American football.

To start the fourth quarter, Wood launched a perfect punt, angling the ball away from Stuhldreher and out of bounds at the Irish 5-yard line. Layden, kicking from deep in his end zone, attempted to pin Army back by lofting a high punt. Wilson signaled a fair catch at the Notre Dame 35, but the hard-charging Irish flankers missed the signal and plowed into the Cadet star. A 15-yard penalty put the Cadets at the Irish 20, and Chick Harding took over signal calling for Army.

On first down, Wilson sprinted to the left and starting circling end, only to be felled by John Weibel for a gain of two. Wood smashed into the line, where Walsh and Layden stopped him after three yards. On third down, Joe Bach stopped Wood for no gain. On fourth down and five from the 15, the snap went to Harding, who faked a handoff to Wood and pulled away with the ball. Wood dove into the right side of the line, while Harding circled left end and raced untouched to the end zone, sending the Army rooters into a frenzy.

Garbisch drop-kicked the point, and Army was back in it, trailing 13-7 with 10 minutes left. He then went from teammate to teammate, encouraging them to keep fighting because victory was within sight.

Garbisch kicked off to the Irish 13, and three plays later Layden punted the ball back to Garbisch, who was downed on the Army 46. The Army, looking spent, couldn't mount a drive. After each play, Adam Walsh dragged himself to his feet, took his position, called the defensive signal and, more often than not, made the next tackle.

Wood punted out of bounds to the ND 22, and the Irish went backward in two plays. On third-and-13, Miller was forced out of bounds on an attempted end run. Layden punted to Wilson, who was corralled at midfield on a nice stop by Eaton. Two line plunges gained two yards, setting up third-and-8. The corps of cadets hollered in unison, hoping there was more magic left in Wilson's legs. On third down, the Army star got the ball but was hauled down by Walsh far short of a first down.

Wood punted, again sending the ball out of bounds at the Irish 25. The Irish by now had gone to mostly line plunges, not risking anything wide. Three runs netted nothing, and Layden punted again to Wilson, who was stopped at the Army 35 by Joe Bach.

The Irish line stopped Wood's run off tackle. Then Tom Trapnell went in at quarterback for the Army, now desperate to get the ball downfield. Surely a pass would be coming. In a surprise move, though, it was Wilson who would launch it. He had a bead on a receiver, but Adam Walsh leaped into the air and came down with the leather cradled in his smashed hands. The final serious Army threat was vanquished. From the Army 35, the Irish ran three more safe plays before Layden missed on a drop-kick attempt.

Now 80 yards from the goal, Army needed a miracle. Harding tried to find room around right end, but Hanousek dropped him for a three-yard loss. Two Army passes fell incomplete, and a punt advanced the ball into Notre Dame territory as referee Thorp's pistol signaled the end. Two exhausted teams left the field to the appreciative cheers of fans who realized they had seen a battle of two giants. It was Notre Dame's quick-striking precision and speed that dominated the second and third periods and knocked the Cadets back on their heels from where they could never fully recover.

Both captains, the centers, had given their all. Garbisch wanted to enter the Notre Dame locker room to congratulate Walsh, but Rockne intercepted him. Thanks for the thought, the coach told him, but Walsh was in no shape to see anyone but a doctor.

Walsh was taken to Roosevelt Hospital on 10th Avenue where an X-ray showed two small broken bones in his left hand to go with the three he already had in his right hand. Doctors urged Walsh to remain in New York for treatment, but he insisted on returning home with his team.

13

A Blue-Gray October Sky

THE CROWD OF 1,200 that packed the Palais Royale in South Bend for the News-Times' grid-graph whooped, clapped and sang along with the Lucky Seven as the combo played the Victory March over and over. It had been a raucous afternoon, and the experiment was dubbed a huge success. Fans didn't have to stand outside straining to hear an announcer from a megaphone; they had a complete description of the game, lots of lively music and like-minded Notre Dame fans with whom to cheer.

The newspaper enthused: "Had Captain Adam Walsh and his ... fighting gridders heard the cheers that went up for them here, who knows but that the Notre Dame score might have mounted." Fans were encouraged to come back for the description of next Saturday's game at Princeton and the remaining away contests at Wisconsin, Northwestern and Carnegie Tech.

The student body on campus packed the gym, shouting themselves hoarse in the excitement. The Notre Dame band kept playing. Spilling out of the gym, students cheered and shrieked in a celebration that lasted into the night. It was reported that "echoes reverberated over the university buildings as the student body in true Notre Dame fashion celebrated the impressive victory of the Fighting Irish." The students, led by the band, paraded across campus, hailing their heroes. The march culminated at the Main building, where the crowd was addressed by their president, Father Walsh. Standing atop the building's steps, what a different feeling he had than that of five months earlier, addressing students from atop the Civil War statue downtown during the Klan incident. As was his custom, in hailing today's heroes, Father Walsh recounted the famous 1909 Michigan game and Vaughan's reputed smashing of the goal post to claim an Irish victory. After the demonstration, plans were made for a welcoming ceremony to greet the team on its arrival back in South Bend Sunday afternoon.

Another bit of news from the day could also have explained Father Walsh's exuberance. Since the end of September, the Ku Klux Klan had circulated rumors that they were planning a return trip to South Bend – for Saturday, October 18. Neither South Bend city officials nor members of the Notre Dame administration knew for sure whether the planned march was fact or Klan hyperbole. By October 11, Father Walsh felt confident that the Klan would bypass another trip to South Bend and assured Father Charles O'Donnell, the provincial superior, that O'Donnell could keep his scheduled date at the Polo Grounds to watch the Army-Notre Dame game. O'Donnell, who had promised to deliver five tickets to the game to New York City Archbishop John Cardinal Hayes, trusted Walsh's assessment of the situation and continued a planned trip to Washington, D.C. before heading to New York in time for what promised to be an important day on the field. By nightfall on October 18, no Klansmen had arrived in town, and no Klan rally occurred.

AS HAD BEEN the case in 1923, Rockne determined it was best to have the team start for home Saturday evening, following a post-game meal. With the short week and quick return trip out East, it was important to get back to campus. After the Princeton game the following Saturday, there might be more time to enjoy the sights and sounds of New York City. The players, tired and banged-up from the exhausting battle, were anxious to head home. With Captain Walsh back from the hospital, his hands heavily bandaged, and with the team fed, they boarded their train at the New York Central station to begin the 20-hour journey home.

At newspaper offices around New York, as across the country, columns of coverage of the big college games were being prepared for the Sunday papers. It had been a monumental day for the sport. In Urbana, Illinois, "a flashing, red haired youngster, running and dodging with the speed of a deer, gave 67,000 spectators jammed into the new $1,700,000 Illinois Memorial stadium, the thrill of their lives when Illinois vanquished Michigan 39 to 14 in what probably will be the outstanding game of the 1924 gridiron season in the west."

Harold "Red" Grange had taken the opening kickoff and raced 95 yards for a touchdown to christen the new edifice. He then broke loose for touchdown runs of 65, 55 and 45 yards – all before the first quarter ended. Grange finished the day with five touchdowns and 402 total yards. His feat was "declared by gridiron experts to be one of the most phenomenal in the history of the game." Newspapers scrambled to find pictures and sketches of the Illinois star to run with their game coverage.

It had been an extraordinary day at the turnstiles for college football. In addition to the 67,000 at Illinois and 60,000 in the Polo Grounds, 50,000 gathered in Cambridge to see Harvard defeat Holy Cross, 12-6, and crowds of 45,000 were tallied for both the Yale-Dartmouth and Penn-Columbia games. Three upcoming Notre Dame opponents played in front of impressive crowds of 25,000 – Princeton, a 17-14 victor over Navy; Georgia Tech, which edged Penn State, 15-13; and Nebraska, triumphant over a good Colgate squad, 34-7, at Lincoln.

Reporters covering the Army-Notre Dame batted out stories that covered a variety of elements of the big game. The New York Times, in addition to expansive game coverage, went into great detail on the arrival of the West Point band and corps of cadets, the pageantry and atmosphere of the contest.

Westbrook Pegler, whose account was dispatched to a number of papers nationwide, commented on the make-up of the 60,000: "It was a strange crowd which filled the permanent stands and bleachers because Notre Dame had brought only a few non-combatants along to kick up a noise, and the Army's cadets filled only a pocket of the capacious stadium. It was largely a non-partisan crowd, come to see a good game of football."

Chicago's Walter Eckersall, who served as linesman, was able to dash off a detailed dispatch that included his up-close, blunt observations of the match.

"It was a fierce, aggressive struggle, but remarkably clean. The tackling and blocking was about the hardest seen in the these parts in years…Notre Dame's slashing attack, directed at the Army flanks, was the turning point of the game. The cadet ends and tackles failed to shift fast enough with the westerner's backfield shift. The (Army) ends on most occasions played a waiting game and were made to look bad. The tackles, who failed to move out far enough, were partially responsible for the Notre Dame backs getting around the ends or cutting in just off the tackles."

Damon Runyon, writing for the *New York American* and the Hearst syndicate, took a different tack, opting to focus on the Army mule and the blanket that draped the mule. He thought Notre Dame fans would emulate the tradition shown by victorious Navy fans, who would charge from the stands after defeating the Cadets and snatch the mule's blanket. Although the enthusiastic ND fans never approached the mule, Runyon stuck with his idea for the lead. Young Frank Wallace was torn between his allegiance to Notre Dame and the need to write a lead for the Associated Press that would appeal to a diverse reader base. He managed to do both when he wrote: "The brilliant Notre Dame backfield dazzled the Army line today and romped away with a 13 to 7 victory in one of the hardest-fought of the intersectional series between the two teams. More than 50,000 people saw the game at the Polo Grounds."

Grantland Rice, in the evening twilight and gathering chill, sat at his typewriter in the Polo Grounds press box and pondered his opening. National readers of his *Sportlight* column were used to Rice's poems, odes and flowery speech. He regularly made an effort to liven the mundane with a clever turn of the phrase. He was well-read in classical literature, having majored in Greek and Latin at Vanderbilt.

Something about Strickler's halftime comment and the imagery of horses stuck in Rice's mind when he reflected on the Notre Dame backfield. He recalled the 1923 game at Ebbets Field, which he took in from field level. At one point, he recalled, the charge of the players on an out-of-bounds play brought to mind the possibility of being trampled by a runaway team of horses. It all clicked. His fingers hit the typewriter keys:

> "Outlined against a blue-gray October sky, the Four Horsemen rode again. In dramatic lore they are known as Famine, Pestilence, Destruction and Death. These are only aliases. Their real names are Stuhldreher, Miller, Crowley and Layden. They formed the crest of the South Bend cyclone before which another fighting Army football team was swept over the precipice at the Polo Grounds yesterday afternoon as 55,000 spectators peered down on the bewildering panorama spread on the green plain below.
>
> A cyclone can't be snared. It may be surrounded, but somewhere it breaks through to keep on going. When the cyclone starts from South Bend, where the candle lights still gleam through the Indiana sycamores, those in the way must take to storm cellars at top speed. Yesterday the cyclone struck again, as Notre Dame beat the Army, 13 to 7, with a set of backfield stars that ripped and crashed through a strong Army defense with more speed and power than the warring cadets could meet."

From there, Rice described "the driving power of one of the greatest backfields that ever churned up the turf of any gridiron in any football age." He noted the following on the second quarter scoring drives: "the unwavering power of the Western attack that hammered relentlessly and remorselessly without easing up for a second's breath." Rice paid particular homage to the speed of the Irish attack, the precision with which it worked, and the consistently effective blocking it used to advance the ball on the ground.

"Always in front of these offensive drives could be found the whirling form of Stuhldreher, taking the first man out of the play as cleanly as if he had used a hand grenade at close range," Rice wrote. "This Notre Dame interference was a marvelous thing to look upon."

He also had high praise for ND's defensive play.

"When a back such as Harry Wilson finds few chances to get started you can figure upon the defensive strength that is barricading the road. Wilson is one of the hardest backs in the game to suppress, but he found few chances yesterday to show his broken field ability. You can't run through a broken field until you get there."

He concluded by stating that "we doubt that any team in the country could have beaten Rockne's array yesterday afternoon, East or West. It was a great football team brilliantly directed, a team of speed, power and team play. The Army has no cause for gloom over its showing. It played first class football against more speed than it could match.

"Those who have tackled a cyclone can understand."

The editors at the *Herald Tribune* felt the quality of Rice's piece, and the significance of the game merited front-page play, and so the story ran on the front of Sunday's paper – page one, column one at the top left-hand corner.

Rice was not totally alone in developing the equine theme. Heywood Broun, a fine wordsmith writing in the New York World, wrote that Notre Dame "defeated the West Pointers with sweeping cavalry charges around the ends...They were light horsemen, these running backs of Notre Dame, but they swung against the Army ends with speed and numbers. The players were run wide and again and again, some unfortunate solider sentinel would race all the way across the gridiron and over the sidelines without ever getting contact with any one but one of the interfering outposts."

Before boarding the train home, Strickler stopped at a newsstand and grabbed copies of the "bulldog" early editions of the Sunday papers. Reading Rice's lead, he could barely believe his eyes. According to Strickler, he sent a wire to his father back in South Bend, advising

Mr. Strickler to round up four horses for a publicity photo he wanted to have taken.

At the New York Central station in South Bend late Sunday afternoon, thousands gathered to greet the returning heroes. While the train was still several minutes out, "bedlam broke loose at the railroad station and increased in volume as the train pulled in." With the Notre Dame Band playing the Victory March, some three thousand students and townspeople clapped, whooped and hollered. They encircled the players and marched down Michigan Avenue from the station to the Oliver Hotel, while they "split the heavens with volume after volume of cheers for Rockne's fighting men."

Outside the Oliver, cheer leader Luther stood and addressed the demonstration, giving his eyewitness account of the previous day's goings-on. Luther told the cheering crowd of the "magnificent courage despite agonizing injuries" shown by Captain Walsh, and that his game was the "greatest exhibition of courage and power" that the New York crowd had ever seen. One by one, Luther spoke out the names of the Irish players involved in the battle, and the throng responded with deafening cheers. The spirited rooters implored Luther to introduce Coach Rockne, but it seemed that the "wonder coach" had slipped away from the pack somewhere in the vicinity of the train station. This evening would be strictly for students.

Layden and Walsh represented the team in appearing before the crowd on the street. Layden simply bowed to the masses, eliciting a "wild outburst of applause." It was up to Walsh to say a few words on behalf of his teammates. He praised the efforts of his fellow Irish, saying they were worthy of the current outpouring of affection.

"The fellows played real football against the Army," Walsh concluded. "They had to play real football, or else they'd have been carried off the field in stretchers."

The cascading cheers of the fans met the competing noise of car horns honking in the October evening. For three solid minutes, the din filled the streets. Luther's final words set the stage for the weeks ahead: "Notre Dame will defeat Princeton, Georgia Tech, Wisconsin, Nebraska, Northwestern and Carnegie Tech!" he screamed.

All would be challenging games, starting with Princeton, whom the

Irish would face without their stalwart captain. It was announced that evening that Walsh would definitely not be able to play.

IN THE COMING days and weeks, the notion of Notre Dame having not only a "wonder team" but a backfield of biblical proportions would sweep across the country. Rice's phraseology would gradually make its way into other sports writers' descriptions. William F. "Bill" Fox, Jr., a 1920 Notre Dame graduate, had gone on to become a reporter and then joined the sports staff of the *Indianapolis News*. He saw the 1924 team, as long as it continued to perform at a high level, as a major national sports story. Fox strongly encouraged Strickler to take advantage of the opportunity Rice's story presented, and Fox offered to help in any way he could.

Strickler enlisted his father, who had more experience around animals because of his job on the university farm, to help with the publicity photo shoot. His assignment was to round up four riding horses for the famous backfield to mount. Instead, he came up with four very well-worn work horses, of different sizes and condition. Mr. Strickler had them saddled and ready to go at the coal-and-ice business just down the street from his favorite tavern downtown.

George Strickler rode one horse and held the reigns of the other three. It was a tough slog to campus. He was pulled off the horse he was riding as the other three strained against the reigns. Finally, he arrived at the practice field, explained the stunt to the guard, and brought the horses onto the field. The commercial photographer Strickler hired for the shoot, Mr. Christman, was already there. The four players were summoned, and they began to look askance at one another.

Except for Stuhldreher, who had handled horses while delivering groceries for his father's store, the four had little equine expertise. But more than that, each knew that being thrown from a horse could cause an injury that would, in an instant, put an end to their participation in a magical season. All that risk to get photographed upon a horse?

With the players anxious, and Rockne not wanting his practice interrupted any more than necessary, it was a quick photo shoot. A couple of shots were taken, the players were on their way, and Strickler guided the horses off the field.

Once the prints became available, Strickler went to work distributing the photo. His first sale was to Pacific & Atlantic, a national news photo agency. Every time P&A syndicated the photo in another newspaper, Strickler received a royalty. One by one, the major newspapers in the country ran the photo. The nickname and photo became vehicles for the sporting public to connect a personal story to the feats of a team which was picking up admirers by the thousands. The efforts of Rice, Strickler, Fox and others aside, a rapidly growing fan base, especially one of Irish-Americans, was eager to embrace the story of the college boys representing the school in South Bend.

THE NEW-FOUND fame seemed to have little direct impact on the Irish players. There were injuries to heal, exams for which to study, and daily activities that demanded their attention. The fellows also possessed a natural modesty of a group of down-to-earth players who simply loved the game of football. They cherished the time spent together as a group of 22 seniors having their 'final fling' with the college game.

After returning from the Army game, Layden wrote his romantic interest, Evelyn Byrne, back home that "against the Army, I played a few minutes, and was fortunate enough to score a touchdown." As for the upcoming Princeton game, Layden wrote, "I hope I am again fortunate enough to make the trip."

The players' fellow ND students were not shy with their praise. The Scholastic that week summarized Walsh's performance:

"Standing man to man, leader against leader, Walsh and Garbisch fought supreme, the battle of their lives, calling occasional 'time out' that they might cool the heated blood and relax the tightened muscles. With two almost useless hands, the Irish captain went down, under and up, time and again 'smearing' plays – in defense, a polished center of a granite wall. To Captain Garbisch, a true Cadet, a leader of high caliber, a fighter from the sound of the whistle to the report of the gun, due respect is given. Only an Adam Walsh could hinder his all around play."

IN A FRIGHTENING postscript to the New York trip, the "Smith and Davis" blimp, meant to fly over the game, exploded during its test run Sunday, bursting into flames and setting fire to a 30-foot section of roofing over the Polo Grounds grandstand. The blimp was released from a 10-ton truck Sunday and soared to a height of 400 feet, its political message visible to thousands in the area. When its safety had been proven, handlers began hauling it down. The blimp bucked, shifted course and crashed into the upper grandstand, shooting flames into the sky and setting the roof ablaze.

Nobody was injured.

14
Headed East Again

THE IRISH, TIRED from the Army trip, held workouts in their brief three-day stay back in South Bend. Some questioned whether the team should have remained in the New York-New Jersey area for the entire week. But Rockne knew school officials would not want to invite charges of shirking academics that such a travel plan could attract. The traveling squad changed slightly between games.

Adam Walsh, hands bandaged, led the entourage onto the train Thursday afternoon, ready to take on his role as non-playing captain. Joe Harmon was expected to play in Walsh's place with Arndt and Maxwell in reserve. The squad arrived in the Asbury Park, New Jersey, area at mid-morning Friday, October 24, checking into their headquarters at the Coleman House. The resort season in the area of beaches, boardwalks and golf clubs was over, providing Rockne and his men with the desired level of quietude. The next destination was the Deal Golf Club, where ND's "eastern representative" Joe Byrne, a member and former president of the club, had arranged for the team to practice on the polo field.

Before that, Rockne had another brief stop planned. Just outside

132

the Deal Club stood a grain scale, and Rockne took several of his players, most notably his star backfield, and met members of the New York sporting press at the scale. Some press members questioned whether the Irish backfield was really as light as advertised. Rockne had Granny Rice call each of the backs, one-by-one, up to the scale. The results matched the reported weights of the players: Layden was the heaviest at 161 pounds, Crowley and Don Miller were both close to 157 pounds, and Stuhldreher came up a few ounces short of 152 pounds. After practice, the team took a stroll on the boardwalk, had dinner and retired early.

Plans for the return trip differed from the previous week. The team was scheduled to attend a "theatre party" Saturday night, stay over in the city, and leave after Mass and breakfast Sunday morning. Rockne, though, reserved the right to change plans and order a Saturday evening return to South Bend if the game didn't go according to his wishes.

IT HAD BEEN nearly 55 years since the afternoon of November 6, 1869, when a group of 25 Princeton students traveled the short distance north to New Brunswick, New Jersey, to take on a similar number of Rutgers men in the first game of intercollegiate football. The site was a meadow across the street from the residence of the late President Grover Cleveland. The home team prevailed that day, reaching the six goals required for victory, while holding Princeton to four. There was joy along the banks of the Old Raritan. But in the next few decades, as the game grew, Princeton took its place as one of the pioneers, and for generations had been part of The Big Three – with rivals Yale and Harvard. It hadn't lost to Rutgers since that historic opener.

Yale was the first true power in college football. In an 18-year stretch, from 1883 through 1900, the Elis' domination was staggering. They suffered only nine losses those years, six coming against Princeton, while winning 197. The Yalies had seven perfect seasons and four others nicked only by ties. Three times they held opponents scoreless for the entire season, while scoring 694, 488 and 435 points, respectively.

Princeton's mark during the same period was strong in its own right. The Tigers lost only 16 games in those 18 years, and 10 of those were to Yale. Princeton's 175 wins included three perfect seasons and four others in which they were tied only once. The battles between the Bulldogs and Tigers were epic, nearly all coming as the final game of the season. Six times, Yale handed Princeton its only loss of the season; on four other occasions, the Tigers did the same to Yale. For many years, it was the most intense rivalry in college sports. Only later did Yale shift its attention from Princeton to Harvard as its chief rival.

In 1924, Princeton's coach, 44-year-old Bill Roper, was a veteran of the football wars, a link back to the prime Yale-Princeton battles. The Philadelphia native played for Princeton's unbeaten 1899 team and was in his third stint as the Tigers' head coach. Roper coached unbeaten squads in 1906 and 1911, in his first two stops as the leader at Old Nassau. In 1911, he had coached the "wonder athlete" of the age – the incomparable Hobart Amory Hare – better known as "Hobey" – Baker. In addition to his starring role on the gridiron, Baker was considered the finest hockey player of his era.

In between coaching stints, Roper officiated college football games. He worked as the umpire in the famous 1913 Army-Notre Dame game, and commented later that he had always believed that such playing was possible under the new rules, but that he had never seen the forward pass developed to such a state of perfection. Roper was in his sixth year of his current stretch at Princeton and had guided the Tigers to two more perfect campaigns – 1920 and 1922. Roper's 1922 team had come to be known as "The Team of Destiny" – mostly for one memorable afternoon at Stagg Field in Chicago.

Princeton made headlines simply by agreeing to make the long trip to the Midwest, its first such journey. The Tigers were unbeaten, despite being considered the underdog in most of its games. They were not expected to beat the University of Chicago juggernaut. A crowd of 32,000 jammed Stagg Field, named for the great Amos Alonzo Stagg, then in his 32nd season as head coach of the Maroons and with another undefeated powerhouse. Three touchdowns by Chicago's All-American fullback, John Thomas, gave the Maroons an 18-7 fourth quarter lead. Minutes later, the Tigers' hopes appeared to fade as John Cleaves lined up to punt from the back of his own end zone. But he faked the kick, and lofted a pass that brought Princeton to midfield. Then Chicago fumbled a punt, and Princeton scored to close within four points.

The fighting Tigers, inspired by Roper's typical never-say-die attitude, stiffened on defense, got the ball back and drove down the field with the clock ticking down. On fourth-and-goal from the three, Harry Crum wrestled his way out of the grasp of Chicago's defense and scored. Princeton converted and led, 21-18. Stagg's Maroons, stunned by the reversal, took to the air and made a desperate attempt to pull out the victory they thought should be theirs. Down the field they drove, to the Princeton one-yard-line. Only seconds remained. John Thomas, as expected, would get the ball and a chance for his fourth touchdown of the day. But the Orange and Black line, anchored by All-American tackle Herb Treat, rose up as one, smothered Thomas and left him a foot shy of the goal line. Princeton won, 21-18.

Back in Princeton, hundreds of students celebrated the dramatic victory, lighting bonfires and parading the length of Nassau Street singing and cheering. The school's famous bell rang out the sounds of the "Glory of Old Nassau." Among the great Princeton victories of the past half-century, there had never been one bigger or more dramatic. The "Team of Destiny" finished 8-0, concluding the '22 season with another dramatic duel, coming away with a 3-0 win over the Elis. Roper was hailed as a genius coach, not for his strategy or technique, but rather for his ability to instill a fighting spirit into his players, which fueled the heroic upset victory.

The Tigers' fortunes took a decided downturn in 1923, starting with Notre Dame's first visit to Palmer Stadium on October 20. Princeton's 2-0 record included wins over Johns Hopkins and Georgetown, while the Irish were 3-0 coming off their Ebbets Field shutout of Army, 13-0. Led by the dazzling moves of Don Miller and Crowley, the Irish handed the Tigers "one of the worst trouncings in the history of Nassau," a 25-2 pasting, in which a blocked Notre Dame punt into its own end zone was the only Princeton score. The margin in first downs was similar, 25-4, as "Rockne's pupils were so superior that the big hopeful Princeton crowd was awed."

The 32,000 fans knew that Notre Dame was on a roll, and

Princeton was unproven after losing several of its top stars from '22. "The defeat was not unexpected," wrote one Eastern scribe, "but after the sensational record of the Tiger eleven of last year, the crowd still hoped for miracles." The '23 Tigers would go down as a mediocre unit by Princeton standards, finishing 3-3-1, including a 27-0 drubbing at the hands of Yale.

Things had to be better this year, most Princetonians thought. Rumors began to circulate that Coach Roper was considering making this his last season at the Tiger helm, and all involved wanted to send him out with a great year. An end, E.C. "Buzz" Stout Jr., took his role as captain seriously and exhorted his fellow students to give their all in supporting the team. Sophomore quarterback Jake Slagle quickly emerged as the expected star of the Tiger backfield. Slagle opened strong, scoring two touchdowns in a 40-6 rout of outmanned Amherst. Lehigh was the next visitor to Palmer Stadium, and they battled Princeton in a defensive struggle that ended in a scoreless tie. Roper needed to do something to pull his squad together. On Wednesday, October 15, Roper surprised his varsity at practice. The coach had assembled an "all-star" team of former Princetonians, including '23 star lineman Treat, to scrimmage the current squad.

On Saturday, October 18, while Notre Dame was taking on the Army in New York City, Princeton entertained the Naval Academy. Capt. George W. Steele, U. S. officer on the German dirigible ZR-3, attended the game cheering wildly for Navy. The Navy band, 1,600 midshipmen, and their goat mascot paraded at Palmer.

It was another intense, battering contest – no fewer than five Navy players had their noses badly injured, including two that were broken. The Middies were knocking down every charge Princeton made and led, 14-7, midway through the fourth quarter. A promising season for the Tigers seemed on the verge of slipping away. But on a fourth-and-goal from the 5, Slagle faked, dropped back and hit Tillson with a touchdown pass. The point tied it, 14-14. Moments later, little-used sophomore Sam Ewing calmly dropkicked the ball from 18 yards out, and Princeton held on, 17-14. It was yet another dramatic, come-from-behind victory for Roper's men, and it put them in a confident state for their next game – Notre Dame.

THE TIGERS GARNERED attention not just as comeback specialists, but because of another unique aspect of their game plan. One press box wag gave this sardonic description of the scene from the Navy game:

"The Navy men were somewhat annoyed by the Princeton system of signaling (plays). Before each play, the Princeton eleven would retire to the backfield and go into conference, apparently taking a vote on the play. Mr. Bill Roper favors this parliamentary procedure, but many experts are squawking vociferously about it. On the whole, it seemed to work favorably."

In his weekly column, Rockne commented on the "rumpus over the 'huddle'…in the East." He cited the fact it might be helpful to a team whose signals are being called by a lineman, or one whose quarterback lacks a "sharp, decisive way of snapping out his signals." Rockne's take was that a delay could occur if the team started arguing over which play was called. He noted that when used by a fast-moving team that comes quickly out of the huddle and starts its plays before the opponent has time to digest the formation, "in that respect it touches upon the purpose of the shift."

A former Princeton star from the class of 1893, Parke H. Davis, provided football commentary for The Daily Princetonian and gave Tiger fans hope for a much different result than the 25-2 shellacking of '23. "Notre Dame can not be rated as strong this fall as in 1923," he noted. While pointing out that ND's backfield returned intact, he said of the new linemen, "it seems improbable that this green line can furnish the basis for such performances as the veteran line provided in Palmer Stadium one year ago."

For the first time all season, Roper operated practice behind closed doors. He felt that the close call against Navy drew out several of his better plays, which were planned for the Irish. He decided a new set of plays needed to be developed. He once again assembled several players off his '22 squad to scrimmage his varsity. The mission was to solve the defensive problems evident in the Navy game, and his charges looked better in holding the "all-stars" to a scoreless tie in Tuesday's work.

He also shifted Dinsmore to quarterback, moving Slagle to one of the halves. Dinsmore, who had been hampered by illness, was also selected to call the signals, replacing Captain Stout in that role. After three days of intense defensive drills aimed to combat the Irish attack, Roper turned his attention to offense by Thursday's workout. In Dinsmore, he had a quarterback with two years experience, and the veteran led the Tigers in a series of sharp signal drills.

SATURDAY, OCTOBER 25, was billed as an extravaganza of college football in New York City and environs. All three major league ballparks would be put to use: West Virginia was taking on the "Prayin' Colonels" of Kentucky's Centre College at the Polo Grounds; Yankee Stadium was hosting Lafayette against Washington & Jefferson; and Ebbetts Field was the site for the St. John's-Villanova tussle.

Not to be overlooked was the much-awaited Columbia-Williams tussle at Baker Field, where a capacity crowd pushing 20,000 would see whether the amazing Ephs could duplicate their stunning, streak-ending upset of Cornell three weeks earlier. Two of the finest coaches in the game, Percy Wendell of Williams and Columbia's Percy Haughton, would match wits.

In Princeton, Saturday's weather was pleasant and perfect for football. Raccoon coats, advertised by several New York clothiers who made frequent stops at Princeton to take orders, would be more a fashion statement than a meteorological necessity. At the grand Palmer Stadium, workers had erected temporary seating in the south, open end of the field to accommodate any spillover from the permanent seats. Through Saturday morning, special trains put up by the Pennsylvania Railroad ran from Penn Station in the city, Hudson Terminal, Jersey City and Newark, depositing thousands of fans for the big game. Atop Palmer, the same radio crews that called the Army-ND game were setting up to broadcast over WJZ and WEAF.

Palmer's field was in perfect condition as the two teams entered the stadium for the 2:30 kickoff. Princeton's band marched down the field in front of the Notre Dame section and then across to their game position. Notre Dame started its Shock Troops, with two of its sophomores from Philadelphia in the lineup – Joe Boland at left tackle and Joe Maxwell at center. Scherer, O'Boyle, Connell and Cerney were in the backfield. O'Boyle kicked off to the Princeton 5, and Connell stopped the Tiger return at the 15. Slagle immediately punted, setting the pace for the first quarter. Before it was over, there would be 13 punts – seven by Slagle and six by Cerney.

The Shock Troops performed as expected, taking Princeton's best punches and holding the Tigers in check. Boland, Maxwell, Connell and Cerney consistently bottled up their Black and Orange counterparts, and Maxwell broke through to block Slagle's attempted punts. Late in the quarter, Princeton had the ball at ND's 40. But Cerney broke through and nailed Prendergast for a 10-yard loss to midfield. On the next play, Princeton was called for unnecessary roughness and was pushed far out of scoring range.

The first quarter ended, and Rockne rose from the bench, gestured with his right hand and, as one, the eleven Notre Dame regulars dropped their blankets and bolted onto the field. The Irish fans gave a great ovation at the quarter's end, in appreciation of the second team's work, and in excitement over the regulars hitting the field. As the Shock Troops, drenched in sweat, trotted off the field, Captain Adam Walsh slapped each man on the back, thanking him for his tremendous effort. They had not only worn down the Tigers and drawn out some of their strategy, but they had also left the home team with a psychological disadvantage, knowing they had done no better than tie the ND subs.

The first-teamers started tentatively, and Layden punted to Dinsmore on the Princeton 10, where he was thrown out of bounds by Hunsinger and Kizer. Weibel then stopped Dinsmore's run, and Slagle punted to Stuhldreher, who weaved through the defense on a 39-yard punt return, with only a tackle by Slagle preventing a touchdown. From the Tiger 26, ND advanced with Miller hauling it around end for seven yards. On fourth-and-inches, Layden drove through an opening, but the ball squirted loose, and Princeton recovered on its eight-yard-line. Collins and then Weibel stopped Tiger rushes for short gains, forcing another Slagle punt. Stuhldreher was downed immediately at the ND 47. Crowley made a yard, and on second-and-nine, Stuhldreher faded back and hit Miller for 22 yards to the Tiger 30.

A low-driving charge by Layden was good for 10 more and then Miller added three. From the 17, Crowley shot through an opening between Kizer and Rip Miller, twisted out of several attempted tackles and hauled two defenders into the end zone. Crowley's kick attempt was blocked, but ND led, 6-0.

Princeton chose to kick off, and Miller returned it to his 23. Dinsmore was shaken up on the play, and Dignan took his place. Miller spun around right end for a first down out at the 35. Princeton's Slagle stopped the Irish with an interception, and the Tigers had the ball in ND territory.

Slagle made a nifty fake and hit Drews with a nine-yard pass. Dignan plunged for a first down at the Irish 35. Cradling the ball in the pileup, Dignan felt he had been hit in the throat and slugged an Irish player. Referee Vic Schwartz immediately ejected Dignan and penalized Princeton half the distance to its goal – 33 yards. Weeks got 10 yards back on a nice run, but on the next play he was clobbered by Collins, and the ball popped loose, with three ND defenders covering it at the Princeton 40. But a holding penalty and two incomplete passes stalled any advance, and the half ended with ND ahead, 6-0.

Princeton received the second half kickoff, but again could not move against the center of the Notre Dame line. Slagle punted to Stuhldreher, who fumbled. Princeton recovered at ND's 35 for its first big break of the game. The Tigers again attempted to dent the interior, but Harmon, Kizer and Glueckert held. A third-down pass was incomplete, and Slagle punted into the end zone.

With Notre Dame's ball at the 20, the Irish came alive. It was at these times that Stuhldreher's ability to be commander on the field proved the most successful. A master of sound quarterback play, Stuhldreher noticed that the Princeton tackle and end on each side were playing wide. With that type of setting and a Notre Dame backfield loaded with the talent it possessed, Stuhldreher confined his play calling to sharp thrusts by Layden through the thinned-out line and cutbacks by Crowley and Miller. It worked to perfection.

Left tackle Bach sprung Crowley for 15 yards. Next it was Layden, who, one Eastern writer observed, "leans so far forward that he seems to be nose diving instead of running." Six yards for Elmer. Don Miller broke free off Rip Miller's block and went for nine more, to midfield. It was a dizzying array of fakes, feints, misdirections, and phantom ball-carriers – all with solid interference in front. Layden broke tackles and roared for 22 more, to the Princeton 28. The Tigers called time, trying to regroup. The thousands of proud Catholics in the west stands waived blue banners and shrieked hysterically.

The yards came in smaller chunks. Crowley hit left tackle for three; Layden got another three through center, then three more. On fourth down, Layden plunged for the needed yard. Four more carries gained another first down at the Princeton six. A decisive touchdown looked inevitable as the Irish advanced methodically. But a different fate awaited the charge.

Miller burst through for an apparent touchdown, but ND was penalized for holding, pushing the ball back to the 20. Two plays later, a holding call knocked the Irish further back, to the 40, and Layden ended up punting. A 74-yard advance had netted nothing. There was no time for disappointment, however, as the Irish defense took over and stopped Weekes on three runs, forcing yet another Slagle punt. Stuhldreher ripped off a 12-yard return, and Layden broke free for 13 yards, to midfield.

At this point, the Tigers became inspired, digging deep to play heroic defense. Princeton's Gates and Stout threw Crowley for a three-yard loss. Miller was held to no gain. A pass from Stuhldreher to Hunsinger was broken up. Layden then launched a magnificent punt into the Princeton end zone. After another quick exchange of punts, the quarter ended, with Princeton in possession at its own 22, still trailing by just six points. Anything was possible.

From the bench, Notre Dame's Walsh had a look of grim concern. Harmon was playing wonderfully in his stead, and the whole line was stout, but the fellows seemed to need something extra to put this one away. Weekes started the final quarter with a plunge for three yards. Slagle was stopped for no gain, and then Weekes went for five before the Irish backs ganged up to stop him two yards short of first down. A poor, low punt by Slagle set ND up at its own 42.

The "South Bend cyclone" cranked up, with Crowley driving out to midfield. Layden hammered for seven. Crowley, whirling and pivoting, danced 17 yards to the Princeton 25. "Crowley the fighter," he was described, "who deliberately offers a tackler his foot and then withdraws it; Crowley, who refuses to be stopped even when three pairs of orange-striped arms are clutching his blue jersey."

Layden, Crowley and Miller each took another crack, but gained just five yards total, leaving fourth-and-five at the 20. Stuhldreher calmly surveyed the field, found Crowley open and hit him for a 10-yard gain to the Princeton 10 for a first down. Two plays later, Crowley drove behind Bach, fought off a wall of tacklers – twisting away from one after another with knees flying high – and slipped free to cross the goal line under the crossbar. His kick was blocked, but a 12-0 lead suddenly looked insurmountable, especially with the Irish defense on top of its game.

Slagle kicked off, hoping for a quick turnaround deep in the Notre Dame end. He drove the ball to the Irish 5, but Layden picked up steam for an 18-yard return to the 23. With the clock winding down, the Irish goal was simple: get another march and put the game away. Layden dove for several yards, and Miller rambled to within a foot of first down. Layden gained the needed yardage to the 35. On first down, Crowley burst through the right side of the line behind Rip Miller, and danced 25 yards to the Princeton 40. The roar again went up from the ND rooters, now sensing the final blow.

The Blue-and-Gold machine continued marching. A Crowley-to-Miller pass earned a first down at the Tiger 25. Layden bulled on three rushes for another first down at the 15. Crowley made another eight. On fourth down, Crowley was stopped inches short at the 5, and the ball went over to Princeton, who could muster no offensive movement. Slagle punted out of his end zone, Miller got loose on a couple of runs, and, after a Layden punt was blocked, Princeton fumbled, with Bach recovering, and the whistle sounded.

NOTRE DAME'S 12-0 victory might not have impressed those just looking at Saturday's scores, but anyone taking a closer view at the game would notice the one-sidedness of the contest. The Irish racked up 374 yards, 326 on rushes. The beleaguered Tigers mustered only 97 total yards. First downs told a similar tale, with an 18-4 advantage for

ND. The reviews from the Eastern press told the tale.

"Princeton was lucky that the score was not twice as much," observed the New York World. "This was no sluggish, poorly equipped Navy team that the jungle cats were up against, but a first class, splendidly drilled and conditioned aggregation with a consistent running attack built on speed and deception."

Despite the penalties and fumbles that kept the score down, Rockne and the lads were in a celebratory mood Saturday night. Two tough battles against two of the East's best had resulted in clear victories. The boys earned their "theatre party," and were taken to the New Amsterdam Theatre on West 42nd Street for a show featuring Will Rogers and the Ziegfeld Follies.

Rogers, a great friend of Rockne and the Irish, came out on the stage with a blue Notre Dame sweater and the interlocking ND monogram. The crowd went crazy. Another member of the cast shouted from the side of the stage, "What's going on out there?"

"I don't know," Rogers said, trying to act befuddled. "Unless they're cheering my North Dakota sweater." The Irish fans loved it.

The Irish returned to the Belmont Hotel with just enough time to catch some sleep before Sunday morning Mass at St. Patrick's Cathedral. It was then off to the Pennsylvania station and the trip back to South Bend.

A few of the boys were allowed an extra day on the trip. Rip Miller was given permission to take a train to Boston to see Esther Templin, now a student at Simmons College. And the Philly sophomores, Boland and Maxwell, received permission to spend the day with their families and take a later train back west.

15
Homecoming

ON MONDAY, OCTOBER 27, Coach Percy Haughton was directing his Columbia University team's practice at Baker Field when he complained of feeling ill. He was taken by taxicab to St. Luke's Hospital in Manhattan and died a few minutes after arrival of what was called "acute indigestion." Haughton was 48.

Haughton was considered one of the giants in college football coaching, along with Rockne, Pop Warner and Fielding Yost. A former Harvard lineman, Haughton had taken the reigns at his alma mater in 1908 and lifted its fortunes to unprecedented heights, including undefeated seasons in 1912 and 1913. He came out of football retirement in 1923 to take over at Columbia. It was said of Haughton that he "took students, and made football players out of them."

"He was something more than a great coach," wrote Grantland Rice, who had watched Haughton coach his last game against Williams just days before. "He was an inspiration such as few may ever chance to know. He did something more than give his teams winning plays — he gave them morale beyond any leader we have ever known." Bob Williams, the referee for Columbia's final game under Haughton, commented, "Columbia played great football, but above that I have never seen a team fight with finer, fairer spirit. It was an inspiration to see the soul they put into their play."

For Rockne and his players, who were preparing for their homecoming game against Georgia Tech, it was another reminder of life's frailty.

Another homecoming, this one at Cornell, took on a different flavor. The school was scheduled to dedicate the Cornell Crescent, the distinctive new grandstand at Schoellkopf Field, in its homecoming game against Columbia. Out of respect for Columbia, ceremonies were cancelled, flags flew at half-mast, and much of the usual "color and pageantry" was shelved.

THE IRISH WERE a tired bunch on the train ride home from New York, and another major injury surfaced. Stuhldreher had badly injured his shoulder, and it was feared he could miss the next two games. The toll of leading interference for Crowley, Miller and Layden play after play was clearly taking its toll on his 150-pound frame. Stuhldreher excelled at his grueling role as a blocking back, whether it was making contact with an opposing lineman or finding the angle on a would-be tackler downfield.

Stuhldreher "can come closer to hitting a tackler's kneecap with his own shoulder blade, starting fifteen feet away, than almost anyone we ever saw," Rice wrote, naming the Irish quarterback as one of the top three at this "most intricate of all the gridiron sciences. When he lets fly the first man in the path goes down, and stays down until Layden, Miller or Crowley have passed on by. Stuhldreher is…a wizard at interference."

Homecoming week activities at Notre Dame began with Eddie Luther conducting a noon meeting Wednesday in the gymnasium. Students were given instructions for their part in the celebration. After the final cheers and with the sounds of the "Hike" song still in the air, the men charged onto the field south of the gym to begin the wood piling contest. A set of stakes, each painted with the name of a residence hall, were planted in the field. The men from each hall scurried to find available timber in the surrounding fields to pile up at their hall's stake. "Before nightfall, the rivalry was aroused to a fighting pitch."

Rockne excused the regulars from scrimmages Monday and Tuesday because of the recent back-to-back road trips. At quarterback, Scharer, Edwards and Reese took turns operating with the first unit in place of Stuhldreher. Harmon and Maxwell again worked in place of Walsh. In Georgia Tech, the fellows would be facing one of the South's consistently strong teams. Bill Alexander, who graduated from Tech in 1912 as class valedictorian, had taken over as head coach from John Heisman in 1920, after a 16-year stint in which Heisman and Tech rolled up a 102-29-7 record, including four undefeated teams. Since then, Alexander had built an imposing 29-7-5 record, and the Yellow Jackets claimed Southern championships in 1920, 1921 and 1922 before falling off a bit in '23.

Tech headed to South Bend with a record of 3-1-1. They started with shutout victories over Oglethorpe and Virginia Military, then tied Florida, 7-7. On October 18, in one of the other big intersectional games, Alexander's squad edged Penn State, 15-13, scoring a major victory for Southern football. The next week brought a stumble against Alabama, and the Jackets were eager to erase the sting of the 14-0 setback. They also brought a memory of last year's visit to Cartier Field, when the Irish ran wild in a 35-7 win. Don Miller showed his amazing agility running, 59 and 23 yards for touchdowns. Miller turned a pass from Crowley into a 30-yard gain and set up another. After it ended, Coach Alexander noted, "The Notre Dame team is the best team that I have ever seen."

ON FRIDAY, OCTOBER 31, the *News-Times* proclaimed that "Notre Dame and South Bend are ready to welcome the crowds of alumni and their families who will attend the greatest Homecoming in the history of the university." ND monograms and blue-and-gold streamers could be seen at nearly every downtown business. Store fronts were decorated with the school colors of both ND and Georgia Tech. Thursday evening, several hundred students and townspeople watched an elimination boxing tournament at the Gymnasium with 13 bouts of 3 two-minute rounds.

Dispatches from Chicago indicated that hundreds of football fans from the Chicago area were passing up the Purdue-Chicago game at Stagg field and the Indiana-Northwestern tussle in Evanston to come to South Bend. Easily the largest crowd in the history of Cartier Field was expected. All but a few reserved-seat tickets were gone by Thursday. Al Ryan, director of ticket sales, said that 4,000 general admission tickets would be sold Saturday starting at 1 p.m. Thursday also saw a crew hastily construct temporary bleachers at the south end of the stadium to seat an additional 1,500 fans.

Though this was just Notre Dame's fifth Homecoming, the sense of family – the bond between alumni and current students, between alumni and alma mater – had been a vital part of the university since the school's founding. Father Sorin's vision of a great university was one that carried the benefits of Catholic higher education across America and around the world, creating an ever-widening circle of influence. As educated men went out into the world, they would always remain warmly embraced by Notre Dame.

An 1897 graduate active with the Alumni Association put it this way:

"I have been back to Notre Dame (several) times in a period of twenty-five years. These visits have been delightful, and why?....New faces are observed. You meet the present generation and when these men are told you were at Notre Dame years back, your hand is grasped in genuine friendship and the old boy feels that he's sure enough back again with his own folks. The longer the time is away from Notre Dame, the more keenly will one appreciate the sterling worth of the men of Holy Cross and the splendid spirit that permeates every individual of the Congregation. Their welcome is real and genuine.

....The analogy of a college and a mother of a family is right here thrown out in strong lights. The love of a real mother is never divided – her son who succeeds is loved by her but not more or less than the son who fails."

He concluded by saying: "When it comes to loyalty, first, hand it to the old college and men of Holy Cross – they are the salt of the earth. Win, lose or draw – they are behind you to a man, and that's loyalty."

A classmate of the Four Horsemen, James Armstrong, put it this way: "The diploma here is not a discharge, but simply a passport to travel in the outside world, with the mutual hopes of frequent returns to campus – another ingredient of the spirit of Notre Dame."

The role of the alumni in assisting the University was becoming more formalized. The *Alumnus* magazine started publishing in 1923, keeping alums up-to-date on a variety of campus and alumni activities. In April 1924, a new concept was unveiled – the first Universal Notre Dame Night, on which 40 Notre Dame clubs across the country held simultaneous events celebrating their love of all things Notre Dame.

HOMECOMING 1924 ALSO featured very specific special plans. The game was to be the reunion of the first football team ever to represent Notre Dame. For one game, on November 23, 1887, and back-to-back contests in April of 1888, Michigan came to town and taught their counterparts the new game of football. The captain of the first team, now Dr. H. B. Luhn of Spokane, Washington, spent a year and a half tracking down the other members of the first eleven. He found all but one:

Quarterback Joe Cusack, colonel, U.S. Cavalry, El Paso, Texas
Tackle George Houck, Portland, Oregon
End Joe Hepburn, insurance business, Detroit
Guard Ed Sawkins, sanitary officer, Detroit
Center Frank Fehr, capitalist, Louisville, Kentucky
End F. H. Springer, Columbus, Georgia
Fullback Ed Prudhomme, member Louisiana Legislature, Bermuda, Louisiana
Guard Patrick Nelson, district court judge, Dubuque, Iowa
Tackle Gene Melady, meatpacking business, Omaha, Nebraska
Halfback H. M. Jewett, president, Paige Motor Company, Detroit

It was the first effort to bring these pioneers of Notre Dame

The Notre Dame farms supplied food for the dining halls.

The view of the Golden Dome
from Cartier Field.

Cars parked next to the wooden bleachers at Cartier Field.

Joseph Casasanta helped to reinvigorate the Notre Dame Marching Band. The band traveled to Madison and Chicago in 1924 for games against Wisconsin and Northwestern.

The dining hall facilities in the basement of Badin Hall.

Left to Right, the Seven Mules: Ed Hunsinger, Rip Miller, Noble Kizer, Adam Walsh, John Weibel, Joe Bach and Chuck Collins. Harry Struhldreher is at quarterback with Don Miller, Elmer Layden and Jim Crowley in the backfield.

oach Knute Rockne was not hesitant to give a personal demonstration on the right techniques uring practice.

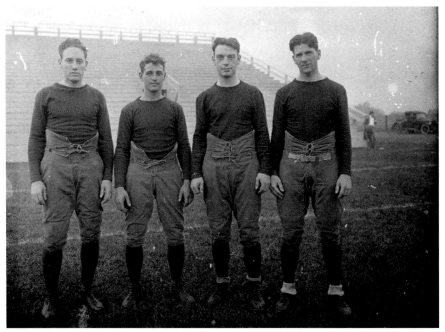

From left: Don Miller, Harry Stuhldreher, Jim Crowley and Elmer Layden.

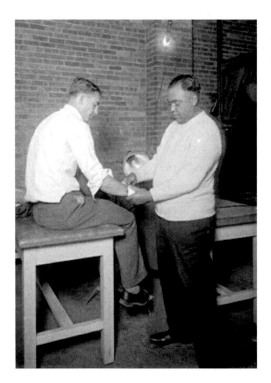

Trainer Verly Smith (left) treats a player. Coach Knute Rockne and Captain Adam Walsh (below).

Notre Dame vs. Army at the Polo Grounds on October 18, 1924.

The Notre Dame traveling party took in the Ziegfeld Follies and Will Rogers in New York City after the game at Princeton.

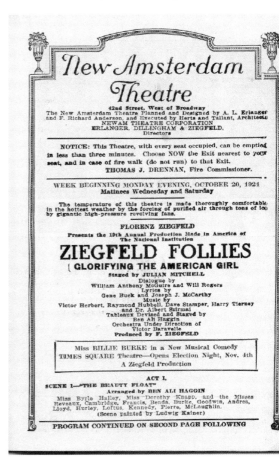

A movie poster for "The Four Horsemen of the Apocalypse."

Notre Dame's
Four Horsemen,
from left to right:
Don Miller,
Elmer Layden,
Jim Crowley
and Harry
Stuhldreher

Joe Bach
Left Tackle
Chisholm, Minnesota

Chuck Collins
Left End
Oak Park, Illinois

Jim Crowley
Left Halfback
Green Bay, Wisconsin

Ed Hunsinger
Right End
Chillicothe, Ohio

Noble Kizer
Right Guard
Plymouth, Indiana

Elmer Layden
Fullback
Davenport, Iowa

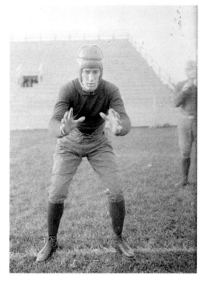

Don Miller
Right Halfback
Defiance, Ohio

Edgar "Rip" Miller
Right Tackle
Canton, Ohio

Harry Stuhldreher
Quarterback
Massillon, Ohio

Adam Walsh
Center
Hollywood, California

John Weibel
Left Guard
Erie, Pennsylvania

Knute Rockne
Head Coach
With Mascot
Tipperary Terrence II

Crowley takes off around end against Princeton. Notre Dame won 12-0.

Notre Dame's Don Miller battles three Georgia Tech defenders.

Notre Dame's first football team from 1887-1888.

Left to right: Joseph Hepburn, of Detroit; Frank Hagenbarth, of Salt Lake City; Dr. Henry B. Luhn, Spokane, Wash.; Col. Wm. Luhn, Omaha, Nebr.; Edward Prudhomme, Bermuda, La.; George Houck, Portland, Oregon; Patrick Nelson, Dubuque, Iowa; Wm. P. McPhee, Denver; Frank Fehr, Louisville; Eugene Melady, Jr., and Eugene Melady, Sr., Omaha. The other members of the team were unable to attend the celebration.

The original team gathered for the first time since 1888 to be honored at Cartier Field during the halftime of the 1924 Homecoming game vs. Georgia Tech.

The Homecoming Dance was held Friday night October 31, 1924.

Notre Dame students who traveled to the away game in Madison received a souvenir postcard.

STUDENT TRIP TO WISCONSIN---Nov. 8, '24

19   24

Notre Dame 38   Wisconsin 3

...s pack Cartier Field for the November 15, 1924 Nebraska game. The Notre Dame ...rching Band performed at halftime.

A cartoon depicts the Charge of the Four Horsemen before the Northwestern game.

The Notre Dame traveling party departs from Chicago, headed for Pasadena, California.

A capacity crowd of 53,000 watched the January 1, 1925 Rose Bowl game.

Jim Crowley rambles for yardage in the Rose Bowl.

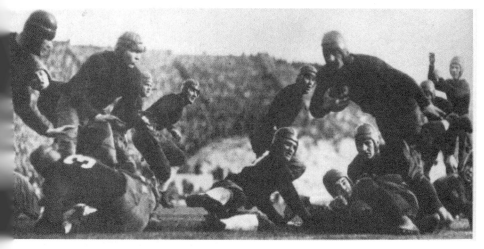

Harry Stuhldreher carries the ball against Stanford.

The team celebrates in Cheyenne, Wyoming after the Rose Bowl.

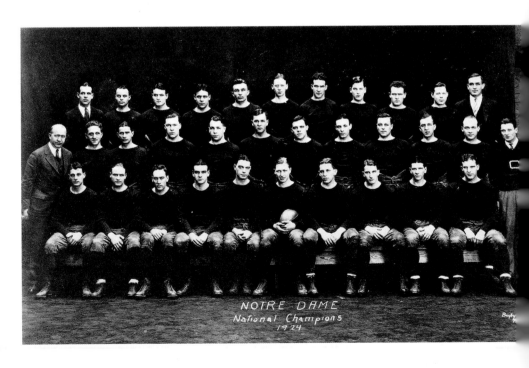

Notre Dame's first national football championship team.

football back to campus as a group in the 36 years since they donned a set of unpadded canvas football suits and, after a brief scrimmage against a team of "scrubs" outfitted in their civilian clothes, took on Michigan. "We had one football, three rule books and no coach," recalled Luhn in preparing for the reunion. "But we did the best we could, and after all, it was the start from which the great Notre Dame teams of later years are the results."

Thousands of Notre Dame alumni, fans, families of current students, and Georgia Tech supporters streamed into South Bend all day Friday. Student volunteers met visitors at each of the train stations and hotels. Information booths, which were of "incalculable worth" to the many visitors, were manned all day. The major hotels – the Oliver, the LaSalle, the Jefferson – were jammed, and townspeople even opened up their homes to some of the overflow.

When the Georgia Tech contingent arrived by train at noon Friday, they were met by a large group from the ND Villagers club. John Stoeckley led a group of some 25 students, who drove the Yellow Jackets in a caravan to the Oliver. Eddie Luther, Max Nikhart, Mike Nykios, Ulysses Rothballer and Ernie Wilhelm drove the Tech team.

At 7 p.m. sharp on Halloween, Friday, October 31, Notre Dame students gathered behind the Band for the Homecoming torchlight parade through campus. "Hundreds of red flares gave the ancient halls of learning a glowing countenance as the voices of hundreds of students cheered the victories of their team." Alumni and fans entered campus under a welcome arch of electric lights, courtesy of engineering students, who also designed an ingenious display of electric lights on their classroom building.

The assembled masses, now including hundreds of alumni, stood in front of a temporary stage just south of the Gymnasium. Eddie Luther introduced Tech Coach Alexander and every member of his team to loud and prolonged applause. Notre Dame men were taking to heart the reminder to provide their visitors with the most cordial of receptions. This contrasted with the less-than-hospitable reception Notre Dame had encountered on recent trips to Atlanta, where anti-Catholicism was strong.

A poem appeared in the *News-Times*, by I.R. Ishers, entitled, "Our Friendly Foes."

Hail, valiant sons of Dixie,
The dearest of our foes;
The whole school bids you welcome;
Each heart with gladness glows.
We trust that as you vision
Once again our Golden Dome,
Your own brave hearts will tell you
That you, too, are coming home.

Of your prowess as fine gridders
There's but little need to tell;
You've proved it clear this season,
As Penn State knows full well.
If we had to lose a battle
(As of course we don't propose)
You'd be our choice as victors –
You gallant Dixie foes.

Coach Alexander addressed the crowd. "We consider it a great honor down south to be included on the Notre Dame football schedule, and we will try to give your team a game tomorrow that will be worthy of your Homecoming." Eddie Luther then gave the starting signal and a swarm of students raced past the alums and out to the field where the firewood was piled. George Wittner from Carroll Hall won the contest to be the first to light his hall's wood; he won an ND scarf. Then all the other wood was added, and the great bonfire roared in the October night, illuminating the entire scene.

Back on the stage, alum Pat Manion, law faculty member, took over as master of ceremonies. He presented a silver loving cup to Brownson Hall for creating the largest woodpile. Brother Alphonsus, for many years the rector of Brownson, accepted proudly. The crowd, now numbering in the thousands, was treated to a vaudeville-style variety show put on by the entertainment committee of the Blue

Circle Club. A rollicking parody of the Ziegfeld's Follies, called "The Fat Man's Follies," brought six of ND's heftier students to the stage. Hogan Morrissey, one of the six, stayed on stage to present several more songs, and the crowd roared with approval.

The highlight of the evening was the presentation of several of the 1887 team members, starting with Dr. Luhn, who was introduced to "riotous cheering." Hepburn, Prudhomme, Melady and Nelson, along with classmates W. P. McPhee and Frank Havenbarth took the stage and were greeted with a huge ovation. More student entertainment followed, and by the time the Band struck up the Victory March, the crowd had nearly shouted itself hoarse. The evening concluded with hundreds filing into the gymnasium to watch the University's boxing finals.

Downtown, hundreds of others gathered for the annual Homecoming Dance at the South Bend Tribune building. Traditionally held on Saturday evening, it was switched because this Saturday was November 1, All Saints Day, a holy day of obligation in the Catholic church. All students would be expected to attend Mass on Saturday.

Class President Don Miller and Elmer Layden served on the committee that organized this dance as well as others. Some of the couples attending the dance included Jim Crowley and Helen Cleary. Helen was a St. Mary's student from Escanaba, Michigan, which was barely a hundred miles up the shore from Jim's hometown of Green Bay. Helen had four brothers, two of whom attended Notre Dame as "minims". Another St. Mary's student, Dorothy Fisher, was the steady girlfriend of Adam Walsh. Some thought that the couple was close to making wedding plans. Don Miller's date was from St. Mary's of the Woods in Terre Haute, Indiana. Mae Lynch had met Don in 1922. Mae's father was a good friend of Coach Rockne. On the way into the game against Butler that fall in Indianapolis, Rockne invited Mae and her father to join him on the bench for the game. The players were puzzled, since they had never seen a girl on the bench. A week later, Don spotted her at a dance and asked her if she was the girl on the bench. They had been a couple ever since.

Because it was Homecoming and a church feast day, Saturday morning classes were canceled. ND students were able to enjoy the buzz of activity that enveloped campus from mid-morning. With a record crowd expected, automobiles started crawling onto campus earlier than usual, following the intricate traffic regulations that had been put into place and published in the newspaper. From downtown, cars were asked to cut over on Howard Street and then proceed up the newly-paved Notre Dame Avenue, just reopened in time for Homecoming. A large field for parking between Notre Dame Avenue and Eddy Street would accommodate hundreds of vehicles. Another field on Eddy and a smaller one near Sophomore Hall would be used for the expected overflow of cars.

At 11 a.m. on a glorious October Saturday, the lunchroom staff from O.A. Clark began serving a barbecue dinner in the field next to the gym, where thousands stood the night before to be entertained. As game time approached, the Notre Dame Band was joined by the Studebaker band and the News-Times Boys Band to entertain the midday diners. Blue and gold banners were everywhere. Women arrived carrying the big yellow chrysanthemums of Notre Dame.

THE IRISH PLAYERS received their final instructions, which included a simple refrain – "Watch Wycoff." The junior fullback from St. Louis presented a triple threat of running, passing and kicking unlike nearly anyone else Notre Dame would face. At 6-feet, 200 pounds, Doug Wycoff was the major force behind Georgia Tech's attack.

Fans were packing the wooden stands when they were treated to a most unusual sight. Slowly rolling onto Cartier Field was a brand new Studebaker Bix Six sedan, the top-of-the-line model. It was driven by George F. Hull, well-known as the former co-proprietor of Hullie & Mike's cigar store, a favorite haunt of ND students for years. When the auto pulled up near the Irish bench, Frank Shaughnessy of the Chicago Notre Dame Club made a quick presentation – the car was a gift of the alumni to coach and athletic director Knute Rockne in appreciation of his years of work in putting Notre Dame on the athletic map of the nation and, indeed, the world.

The players were not overlooked, as Notre Dame monogram blankets were presented to 33 varsity players. They came courtesy of many local businesses and individuals – everyone from the Leroy

Clauer Sports store, Kuehns shoe store and the South Bend Beverage and Ice Assn., to Republican Senator James E. Watson and Republican Congressman Andrew J. Hickey.

With the festivities concluded, the colorful crowd settled back to watch football. ND started its Shock Troops again, and Wycoff took advantage, following perfect blocking, to run for 40 yards on the first play from scrimmage. Scharer, the Irish safety, made a touchdown-saving tackle. The ND subs got their bearings and slowed the Georgia Tech rush, which forced a 25-yard field goal to give the Jackets a 3-0 lead. After a Notre Dame punt, Wycoff started rolling again. The first of the ND regulars, right tackle Rip Miller, entered the game. Wycoff tried an end run around the other side of the line, but Crowe caught him for a nine-yard loss. The Tech star then showed his kicking prowess and launched a 55-yard punt to the ND 27.

Minutes later, after another punt exchange, ND's Wilbur Eaton recovered a fumble on Tech's 37. The Shock Troops found their timing. Doc Connell and Bill Cerney made several strong runs and moved the ball to the Yellow Jacket five. Penalties pushed the Irish back, and they lost the ball on downs at the 13.

Wycoff again got his team out of dangerous territory, this time with a punt of 58 yards. As the quarter was running out, Notre Dame fans spotted a familiar figure tossing off his blanket and entering the game. They could scarcely believe their eyes – it was Adam Walsh. The crowd cheered as their captain took his spot at center. A moment later, he was joined by several other first-stringers.

Cerney and Scharer had remained in the backfield. Don Miller, on his first attempt, broke loose for 32 yards. Crowley, also new in the game, added another 15. Carries by Cerney, Crowley and Miller got the ball to the 5. This time the Irish scored, Crowley passing to Miller, then added the point for a 7-3 lead. Another Wycoff punt gave Rockne's squad the ball at its own 43. Miller's speed and elusiveness were again too much as he went around left end for 18 yards. Crowley burst through Rip Miller's block and zigged for 15 more. Layden, now in the game, ran twice to get it inside the 10, and three plays later crashed through center for a touchdown. In just a few minutes, ND jumped to a 14-3 margin.

Harmon replaced Walsh, and the captain again received great cheers as he left the field. No need to keep Walsh in a game being dominated by Notre Dame. Layden also took a seat, replaced by Bernie Livergood. After a Notre Dame punt, Red Hearden went in for Don Miller, and young Jack Roach replaced Crowley. On just his second carry, Roach tallied a 35-yard run to the Tech five, then scored on the next play. Reese, now in at quarterback, added the kick, and the half ended, 21-3. The crowd, in a convivial mood to start the day, was in even greater cheer. A colorful, unusual halftime show seemed right for the day. Trumpeters dressed in vibrant costumes took to the field, introducing a mock football game of "teahound" players dressed in clown costumes.

The Irish started the second half with a few of its first-unit linemen still in the game. A sub backfield of Edwards, Houser, Connell and Livergood took the field. With a 21-3 lead, Crowley, Miller and Layden were done for the day. Running behind Rip Miller, Joe Bach and John Weibel, the Irish continued to rack up yardage. Livergood went up the middle for 14. Houser circled end for 18. Livergood made another 15 after crashing through the line. But one drive ended with a fumble, another drive when the ball went over to Georgia Tech on downs, and a third drive when Red Edwards' drop-kick attempt from 30 yards went wide. The third quarter ended with no scoring.

Early in the fourth quarter, the remaining regulars in the line exited, and an all-backup squad full of energy against a rapidly-tiring Engineer eleven was raring to show its stuff. Livergood made another 18-yard gain. Doc Connell broke through tackle for 18. The march continued to the Tech 3-yard-line where Scherer passed across to a wide-open Roach for a touchdown. Roach added the point for a 28-3 lead.

More ND players joined the fray, including Gerry Miller, making his first game appearance of the season. Don Miller looked anxiously from the sideline, hoping his brother would get a taste of the success his teammates had been enjoying all afternoon. On his first play, Gerry broke free and hauled in an 18-yard pass from Scherer. Moments later, Joe Rigali entered the game and intercepted a Tech pass at the Engineer 25. Livergood hauled the ball four times, the last time a one-yard plunge for the game's final touchdown. Bernie Livergood, the senior from Stonington, Illinois, had completed his best day as a college football player. And Notre Dame won, 34-3.

Three Saturdays, three intersectional victories – it was an unheard of feat. Notre Dame was winning over fans and the press from coast to coast. And behind the scenes – unbeknownst to most Irish fans, and even the team itself – conversations were underway to arrange for Rockne's "wonder team" to extend its season with a West Coast spectacular. With a 5-0 start, Father O'Hara's hopes to showcase the University were beginning to become a reaility.

16
On to Wisconsin

ALMOST AS LONG as there had been a University of Notre Dame, there had been the Notre Dame Band. The first record of the Band shows that it played for the first commencement in 1846, three years after the founding of the school. The Band played as part of the send-off for students from the Main Circle to both the Union and Confederate Armies. It traveled by horse and wagon to Chicago to play a benefit for victims of the Great Fire in 1871.

For one of the few times in its history, the band was headed to a Notre Dame game away from Cartier Field. The 62-piece band, led by its young director Joseph Casasanta, prepared to join the student contingent making its annual away game trip – to Madison for the game against Western Conference stalwart Wisconsin.

The Band was known for its signature pieces – the Notre Dame Victory March, now 15 years since its composition by Rev. Michael Shea, Class of 1904, but only a few years since being played regularly at athletic events; and the Hike song, a more recent composition by Casasanta.

Only one year earlier, the Band was a struggling organization, its status shaky and its future uncertain. Casasanta, just finishing his undergraduate studies, infused new life into the group. Casasanta attracted new members, and he convinced University officials that the Band was strong and growing. He helped raise funds for impressive new military-style uniforms, which debuted in 1923. The Band earned goodwill for the University by playing benefits, such as the Knights of Columbus concert for St. Joseph's Hospital. In the weeks leading up to the Wisconsin trip, raffle tickets were sold on campus to help raise funds to "send the Band to Madison."

THE MADISON GAME was shaping up as a "second homecoming." Notre Dame alums and fans from across the Midwest – and those simply wanting to see the "Four Horsemen" and their mates – made plans to get to Wisconsin's capital city for the first meeting between the two schools since 1917. For weeks, ticket requests had been pouring into the Wisconsin athletic department for the November 8 game. It was the deepest foray into the West on the Irish schedule and the best chance to see the team that had wowed the East.

"That the crowd at the Notre Dame game will be more evenly divided in support of the two teams than usual is the prediction of Paul F. Hunter director of ticket sales," noted a Madison paper. Notre Dame was expected to fill the entire south half of the east stand with more than 5,000 seats in one block. In addition to the 5,000 tickets sent under registered mail to Notre Dame, several thousands more were sold to Irish followers from the Madison ticket office. Additional bleachers were being constructed, and a record crowd was expected.

"Green Bay is sending down 600 fans to cheer for Crowley," one paper reported. From the Iron Range of Minnesota, a large group was making plans to travel and see Joe Bach play. And Iowans, proud of producing Notre Dame backs Layden and O'Boyle, sent in ticket requests by the hundreds. Wisconsin athletic officials were happy for the sudden wave of business, but realistic about what was drawing the fans' attention.

At the same time, interest was also growing for the Badgers' final two games on the schedule – the Nov. 15 Homecoming clash with Iowa, and the season finale against arch-rival Chicago. On the first day of ticket sales for the Iowa game, students bought 5,119 ducats, the largest single-day sale in Wisconsin football history. Students camped out in the cold, with occasional fistfights over places in the queue, for the chance to buy Chicago tickets.

PERHAPS WISCONSIN FANS were hoping for a big finish for what had been a difficult, sometimes horrifying, set of circumstances the past several weeks. Jack Ryan had come 90 miles west from inter-state rival Marquette to take the reigns at Madison in 1923. From 1917 through 1921, he guided Marquette to an overall record of 28-5-5, including an unbeaten 1917 campaign in which the Golden Avalanche outscored its opponents 348-7. One of his five overall losses was a 21-7 defeat to Notre Dame in 1921.

Wisconsin had been one of the conference's dominant teams in the first decade of the new century, at one point losing only five games in five seasons. After an unbeaten championship team in 1912, the Badgers had a series of seasons hovering around the .500 mark before a post-war resurgence under Coach J. R. Richards. Ryan's first Badger team in 1923 started strong with three wins, including a 52-0 shellacking of Indiana. Wisconsin then scored just nine points in the final four games to finish 3-3-1.

Several key returning players had hopes riding high for the Badgers in 1924. Shutout victories over North Dakota State, 25-0, and Iowa State, 17-0, had the team and fans feeling optimistic. However, on October 11, little Coe College of Cedar Rapids, Iowa, came to Camp Randall and held Wisconsin to a shocking 7-7 tie. Though outgained, the determined Kohawks held twice within their five-yard-line, including a last-minute stand which left the Badgers a yard short of the Coe goal line on the game's final play. The game "was unanimously voted one of the worst exhibitions seen here in years," noted one Madison reporter. The Badgers played better the following week, holding Minnesota to a 7-7 tie.

ON THE MORNING of Thursday, October 23, just hours before the Badgers were to leave for Michigan, senior backup quarterback Herbert Opitz was attending a laboratory class in senior engineering. The class

158

was experimenting in "stepping up" currents of electricity when Opitz accidentally grasped a knife-switch with both hands. More than 700 volts of electricity pulsed through his body, badly burning his hands and partially paralyzing him. After the current was turned off, Opitz was rushed to the campus infirmary, where a team of physicians used every possible means to revive him. After an hour, they spotted signs of consciousness and held out hope for recovery. By late afternoon, however, the effects of the electrocution overcame him, and Opitz died.

The stunned, saddened Badgers boarded the train for Jackson, Michigan, the stopover point en route to Ann Arbor for Saturday's game. Students and townspeople cheered the Badgers on their departure, but the team's thoughts were naturally with their fallen mate. "We haven't forgotten Herb," said one peer. "But we are going to win this football game. We are going to Ann Arbor to play for him as well as the school which we represent." That same evening, Opitz was posthumously awarded an honorary "W" in recognition of his three seasons on the squad.

The next day brought another setback, though not of life-and-death variety. Ed Williams, the Badgers' talented quarterback and passing halfback, was ruled ineligible by Major John L. Griffiths, commissioner of the Big Ten conference. Williams, it was determined, had participated in athletics for two school years at Morningside College in his hometown of Sioux City, Iowa, before coming to Madison and playing football in 1923. Even though he played football just one of the two years at Morningside, he played basketball in both, so his first year at Wisconsin was his third and final year of varsity intercollegiate competition.

Shaken by Opitz' death and missing Williams' skills, the Badgers provided little opposition to a fired-up Michigan team led by sophomore Benny Friedman and lost to the Wolverines, 21-0. The 2-1-2 season had the feel of a losing campaign. Wisconsin looked forward to having an off date on November 1 and an extra week to prepare for the Irish.

INTERPRETING ALL THE happenings of the Wisconsin football season, as well as the sports world in general, was one of the most unusual columnists of the time. Joseph "Roundy" Coughlin of *The Wisconsin State Journal* received plenty of newspaper column inches – and extreme latitude with the English language – to chronicle the day's events. Proper grammar, punctuation and usage were foreign concepts to Roundy, and the paper drew a sizable readership for him by publishing his prose "as is" under the heading "Roundy Says—."

For instance, he summarized Wisconsin's long afternoon in Ann Arbor this way:

"In the Michigan game we had no fight or pepper it was a dead outfit and we a gang that won't go in there and fight no coach in the world can get results. It only takes sixty-minutes on a Saturday afternoon in four big games to fight-fight-fight. Michigan came on the field full of fight that one word made them in this game and it spells f-i-g-h-t. A coach hadn't ought to tell a team to fight that thing they should do on there own hook and be might proud of doing it."

In the same column, Roundy displayed a much different take on the Badger coach, when he penned: "The writer is for Ryan win or lose I know the facts much better than the average fan." Under a subhead reading "Notre Dame," Roundy sized up the next opponent:

"They never beat a conference team in their lifes. We have played them, they never beat us. They play the Eastern teams and they ain't in it at all with Western football. If the Wisconsin team can get it in their heads that they got a chance with this South Benders they might pull the unexpected and beat them. You can't go in there with your daubers down, you got to be on your toes fighting like they do to get their number. If they see your dauber down then a track meet will be a feature of the day."

It was true. In four previous tries, Notre Dame had not beaten Wisconsin; the Irish had not even scored a point. There were three one-sided shutout losses in 1900, 1904 and 1905, then the scoreless tie in 1917. Always a Badger at heart, Roundy wrote a few days before the game that "I'd give my life away to see Wisconsin beat Notre Dame."

THE BADGERS TOOK advantage of their off-date of November 1 with an evening of "recreation in the way of a banquet and theatre party" on Thursday, October 30. A local meat firm, Goeden and Kruger, provided a steak dinner at Fred Hicks' café. The players went to the Orpheum theatre to watch "moving pictures of Knute Rockne's methods of teaching fundamentals." The movies were made for use at Rockne's coaching schools, featuring players demonstrating how the Irish were taught to block, tackle, pass, kick, hold the ball, catch the ball and other movements.

The Badger ranks became further thinned when Austin Straubel, a husky sophomore from Green Bay and a teammate of Crowley's at East High, was told by doctors his season was over. Straubel suffered an injured finger against Michigan, and his hand became infected. Another regular in the line, center Oscar Teckemeyer, suffered an injury to his nose which severely hampered his breathing. With so many linemen out, Coach Ryan took the unusual move of switching Captain Jack Harris, a backfield veteran, to tackle.

Injuries also vexed Notre Dame's week of practice when it was announced Tuesday that quarterback Eddie Scherer, who played so well in Stuhldreher's absence, would be lost for the season with a back injury. If Stuhldreher still could not go against Wisconsin, the job would fall to Red Edwards, with Reese in reserve.

FOR NOTRE DAME, the chance to play a Big Ten opponent other than Purdue and Indiana, who had accounted for 10 of 12 games against conference opponents under Rockne, put an extra shine on the Wisconsin trip. Notre Dame's relationship with the conference had sometimes been a rocky affair. Notre Dame had sought conference admission as early as the late 1890s but was rejected because of stated reasons that the South Bend school was not big enough or serious enough about intercollegiate athletics. Vague references to player eligibility rules were also cited. When the conference added Indiana and Iowa, Notre Dame applied and again and was rejected in 1908. This time Father Thomas Crumley, vice president and chair of the athletic board, injected a possible theological rather than athletic bias.

ND's football success in 1913 again sparked conversation about entry into the Western Conference. The school's growth as an academic institution, its national recognition as a football power, and its tightening of football regulations, including freshmen ineligibility, seemed to counteract any arguments against inclusion into the Big Nine (Michigan had recently withdrawn). However, the conference, led by Chicago and Minnesota representatives, once again denied the application. Student journalists in the Dome editorialized that more than athletics was in play as part of the conference's rejection: "It's easy to understand why Northwestern and Indiana – teams that would end last in our interhall race – objected, but why Chicago and Minnesota, with pretension to Western Championships demurred makes no sense. But the professional prejudices of the conference's 'Academic Men' as well as the growing anti-Catholicism of Midwestern state legislatures were more important factors."

ACROSS THE LANDSCAPE of college football, the first six weeks of the season had weeded out several contenders for top honors. Notre Dame was getting an increasing amount of attention whenever the leaders of the sport got together or otherwise communicated. In the East, Yale and Pennsylvania drew the most interest. In the far west, California, Leland Stanford and Southern California had risen to the top.

Notre Dame had put itself into strong consideration with its 5-0 record. Yet, in the past few years, the Irish and their fans had read and heard about several possible invitations to post-season games that either never materialized, or were declined by the school for a variety of reasons. Early in the week, reports surfaced that Notre Dame would be invited to play in the annual Tournament of Roses game at Pasadena, California. Rockne was quick to tamp down the rumors. "If any such game is being arranged between Notre Dame and a western team, it is news to me," he averred, adding that the report sounded "like the annual bunk." In the next several days, though, the headlines blared: "Fighting Irish Play in California New Year's Day."

On Wednesday night, Gwynn Wilson, graduate manager of the University of Southern California team, announced to the press that his team would meet Notre Dame in the annual Pasadena classic. The announcement followed long distance telephone conversations between Wilson and Rockne late Wednesday night. By noon Thursday, Notre Dame's faculty board of athletics met and ratified negotiations for the game. Southern Cal already had one "post-season" game scheduled, against Syracuse in Los Angeles on December 6. Scheduling Notre Dame, one report noted, "means the opening of athletic relations with Notre Dame that will see a return contest in 1926 or 1927 either at South Bend or at the Grant Park stadium, Chicago."

On the practice field, there was a new bounce in the Irish's step, as described in the *News-Times*:

> "Thirty-six years of football prestige at the school of the Fighting Irish is now preparing to stand validation in one of the greatest football classics of all time. The announcement came with joyous suddenness, but the hugeness and importance of it all is too much for many of the players and students who are still groping through the mist of happy anxiety, hardly daring to trust their senses of sight and hearing and not quite able to reconcile themselves to the fact that the 'wonder team' will be the feature attraction at the Tournament of the Roses. For years the wearers of the Blue and Gold have hoped and waited in vain for the great post-season classic in California....the Tournament of Roses game comes as a fitting finale to the colorful careers of over a score of Notre Dame gridders who are playing their last year of college football."

Some surmised that relationships formed when Rockne held a coaching clinic at Leland Stanford the past summer played a major role in increased west coast interest in the Irish.

In Madison, it was a week of all sorts of gatherings. On Sunday, November 2, a crowd of several thousand massed at the train station to welcome home favorite son Sen. Robert "Fighting Bob" LaFollette, who was returning to his Maple Bluff home upon completion of his quixotic campaign for president under the Progressive Party banner. Tuesday's election would return President Coolidge to office in a landslide victory over Democratic challenger John Davis. LaFollette would win his home state and garner 17 percent of the popular vote.

On Thursday, Madisonians got a rare treat when Lieut. Com. John Philip Sousa and his band performed two shows at the Parkway Theater. It was billed as "a tribute to the supremacy of Conn instruments" and hosted by Forbes-Meagher Music Company, the local agents for Conn instruments. A matinee offered tickets for 50 cents to $1.50; the evening show had seats up to $2. Friday's *State Journal* summed up the evening show:

"Did you hear Sousa play 'On, Wisconsin' Thursday night? Is there anyone in town that couldn't hear him? No tender prelude there; no soothing, haunting tones or charming melody. When the blare of brass as only Sousa can blare broke into the Badger fighting song, the most famous of college tunes, the roof girders looked uneasily at each other and began to doubt their ability to hang together...Let's hire him to stay over Saturday and play just once before the game starts. The subs could then beat Notre Dame, and any Phi Beta on the hill tackle 'Red' Grange."

Elsewhere, the paper noted that "seventy years old was Sousa Thursday, yet his band of skilled musicians played with as much colorful fire and vigor as if they were led by the young commander of 40 years ago."

AT 8:30 FRIDAY morning, the Irish players boarded their train in South Bend. The destination – Beloit, Wisconsin, at the Illinois border. After arriving at 3 p.m., Rockne's men went through a signal drill with the Beloit College varsity, coached by Tom Mills, who had gotten to know Rockne while attending one of his coaching schools.

Beloit was also the hometown of Irish back Ward "Doc" Connell. He was the fourth of five sons of Dr. D.R. Connell, who was one of the founders of a Beloit hospital. They lived next door to the St. Thomas rectory, and the family was very involved in the church. All four of his brothers attended Beloit College, and one went on to get his degree at Notre Dame. Ward, however, attended Notre Dame's prep school before continuing at the University. Saturday began with team Mass at St. Thomas, followed by the resumption of the train trip, directly to the gates of Camp Randall by 11:00 a.m.

Or, as Roundy put it: "The whole team will go to church in Beloit early Saturday morning and then right after come direct to Madison if present plans ain't changed." Roundy's final thoughts on the game were "Ryan has showed the team lots of stuff this week – if the team don't forget it Saturday and will go out and do their stuff with speed and pepper the Wisconsin team in defeat should look rather good. What more could be fairer."

And there was this: "We ain't looking for no win but if this team gets going the way they can and will do it Saturday it should be a darn sight better game than most think."

All day Friday in Madison, football fans arrived by train or automobile and jammed area hotels. Ten special trains carrying Notre Dame alumni and fans were expected from various points in the Midwest. It was reported that "the Wisconsin capital tonight has been brought to the fever point more because of the presence of the Fighting Irish than in hope of a Wisconsin victory."

FIVE HUNDRED NOTRE Dame students, chattering with enthusiasm and laden with "several tons of overcoats and ribbons" and a banner reading "Madison or Bust," boarded the Student Special at 11:30 Friday night in South Bend. Crammed two and three to a sleeping berth, they eventually drifted off to sleep, but awoke to stories of "the brakemen's wanderings of several hours wherein they combed the countryside in search of a new locomotive to replace the crippled engine which headed the caravan at the beginning of the trip."

The trip continued, rolling along the traction line of the Chicago, Milwaukee and St. Paul, and daylight brought a final ramble along the fields of southern Wisconsin farms, icy white with frost. Upon arrival in Madison, the group had a brisk three-block walk to St. Patrick's church, were Father Carey said Mass. After Mass, the Band led a march of the 500 students, cheering and singing, through the streets of downtown Madison. Around the capital square they marched, oblivious to traffic signs, until they reached the Park Hotel and its enormous banner proclaiming "Notre Dame Headquarters." There cheer leader Eddie Luther took his usual perch, on a third-story balcony, and led the crowd in some boisterous yells and songs before adjourning the mob for a much-anticipated breakfast.

As fans filed into Camp Randall for the 2:00 game, it was obvious this would be a different crowd than the ones that typically filled the stadium. ND blankets and banners and Blue and Gold overwhelmed the Badger fans. The crisp fall weather was perfect for overcoats, with the occasional fur coat worn by Wisconsin coeds and others.

Both teams took the field to loud ovations from the split crowd. Wisconsin won the toss and chose to defend the south goal. O'Boyle kicked off for Notre Dame, and the Irish quickly forced a punt by Wisconsin's Doyle Harmon. Don Miller ran for a first down, then another eight yards on two carries, before the Irish's Bill Cerney punted. Cerney's punt was touched by a Wisconsin player, then corralled by Notre Dame before going out of bounds at the Badger 15. Notre Dame found the going tough from there, but Cerney made a 20-yard place kick for a 3-0 Irish lead.

Trailing, Wisconsin chose to kick off and held the ND backups deep in their end. The Badgers partially blocked a Cerney punt and recovered at their 45-yard line. Harmon advanced the ball to Notre Dame's 45, but the Irish stopped the advance. Twice in the next few minutes, on almost identical plays, Notre Dame broke through the line and blocked place-kick attempts by Harmon from the Irish 45 and 40 – both times Wisconsin recovered the loose football, good for a first down.

On a third-and-four from the ND 41, Harmon hit Steve Pulaski on a 23-yard pass play, giving the Badgers a first down at the 18. A double-pass play gained five more. The Badgers were rolling and ready to strike for an early lead. But Rockne rushed his first team into the game – Layden, Don Miller, Crowley and a rejuvenated Stuhldreher in the backfield; Walsh, Weibel, Bach, Collins and the others into the line. The Notre Dame cheering section let loose a mighty roar as the regulars took their positions.

The Badgers secured a first down at the 7-yard line and pushed for another five yards before Harmon dropped back to the 15 and lofted a dropkick squarely between the uprights, tying the game 3-3. The Wisconsin fans went wild, with hats flying in the air through the stands. The Badgers were tied with the "wonder team" after one quarter of play.

A Wisconsin penalty on Notre Dame's first play of the second quarter started the Irish on a quick drive. Crowley went around left end for five yards, then circled the right side for 15 more. Don Miller added six on an end run, but the center of the Wisconsin line stopped the next rushes. Layden's punt went out of bounds inside the Wisconsin 1-yard-line, burying the Badgers deep within their own end of the field. Harmon immediately punted from deep in his end zone, and Stuhldreher was downed at the 40. A penalty pushed Notre Dame back into its own territory.

Layden fumbled, but a teammate recovered. Another run play failed. A pass from Layden to Miller went incomplete. Now the Wisconsin partisans were delirious with cheering. It was the real "four horsemen" the Badgers were frustrating. Layden rocketed a long punt over the Wisconsin goal line, putting the ball at the 20. The middle of the ND line smothered a pair of Badger runs, and Doyle Harmon was again punting to Stuhldreher. This time, the "little general" took the kick at his own 40, dodged tacklers and spun out of bounds on Wisconsin's 34, a return of 26 yards.

The Badger backs, fighting to prevent the game from turning into a track meet, gave each other some quick encouragement. On first down, Don Miller raced around left end and planted the ball near the Wisconsin 20. Two plays later, following perfect interference from Crowley and Layden, Miller again went around left end, this time for the game's first touchdown. Notre Dame students and alums let out a mighty roar, as Crowley's kick made it 10-3, Irish.

The track meet was on.

Wisconsin tried the field-position strategy of kicking off, but Rip Miller came up with the ball and brought it out to the ND 25. Two runs and a Wisconsin penalty advanced the ball to the Irish 40. Then Stuhldreher hit Miller with a pass to midfield. Miller broke free for 22 yards to the Badger 28. Two plays later, Stuhldreher spotted Crowley crossing over the middle, passed 10 yards to him, and Sleepy Jim took it the rest of the way for another score. He added the kick for a 17-3 lead. The crowd reacted with appreciation of the precision and flow of the Irish attack.

This time Wisconsin received the kickoff, and on the second play, track star Harry McAndrews tried to circle the end, but was hauled down for a seven-yard loss by Ed Hunsinger. Stuhldreher fielded the ensuing punt at midfield, and a minute later Don Miller was off again on a 25-yard gallop to the Wisconsin 17. This time the drive fizzled, as a fourth-down pass from Crowley to Layden failed. Wisconsin showed a little life before the half ended, with the Harmon brothers – Leo to Doyle connecting on a 20-yard pass. But the Badgers were again forced to punt, and the half ended, 17-3. The halftime show was a lively affair, with both bands taking to the field and joining forces for some numbers, and with the Wisconsin band marching around the playing field. In the stands, there was an air of frivolity as Irish backers gave out chants and cheers.

The Irish took the second-half kickoff and, after two penalties, were back at their 16-yard-line. From there, Crowley danced out of the shift, eluded tacklers and broke into the clear, racing 59 yards to the Wisconsin 25 before Doyle Harmon brought him down. Two plays later, Crowley made another 12 yards to the 8, and Layden plowed over from the 4 for another Irish touchdown. Notre Dame's juggernaut was on display, 24-3.

As one account described, "the wild applause that greeted the performance would beggar description at this point in the game, partisanship was almost forgotten and the Badger supporters as well as their Irish delegation was unanimous in their praise for the Notre Dame scoring machine."

The Badgers were demoralized by the onslaught but never quit. They held Notre Dame to force punts on the next two possessions and controlled the ball at midfield. Wisconsin attempted a pass, but Don Miller intercepted at his own 45 and blew through a maze of Badger defenders for 40 yards, to Wisconsin's 15. Two plays later, Crowley followed Joe Bach's block for 8-yards into the end zone. Layden's kick made it 31-3.

The first team, except for Adam Walsh and Chuck Collins, left the field to wild cheering. The Irish attack was everything advertised. Several of the Notre Dame regulars went to shower, and it was said Crowley spent part of the fourth quarter in the stands with his mother, who had made the trip with the Green Bay contingent. "That Rockne would send his first team to the showers after a comfortable margin had been secured was cause for wonderment by the fans," the *News-Times* observed. "Never before had the sporting populace witnessed such an exhibition as was today's game."

The remaining minutes belonged to the second and third units, anxious to contribute to the victory. Beloit's Doc Connell closed out the third quarter with a nifty 25-yard run and opened the fourth quarter with a 30-yard burst. Sophomore Red Hearden, another Green Bay East High graduate, entered the game and reeled off several decent runs. Yet another Wisconsin native, Appleton's Jack Roach, closed out the scoring with a 13-yard touchdown scamper.

After the final 38-3 score was posted, the Notre Dame Band led the students on a march down the field and through the goal posts, where "hats were tossed up and over in token of the conquest." A final chorus of the Victory March reverberated among the emptying stands. Then the parade continued toward downtown, where traffic was again stopped and car horns blared triumphantly.

Saturday night, the Crystal Room of the Loraine Hotel was packed for a banquet sponsored by the Knights of Columbus to honor Rockne and his team. Tributes came from Judge "Ikey" Karel, former Wisconsin football star; Badger basketball coach Doc Meanwell, a good friend of Rockne's; and Notre Dame alums such as Warren Cartier and Willie "Red" Maher, the former Madison high school star who was an Irish teammate of the current players in 1922 and 1923. Rockne and Adam Walsh thanked the local KC Council and praised Wisconsin's sportsmanship.

17
Redemption

IN ATTENDANCE AT the November 8 Notre Dame-Wisconsin game were Nebraska Coach Fred T. Dawson and several of his key players, since the Cornhuskers were idle that day. Upon returning to Lincoln, Coach Dawson was diplomatic in his comments to a Nebraska paper.

"Notre Dame has everything," he said. "They are fast – every man – and work like a well-oiled machine. I believe they could have beaten Wisconsin 50 to nothing if they had wanted to. The backfield gets its plays off in good shape; their passing is good and their generalship excellent. Rockne started his entire second string, and then ran in his regulars to pile up a score after which he again sent in his second string. The regular team played about half the game but the scrubs seemed as good as the first string."

Huskers captain Ed Weir was more direct: "Notre Dame has a great team, but Nebraska can and will beat them next Saturday," said Weir, who noted that he felt Wisconsin was not the stiffest test, and that the Badger ends and tackles were particularly weak.

If Weir's comments made it back to South Bend, they could add little to the fervor the Fighting Irish felt about this game. Ever since the

1924 schedule was released, Rockne's players were intensely focused on November 15 and the chance for revenge with their prime nemesis of the past two years. It was said that in the Irish dressing room, lockers were adorned with all manner of signs such as:

"Get the Cornhuskers."

"Remember the last two defeats."

"This year, we ought to beat 'em, got to beat 'em, WILL beat 'em"

IN LESS THAN a decade, the Nebraska-Notre Dame rivalry had become as fierce as any the two schools played. It started in 1915 and saw the Huskers go 2-1-1 against the Irish in the first four games. Then Notre Dame dominated, taking hard-fought victories with George Gipp-led teams in 1919 (14-9) and 1920 (16-7) and a 7-0 triumph in Nebraska's first visit to Cartier Field for Homecoming in 1921. In 1922, sophomores Stuhldreher, Crowley, Layden and Don Miller combined in the Irish backfield for their first start November 25 against Carnegie Tech in Pittsburgh, winning 19-0. With almost no preparation time, the Irish had to turn around and travel to Lincoln for their season-ending clash with the Huskers on Thanksgiving Day, November 30.

In the final game ever played at Nebraska Field, a crowd estimated at 16,000 crammed the old park to see the classic battle. Notre Dame was 8-0-1, having played the scoreless tie at Army on Armistice Day. Going into Lincoln, the Irish had allowed only 13 points the entire season, with five shutout victories, including wins over Purdue (20-0) and Indiana (27-0). Dawson's Huskers came in with four shutouts and the Missouri Valley championship sewn up with a 5-0 conference record; overall, the Huskers were 6-1, having dropped a 9-6 decision at Syracuse.

The Irish players had to contend with the talented Cornhuskers and with the incessant anti-Catholic taunts and jeers of the Nebraska fans. Each Irish visit to Lincoln, it seemed, was greeted by a mob more vociferous in its antagonism. In that 1922 clash, after a scoreless first period, the powerful Huskers dominated. Nebraska, led by the running of Chick Hartley, Dave Noble and Verne Lewellen, marched down the field. Hartley scored on a short run for a 7-0 lead. Before the half ended, he connected with Noble, and the 200-pounder known as "Big Moose" rambled for another score and a 14-0 halftime lead. The Irish took to the air and cut the margin to 14-6 when Don Miller took a Layden pass and went 38 yards for a score. But a final Irish drive was thwarted inside the Cornhusker 10-yard-line, and the game ended 14-6, Nebraska. The young Irish team that had seemingly overcome the loss to injury of its leader, senior captain Paul Castner, was disheartened.

In 1923, everything was setting up for a Notre Dame squad second to none, and the chances to retake command of the Nebraska series were strong. The Irish plowed through their first six opponents by a combined score of 195-16. This record included wins over Army, Princeton, Georgia Tech and Purdue before the November 10 trip to Lincoln. The reception was typical, with a headline screaming "Horrible Hibernians Arrive Today." At Notre Dame's practice in Lincoln, supposedly closed to all onlookers, several green-clad Nebraska freshmen sat in the bleachers and hurled insults at Rockne and his players. Students and townspeople kept up the banter around Notre Dame's hotel. Banners encouraged the home team to "Beat the Papists" and "Maul the Mackerel Snappers."

This time the venue was the new Memorial Stadium, which the Huskers had opened a month earlier with a 24-0 whipping of Oklahoma. That game, however, was Nebraska's only victory to date; a trip to Illinois had ended in a 24-7 loss, and the previous two weeks brought ties with Kansas (0-0) and Missouri (7-7). Dawson's 1-1-2 squad didn't appear on the surface to be a strong contender to upset the Fighting Irish, even with the support of 30,000 full-throated backers. Yet somehow the Cornhuskers rose up to form a defensive front that frustrated the Irish on the ground and in the air all day. Weir, a converted fullback, led the way from his tackle position. Early in the second quarter, Nebraska's Noble caught a pass at the Notre Dame five-yard-line and dragged two defenders into the end zone to stake the Huskers to a 7-0 lead.

The score held until the fourth quarter, when big Noble again made the deciding play. He broke through the line and raced 24 yards for a score and a 14-0 Nebraska lead. The crowd went berserk, and the game had a similar feel to the previous year. The Irish battled back and scored a late touchdown on a pass from Stuhldreher to backup Bill Cerney but could come no closer. The Huskers left the field in delirious triumph, the Irish in bitter defeat. A season that held the promise of perfection was shattered on the unfriendly turf of Lincoln.

Said one Nebraska account: "The Cornhuskers played over their heads….and as the tide of the grueling battle wended their way, the moleskin warriors from the wheat plain of Nebraska went wild with fight and played the game with the savage attack that had been smoldering in their hearts for many weeks…The Husker warriors were seething with that frenzied fighting temper, that has rent many a football machine to victory over great odds."

Nobody was more disappointed than Harry Stuhldreher. He had played his heart out, completing several passes and intercepting three Husker aerials. He swore to himself that day, and to his teammates, that "we would beat Nebraska in 1924, even if we lost every other game" of the season.

TWO-THIRDS OF the way through the 1924 season, it was clear the Irish didn't have to sacrifice any other games in an attempt to beat Nebraska and stay unbeaten. Notre Dame had started strong and built confidence through each game of its 6-0 start. The wins over Lombard and Wabash didn't come easily at first and had required persistence; the long trips to Army and Princeton, with their attendant hoopla, provided another level of testing that the Irish passed convincingly; and the one-sided victories over Georgia Tech and Wisconsin proved the team, at its best, was nearly unstoppable.

Now, finally, it was time for Nebraska.

IN THE LOBBY of the Oliver Hotel, up and down the cigar shops and haberdasheries that lined Michigan and Washington avenues, in every barber shop in town, the talk was the same: Can they beat Nebraska this time? The sting of the two losses at Lincoln hung heavily over the town and campus. Wrote one observer, "The memories of these two games will live long with the score of men whose college football careers end at the Tournament of Roses on New Year's Day."

The Irish, it was said, had two obligations in the Nebraska game:

"One to themselves to wipe out the defeats of the past two years, and the other to the men who built up Notre Dame's football traditions during a period of 36 years." Perhaps never before, it was suggested, "did the reputation of a football team depend so much on the outcome of a (single) game." A third consecutive loss to the Huskers – before an expected record crowd at Cartier Field, with this team of seniors – was too much for many Irish fans.

GROUPS SUCH AS the South Bend Chamber of Commerce and the university's Blue Circle, meanwhile, felt it vital to remind everyone in town and on campus of the importance of showing visitors, especially Nebraskans, a warm welcome to the area. Preparations began to take on the air of a "second homecoming," as thousands were expected to pour into South Bend on special trains and by automobile. Football games at Notre Dame were becoming "an event." Local groups made plans to handle the overflow of guests, arranging private homes that could accommodate visitors unable to find hotel rooms. Information booths and greeters would again welcome visitors at the train stations and hotels. The attention of the middle west, and indeed the nation, would fall on South Bend and Notre Dame this Saturday. Both wanted to show their best side.

In the midst of Nebraska preparation, it might have been easy for the locals to miss an important development coming out of Chicago on Monday. Officials at Northwestern University, Notre Dame's next opponent on November 22, announced that the game had been moved from the school's field in Evanston and would be played in the mammoth new stadium at Grant Park in Chicago, which could accommodate 55,000 fans.

Meanwhile, contrary to rumblings among some fans and newspapermen that Illinois and Notre Dame should schedule an extra game to decide the middle west championship, word came from Urbana that "there is no possible chance for a post-season game with Notre Dame or anyone else," according to George Huff, director of athletics at Illinois. Huff cited a conference rule that banned post-season games, citing that such games kept players in training too long, and that the required trips kept them away from their studies.

Rockne began the week by releasing his first team from practice Monday and sending his second unit from the field after a brief workout, leaving reserves to battle one another in a scrimmage. On Tuesday, preparations began in earnest. Still, Rockne kept an appointment to give a banquet address at the LaSalle hotel to 150 members of Lions clubs from South Bend, Mishawaka, Elkhart, Gary and Hammond. "The things a coach expects from his men are no more than the qualities an employer expects from an employee, that the world expects from those who endeavor to succeed," the coach said. "First of these is brains. A successful player must be able to analyze; he must be resourceful." The coach went on to describe the other key attributes he sought in players – ambition, energy and dependability: "The price of success on the gridiron is effort, self-denial and perseverance."

Perseverance could also describe the football fans attempting to gain entry to Saturday's big game. The clamor for tickets to an Irish home game had never been greater. Everywhere one went, there was someone looking for another pair of pasteboards. Wrote one local columnist: "The telegrams from out of town asking for Nebraska tickets are beginning to get so numerous around this office that we have a notion to see if we can't stage an overflow football game Saturday afternoon." In years past, the Notre Dame ticket operation essentially worked out of Rockne's pockets; he would physically carry tickets with him which could be sold or given away on the spot. The Tuesday before the Nebraska game, he announced that all tickets, reserved and general admission, were completely sold out. "Never before in the history of Cartier field has there been such a demand for tickets," a local newspaper declared. According to reports, the few ticket-holders willing to part with their passes were asking $7.50 to $15 apiece; in Chicago, choice seats were changing hands for as much as $32.50 each, more than 10 times face value.

THE *NEWS-TIMES* also reported that "Coach Rockne has been flooded with applications for press reservations. Additional facilities to take care of the small army of newspaper men have been provided, the second time that the press coop has been enlarged this season." Station WGN of Chicago requested and received permission to broadcast its first game ever from Cartier Field.

The intense interest in the game was evident across the Midwest. Illinois athletic director Huff had written Rockne weeks earlier seeking accommodations to the game. His plans sparked some of the speculation that a game between the Illini and Irish might be brewing, but Rockne said Huff merely wanted "to see a good football game." Extra police were ordered to be on hand to help control the crowd, and a battalion of students was expected to serve as ushers. In expectation of the crowds, Thomas A. Hynes, president of the South Bend Chamber of Commerce, issued a statement Thursday that read in part:

"Friday a gala crowd will begin to pour into South Bend, larger than we have ever seen. They are coming to see the greatest exhibition of football in history. And at this time we cannot too highly stress the great spirit of hospitality which has always been shown by the people of South Bend to visitors in our city. We are all aware of the appreciation that we have of cordial hospitality extended to us in visits to football games in other cities, and how easily the lack of that hospitality can be noticed. We all know how the Georgia Tech team has been so cordially welcomed by South Bend and by Notre Dame for the last two years. The Atlanta press has stressed this spirit of cordiality…in flowing words.

"Notre Dame has a cordial welcome for Nebraska. They will render much the same service for the Nebraska game as they gave to the Homecoming crowds….South Bend also has the most cordial greeting for Nebraska men and for visitors to the game from every city and every state. We must outdo ourselves in hospitality. We must leave no doubt and no uncertainties in the minds of anyone as to where South Bend really stands. South Bend is coming to be known throughout the country for its welcome and its service to visitors. We will build upon this foundation so soundly that every time the name of our city is mentioned it will bring to mind the happy thoughts of welcome and of hospitality."

BY MIDWEEK, WEIR, the Nebraska captain, had toned his rhetoric to humbly state, "We will play our best." The Huskers' best might have come in the season opener, when they played host to mighty Illinois and bottled up the great Red Grange all day before falling 9-6. Nebraska dropped to 0-2 when it traveled to Norman, Oklahoma and lost to the Sooners, 14-7. From there, they bounced back by drilling Colgate, 33-7, and downing Kansas, 14-7, and Missouri, 14-6.

The Cornhuskers entrained Thursday night, serenaded at the Lincoln station by several of their undergraduate classmates chanting the school cry, "Go, gang, go." Coach Dawson and company traveled through the night to Chicago, where they held a light signal drill Friday afternoon at Stagg Field. They continued on to South Bend and could not have imagined what awaited them.

Pulling into the New York Central station a little after 7 p.m., the Nebraska contingent noticed the lineup of automobiles decked out in the colors of both schools. To the cheers of onlookers, the Huskers were escorted to the vehicles, which were operated by Notre Dame's Villagers Club. The caravan, with horns blaring, wound through downtown and brought the Huskers to the Notre Dame campus, where a huge pep fest was waiting to honor the visitors. The *News-Times* described the scene:

"Eddie Luther, Notre Dame cheer leader, introduced the Nebraska coach and players amid a greeting of the wildest cheering that ever resounded in the Notre Dame gymnasium. Coach Dawson, appearing first in the gallery, was greeted with a full three minutes of din and noise that brought forth unstinted praise from the coach whose mission here is to defend the famous jinx of the Notre Dame-Nebraska game.

What Coach Dawson said to the huge assembly which awaited him bespoke the greatest of feeling for the Notre Dame team and its enviable record. He made no predictions and voiced no claims but after eulogizing the merits of both elevens, he concluded with the hope that the best team might win.

The members of the team were introduced individually and were greeted with thunderous applause, but the shouts and cheers that were unleashed for the benefit of Dave Noble equaled the noisy welcome extended the coach. Noble was introduced as the man who scored the two touchdowns that beat Notre Dame at Lincoln last year."

The welcome, the paper noted, was "one of the most elaborate demonstrations yet staged in honor of a visiting football team" and predicted it "will live long in the memories of the men who will meet Notre Dame on the gridiron Saturday afternoon."

After the rally, the Cornhuskers departed for their headquarters at the Mishawaka Hotel.

IN SOUTH BEND, more than a thousand guests were registered at the Oliver, another 500 or more at the LaSalle and 350 at the Jefferson. Even the lesser hotels were filled to overflowing. It was said that even business travelers "caught the spirit of the occasion and cheerfully surrendered their rooms….and doubled up that visitors for the gala event might be taken care of." Hotel clerks directed late-arriving visitors to private homes listed with the hotels through the courtesy of residents. "No one was without a place to stay Friday…owing to the response of South Bend citizens in opening their homes." All day Friday and especially in the evening, the hotel lobbies and streets were humming with activity. A dozen souvenir vendors hawked miniature footballs and artificial dahlias, and 40 more sellers were expected to come from Chicago by Saturday. Lines were long at packed restaurants not used to such crowds.

Friday afternoon, a long distance telephone call from Detroit came in for Rockne. It was Edsel Ford, son of the famous auto manufacturer, looking for tickets to the game. "I'd like to fix you up," came the reply, "but the only thing I've got left is my place on the coaching bench and I'd give you that only I'm afraid the boys might not like it if I walked off on them right at this time."

Saturday morning, South Bend was inundated with train traffic. Four specials from Chicago came over the New York Central line. One from Detroit arrived on the New Jersey tracks. A special from Indianapolis on the Pennsylvania line brought nearly 200 fans. And the regular New York Central run from the east carried three extra coaches carrying fans from Cleveland. Al Feeney, Rockne's teammate from 1910-13 and now an Indianapolis businessman, arranged for 13 Pullman coaches to bring fans from downstate.

Dozens of "specials" were added to the streetcar lines heading to the University. Taxis were also jammed, and busses were pulled off inter-city lines to take fans to campus. The crowd was expected to be twice the size of the one that saw the same two teams play three years earlier, and the number of automobiles was three times those that had parked for the 1921 game. Despite the huge demand for tickets, Rockne proved true to his word, and more than 500 area Boy Scouts gathered to attend the game as guests of the coach and the university. Members of the Elkhart High School football team were also ushered in as Rockne's guests after an attempt to schedule a preliminary game against a Gary school fell through.

Shortly after noon, the Boy Scout drum and bugle corps led a march of the Scouts to Cartier Field. They marched once around the field and then sat on the ground in front of the north stands. Up in the "press coop," the great crush of newspapermen jockeyed for spots from which to cover the game. One Nebraska paper, it was reported, "is sending an aeroplane here to return with photos for their Sunday paper." Chicago's WGN spent $650 to lay a wire for its first-ever radio broadcast of a Notre Dame home game. The South Bend *News-Times*, which ran its gridgraph only for away games, added a phone line for fans not able to attend the game. By calling Mishawaka 181, fans could get an update on the Notre Dame-Nebraska score, as well as other games from around the country.

FANS IN OVERCOATS and wrapped in blankets tried to ward off the chilling November breeze. Notre Dame won the toss and started the game with its Shock Troops. Harry O'Boyle booted the opening kickoff and the most anticipated game of the season – or many seasons – was underway. At the start, ferocious rushes by both teams were met were tremendous physical resistance. Punts became the order of the day, and Nebraska's Bloodgood pinned Notre Dame deep in its end on one of his first kicks. Rockne sent Layden into the game to punt out of danger, but the ball rolled off his foot and Nebraska's Joe Wostoupal recovered, giving the Huskers the ball at the ND 5-yard line.

Rockne sent in the rest of his regulars to try to stop the Cornhusker charge. Two runs put the ball inside the 1. From there, Myers went over for the touchdown. For the third straight year, Nebraska had taken the first lead of the game, though the try for point hit the goal post and went wide, leaving the score 6-0. The crowd was stirring, expecting the "four horsemen" and their teammates to come out charging. Don Miller started with a 10-yard bolt through tackle. Layden pushed for another first down with a five-yard gain on third down. A penalty slowed the Irish, and Layden punted to Nebraska's 33-yard line. The defensive skills of ND's top eleven went on display; an end run was stopped for a 3-yard loss, and after a Husker penalty, the Irish threw Nebraska for another 3-yard loss. The first quarter ended with Nebraska up, 6-0, but going nowhere against the ND regulars.

Nebraska's punt opened the second quarter. Notre Dame started from its 46, and Crowley got loose on an end run for 21 yards to the Husker 33. Minutes later, Crowley gathered in a Stuhldreher pass and raced 25 yards to the Nebraska 3-yard-line. Crowley and Layden got the ball to the one-foot mark, and Stuhldreher followed a solid wall of blockers into the end zone for a touchdown. Crowley's kick made it 7-6 Irish. Fans of the Blue and Gold cheered crazily – for the first time since 1921, the Irish led Nebraska.

Layden kicked off, and again the ND front wall, led by Walsh, Kizer and Weibel, stuffed the Huskers' charge. ND fielded Nebraska's punt near midfield and started moving again. Crowley passed to Stuhldreher for 13 yards and a first down. Miller smashed off tackle for 15 yards to the 25. Layden made eight yards on a crossbuck. Crowley blasted for six more. The Huskers called time to try to regroup but to no avail. From the 10, Don Miller got the ball, slid off tackle and dodged Nebraska tacklers for a touchdown. Crowley converted for a 14-6 lead – the same score by which Nebraska had crushed Irish hopes for an unbeaten season two years previous. The noise from the Notre Dame fans was ear-splitting.

Layden kicked off; the Cornhuskers netted five yards in three plays. Everything Nebraska tried was finding its match. Irish ends Collins and Hunsinger hemmed in anything headed wide. Rip Miller and Joe Bach fought off the Husker interference and made tackles. The Huskers' final possession of the half went nowhere, and the Irish received a punt at their 34 and started rolling. The timing and unpredictability of ND's plays had Nebraska on its heels. Stuhldreher again played receiver, taking a toss from Layden for 18 yards. Crowley ran for another 18 and then hit Don Miller with a pass for 16 more. Miller ran five yards to the Husker 5, and only the halftime gun stopped the drive. The Irish took a 14-6 lead – and all the better of play – to the dressing room.

AT THE HALF, the Irish dressed an eye wound suffered by Stuhldreher when he was tackled after fielding a punt. They steeled themselves for the second half with a reminder: "This time we beat 'em." For the final time in their college careers, the famous backfield, its rock-solid line and another 11 blue-jerseyed seniors took the turf at jammed Cartier Field. The appreciative crowd, oblivious to the cold, let out a loud, sustained roar. The 1,500 Nebraska rooters in one corner were drowned out by the home team's fans. The final South Bend chapter in a scintillating three-year run – one punctuated by just two losses, both being avenged this afternoon – was about to unfold.

Layden kicked off to start the half, and the Irish smothered three runs by the Huskers. Bloodgood attempted a punt, and it was partially blocked, with Crowley falling on it at the Nebraska 40. Miller promptly found open space around end and rambled 22 yards to the 18. Nebraska called timeout as an injured player, Hutchinson, was carried off the field, replaced by Captain Weir's brother. Two plays later, Miller again raced into the clear around the flank. He cut back to the center and danced 18 yards for a score. Crowley's kick made it 21-6, and the delirious crowd sensed it was over. Nebraska had no answer for the feints, the misdirection and the all-out speed of the Irish.

Still, the scarlet-clad visitors were men of pride, and they would continue to fight despite the score and their wearying muscles. They chose to kick, hoping to pin ND deep in its end. Bloodgood's boot carried nearly to the goal line. Miller ran one way, handed the ball to Crowley, who was headed the other, and Sleepy Jim raced to his 22-yard line. On the first play from scrimmage, Miller yet again burst outside for 18 yards. Crowley darted for eight more, got shaken up but stayed in the game. Layden pounded for six yards up the middle. Miller made a sensational grab of Stuhldreher's pass while lying on the turf. The Irish drove to the Husker eight before losing the ball on downs.

The Huskers were forced to punt, and after Layden missed a field goal, ND forced another punt, this one driving Stuhldreher deep in his own territory. Minutes later, Crowley took a short pass with an open field in front of him and outraced a Nebraska defender for a spectacular 77-yard touchdown, the longest play of the season at Cartier Field. Crowley added the kick for a 28-6 lead, again sending ND rooters into a frenzy.

Two years of pent-up frustration were being loosed upon the outgunned Huskers. The "wonder team" was at its best and was virtually unstoppable.

One Nebraska writer described it succinctly: "At will, literally at will, Rockne's hordes drove, hammered, decoyed their adversaries back, back and back....Rockne hasn't only a marvelous backfield, the smoothest, most beautifully functioning quartet ever assembled, but he has just such an entire first eleven."

Now, one by one, members of that eleven were getting their curtain call, taken out to loud ovations. Connell replaced Don Miller, Crowe went in for Collins, Eggert replaced Weibel. On this afternoon, there had been touchdowns scored by three-fourths of the famous quartet – Stuhldreher, Miller and Crowley. Now it was the fourth member's moment. On a final drive, Elmer Layden carried the ball six straight times, his low profile shooting into openings for four yards, seven yards, five yards. His final burst was a three-yard touchdown that made the final score 34-6. Hats and banners flew into the darkening skies. A din lofted from the wooden grandstands.

Tired. Relieved. Vindicated. The greatest team in Irish history trotted happily to their dressing room. There, an eerie silence prevailed. "When the fellows entered the dressing room," one of the star backs explained, "they couldn't talk, they were so happy over the victory."

Fans went about the campus and city in splendid celebration. The Nebraska jinx had been vanquished. A student writing in the Scholastic gave this wrap-up to the historic day:

"Saturday evening, when the blue-black blanket of night had fallen, and from its eastern entrance the huge, henna, harvest moon began its exodus across the feather-harrowed heavens by a triumphal turn through the airy, arched billows of rolling clouds, it seemed to linger over Cartier Field. Drifts of seeming, celestial, consorting gauziness cut off part of the disk in such a manner that it betook the form of a gold oval balanced in the sky, and it was then that I realized that here was an omen! Hanging over the scene of a late, laborious battle; casting its shimmering silver rays on a cross-barred, battle-scarred arena; pointing to the high golden dome; in the form of a gold football, a symbol of supremacy; banked by the silver of popularity, and thrown into relief by a clear azure sky – the true blue of true Notre Dame men; it was in reality a typification of a great victory.

"Nebraska 6, Notre Dame 34 – it tells its own story. But by way of explanation, we add that if the great dipper of the heavens high, had overturned and allowed a drought of nomadic mercury to splash from the Milky Way into the white-sliced field Saturday afternoon, if such had happened, their quivering, quaking incessant motion would have been shaded by the sure-fire shift, the smashes, runs and all around football presented by the wonder squad. It was the last game on Cartier Field for twenty-two men, and every ounce of their energy was in it. It was a test to determine whether the spirit of Gipp, who never bowed to Nebraska; of McInerney who fell in France in '17, was still alive. Was Notre Dame to crack, to suffer the gall of defeat, to endure the upset that all other great teams had suffered? And the answer came: Notre Dame 34, Nebraska 6."

18
Close Shave In Chicago

FOLLOWING THE NEBRASKA game, Notre Dame was the subject of recognition and adulation in the sporting press from coast to coast. Wrote one visiting scribe from Nebraska: "Notre Dame stands where Notre Dame deserves to stand, where it had stood all this season, as the greatest football team in the republic, possibly the greatest football eleven of all time."

Illinois, whose claim to being the best eleven in the middle west was tarnished by virtue of its 21-21 tie with Chicago on November 8, was now reeling. In one of the most stunning upsets in recent Big Ten history, the Illini ventured to Minneapolis and were spanked, 21-7, by Minnesota at its new Memorial Stadium. The Gophers knocked Red Grange out of the game.

IN THE FAR west, a season of controversy and intrigue was unfolding, putting into doubt Notre Dame's opponent for the game at Pasadena on New Year's Day. Late in October, a major rift over player eligibility pitted the University of Southern California on one side and the Bay Area schools – the University of California and Leland

Stanford – on the other. The conflict centered mainly around Big Bill Cole, the Trojans' star tackle, who was suspected of professionalism and prohibited from playing in the Trojans' showdown with Cal at Berkeley on November 1. USC countered by questioning the eligibility of Cal guard Roy Nerswender, whom the Trojans accused of playing professional baseball in Fresno. It was reported that USC representatives "are engaged in detective duty on the athletic pasts of eight or ten players of both Cal and Stanford."

Minutes before the kickoff at Berkeley, athletic officials from both Cal and Stanford announced they "...regrettably have come to the conclusion that continuance of athletic relations with the University of Southern California is not conducive to the best interests of intercollegiate sport" and that no further contests would be scheduled with USC "after the close of the present football season." Handbills with the decision were distributed in the stands at Berkeley just prior to kickoff. Cal, spurred on by a raucous crowd, upset the Trojans, 7-0.

The loss to Cal didn't immediately dim the Trojans' prospects for playing in Pasadena. The Trojans were a favored pick by several members of the Tournament of Roses committee, due in part to the close friendship between Southern Cal coach Gus Henderson and Rockne. When Southern Cal's graduate manager Gwynn Wilson made his November 5 announcement that the Trojans were set to play Notre Dame in the big game, Tournament president S. W. Creller said he considered the game "practically agreed on," even though no contracts had been signed, and Southern Cal hadn't yet made its formal application.

California took itself out of consideration for the Pasadena game by agreeing to meet the University of Pennsylvania on New Year's Day in Berkeley. Many observers felt the fight for the Pacific coast berth against the Irish would come down to the November 8 battle between Stanford and USC at the Los Angeles Coliseum. But on Monday, November 3, the controversy took another shocking turn when Southern Cal announced its executive committee had voted unanimously to cancel the game with Stanford and gave $50,000 in ticket sales to the Palo Alto school to avoid the threat of a lawsuit. Both teams scrambled to find replacement opponents who could show up to play in five days. Stanford brought in the University of Utah and scored an easy 30-0 victory to improve to 6-0 on the season. Southern Cal figured to do the same against St. Mary's from Oakland, coached by former Notre Dame star Edward "Slip" Madigan. But, as one report noted, "debacle succeeded disaster," and St. Mary's stunned the Trojans and 27,000 fans at the Coliseum, 14-10. Southern Cal had the ball at St. Mary's 1-yard line on third down when the final gun sounded.

The Trojans, who just days earlier had announced they were to play in the Tournament of Roses, now found themselves with back-to-back losses, broken relations with the two northern California schools, and the loss of a major payday from the sale of tickets for the Stanford game. The Los Angeles City Council made a last-ditch attempt to keep Southern Cal headed to Pasadena, but the plea went nowhere. Stanford had all the momentum in the battle for the Pacific coast slot vs. the Irish. Its bid would ride on the outcome of the Big Game against California on November 22 at Berkeley.

IN THE NOTRE Dame administrative offices, the bid to Pasadena and the convincing victories over Wisconsin and Nebraska led to a whirlwind of activity. Memories of the South Bend KKK rally from May still burned within Father O'Hara. He felt the Spirit leading him to do something special with this football season. While President Walsh clearly understood the financial benefits a post-season trip might provide, it was Father O'Hara who recognized the huge potential public relations opportunity the trip held.

O'Hara's deep devotion to the Blessed Sacrament and daily communion helped him see a connection between Catholic religious practice and the success of the Irish football team. Under his watch, daily communion became an integral part of life for Notre Dame athletes, and now those athletes were winning accolades and friends across the country. The trip to Pasadena provided a singular chance to make the school and its Catholic affiliation even more visible.

O'Hara's popularity on campus and his abounding energy and enthusiasm made him a natural to take the lead in planning the preparation for the trip to Pasadena. After Notre Dame accepted the invitation, planning and organization started immediately for a three-week tour to and from the game. The trip would showcase Catholic pride and achievement to alumni, alumni clubs, local Knights of Columbus councils and football fans in the South, Middle West and West.

WHILE THOSE PLANS went on, the team still had two remaining contests on the schedule, the first one against Northwestern on November 22 in a game switched to the new Grant Park stadium. Northwestern was building under the direction of third-year head coach Glenn Thistlethwaite. He was hired before the 1922 season to improve the football fortunes at a school which, despite a number of strong seasons around the turn of the century, had but two winning seasons since 1905. In 1922, Thislethwaite brought the Purple up to .500 at 3-3-1, but they slipped badly in 1923, going 0-6 in the Western Conference and defeating only Beloit and Lake Forest for a 2-6 overall mark.

Another addition to the Evanston campus raised hopes considerably for the 1924 season. Ralph "Moon" Baker, who starred at Rockford High School, enrolled at the University of Illinois in 1922 and played on the freshman football team alongside another Illinois prep standout, Harold Grange from Wheaton. Illini fans salivated over the prospect of a backfield including the likes of Baker and Grange, once they were eligible for the varsity in '23. Those plans were shaken when Baker decided to transfer to Northwestern, where he had to sit out the 1923 season.

A triple-threat back, Baker excelled in all phases and was a player that defenses had to account for on every play. Before the start of Big 10 games, he led the Purple to one-sided victories over South Dakota, 28-0, and Cincinnati. 42-0. The Evanstonians stumbled against Purdue, dropping a hard-fought 7-3 tilt, but then recovered to trim the Michigan Aggies, 13-9, and Indiana, 17-7. Through five games, Baker had tallied five touchdowns, five drop kicks from the field and nine drop kicks for extra points. "His varied abilities," wrote one observer, "have probably brought Coach Thistlethwaite's team more gains than the efforts of the other three backs combined." An excellent open field runner, Baker returned three Purdue punts for 60, 40 and 35 yards. Against Indiana, he intercepted a pass at his own 40 and gained 40 yards.

At 4-1 with three games left, the Purple's prospects for a winning season were looking good. But a trip to Michigan on November 8 turned into a 27-0 nightmare, as Northwestern was unable to contend with Coach Fielding Yost's passing game. The next game, against the arch-rival Chicago Maroons, suddenly looked like an impossible challenge. Coach Stagg's team was riding high from its shocking 21-21 tie of Illinois the previous Saturday and had the Big Ten championship in its sights going into its final two games with Northwestern and Wisconsin.

In front of a packed Stagg Field crowd, Northwestern engaged heavily-favored Chicago in a fierce battle. The Purple's defense came to life and thoroughly knocked down the Maroon's passing game, which connected on only two of eight tries for a total of seven yards. Baker's kicks continually backed up the Maroon attack. Chicago's Bob Curey would do the same to Northwestern. Late in the game, Baker launched a punt that traveled nearly 80 yards. Kicking from his own 15-yard-line, he lofted a ball that sailed over the Maroon safety's head and rolled to the Chicago 7-yard-line. It was from that point, however, that Stagg's forces began their only sustained drive of the game, capped by Curley's perfect 22-yard drop kick. Chicago won, 3-0, but Northwestern's tremendous effort gained them recognition.

Wrote one scribe: "We don't know when we've ever seen a team change as much as Northwestern did in the week following the Michigan game. Against the Wolverines the Purple looked like a fairly good prep aggregation; against the Maroons they acted like a bunch of wildcats ready to tear somebody to pieces. If they can go against Notre Dame in that same condition, Rockne may need everything he's got to stop them."

IN THE FALL of 1924, Chicago was a place of big happenings, big plans and larger-than-life people. It was hard not to get caught up in the whirlwind of activity of the Windy City.

"Start Digging" and "Dig the Subway Now" were rallying cries of aldermen and Mayor Dever, proposing a plan for construction of a massive, municipally owned and operated system of elevated and subway rapid transit. The plan was to unify existing surface and elevated lines and to connect them with newly-planned underground lines. On a single day, the Tribune editorialized that Chicago, for its continued growth and health, must both "dig it now" and find a location of its first – and possibly first two – air ports. "These are pioneer days. The air is the new wilderness. America discovered it. But Chicago has not yet staked out her rightful homestead in the sky." Chicago, already a hub of the nation's railways, was also laying down concrete faster than anyone could imagine, turning gravel or dirt roads into hard-surfaced highways. Like spokes from a great tire, routes such as Rand Road, Roosevelt Road, Archer Avenue and Dixie Highway spread out from the great city.

CRIME IN CHICAGO was also big news. In early September, the city was captivated by the murder trial of Nathan Leopold Jr. and Richard Loeb. The two wealthy young men were accused of murdering a young neighborhood boy.

And where else could a breezy front-page story tell of the recent winnings of some $500,000 by "Big Hearted Al Brown," a well-known figure in Chicago's underworld, also known as Al Capone. Big Al apparently "became friends" with a number of owners and jockeys, meeting them at a cigar store near Hawthorne Park, where he cleaned up in the recent meet. General prohibition agents from the Chicago headquarters of the Illinois-Indiana-Wisconsin enforcement division conducted some of the largest operations in the country, including one raid in southern Wisconsin that dumped 32,000 gallons of beer into sewers.

One of the crowning jewels for Chicago was the opening of the new $5-million Grant Park stadium, along the lakeshore south of the "loop district." Designed by Holabird and Roche, its Classical Revival style used the Greek Doric order, the most distinctive feature being a pair of systole colonnades along the east and west sides. Each colonnade, flanked by tetrastyle templates, was built with a double row of 32 columns. The great edifice was declared ready to use in late summer, with about 35,000 seats completed and construction on seating sections continuing. On September 6 and 7, the stadium was dedicated when crowds of 45,000 and 50,000 gathered for the annual Chicago Police Department track and field meet. In the coming weeks, the stadium would host a great variety of civic events, from a children's parade circus to the Chicago Day program, when men of Troop A of the Fourteenth Cavalry charged with their horses through rings of fire.

A committee of the local American Legion suggested that the new stadium be named in honor of Chicago's soldiers who served in the world war. A group of Gold Star mothers, who had a plan for another memorial nearby, argued against it. On October 17, the Chicago Tribune editorialized that "Soldiers' field is the best name for the Grant park memorial to men of the world war. Soldiers and young men are alike the world over." The name was also backed by the executive committee of the World's War Veterans. "Solders' Field," they said, "where the youth of the nation can compete in health-giving games is the best memorial to a soldier whose first requisite to serving his country is a good physical condition."

The first football game at the mammoth new field was the 1924 Public League High School championship game. Then, on Armistice Day, the "Catholic college championship of the Midwest" was contested between Columbia College of Dubuque, Iowa, coached by ex-Irish star Eddie Anderson, and St. Viator of Bourbonnais, Illinois, a frequent foe of Notre Dame reserve teams. A rainstorm turned the field into a mud hole, and the teams sloshed their way to a scoreless tie.

THE NORTHWESTERN GAME served as a homecoming for Notre Dame's Chicago-area players. At St. Ignatius High School in Chicago, Bill Cerney was the football star gaining attention in 1920 and 1921. When he was approached about the possibility of attending Notre Dame, he agreed, but said, "I'll go only if you take Charlie Collins, too." Thus Chuck Collins became the first in his family to attend college. His father had been opposed to Chuck going to college; as the Collins' patriarch had risen to vice president of the National Car Loading Company, a freight forwarding business, without the benefit of a college education, he presumed his sons could do the same.

Collins came to Notre Dame as a 167-pounder and grew into a solid 198 pounds for his senior year. He was an effective player despite the fact that he was missing the index finger on his right hand. While playing for St Ignatius, an opponent stepped on his hand, and the finger became infected and had to be amputated.

One Chicagoan quoted in the *Evening American* noted "this year Collins has been turning in exhibitions at the wing position that have been subject to no end of comment among coaching circles at Notre Dame. He is the type of player who very seldom waits for action, being better satisfied with himself if he is able to start it. Few men have gained on him this season. His work against the Army, Princeton, Georgia Tech and Nebraska has been the best flank play seen by Notre Dame followers this season.

"The majority of the Army's losses this year (in the Notre Dame game) were directly traceable to Collins' unusual ability. He turned many a threatening end run into a small gain for the mighty Wilson, last year's leading scorer in the East. Chicago may well be proud of its native son."

Crowley, although from Green Bay, Wisconsin, looked at the Chicago game as a homecoming of sorts. Crowley's late father had two brothers who were residents of the city. Uncle John was a physician, and Uncle Jim, after whom Sleepy Jim was named, was a druggist.

IT SEEMED TO some that every Chicagoan who called himself a fan of football was planning to head to the lakefront Saturday for a glimpse at the "four horsemen" and their teammates. True, some 32,000 would pack Stagg Field to watch the Maroons attempt to clinch the Big Ten title against Wisconsin. But the draw of a chance to see the "wonder team" caused a tremendous wave of ticket-seekers. And, as one columnist noted:

"Northwestern hasn't got 'em.
Notre Dame hasn't got 'em.
South Park Board hasn't got 'em.
Where in....ARE the tickets?"

Those unable to score a ducat had the next best thing. WGN was continuing its series of college football broadcasts and made the Northwestern-Notre Dame tussle their game for November 22. Notre Dame was happy to be on the big station again. Quin Ryan, a Notre Dame alum who had broadcast the Nebraska game a week earlier, would call the play-by-play. During the week of the Northwestern game, Ryan asked Rockne if Rockne could bring his famous backfield to WGN studios at the Drake Hotel after the game. Rockne replied that he would be happy to talk for a few minutes, but "the boys on the team are scared to death to talk on the radio, and I wish you would excuse them at this time."

The new stadium was as ready as it could be. During the week, Northwestern's movable bleachers were installed at the north and south ends of the gridiron, adding several thousand seats to the site. Officials decided several thousand more could be admitted to standing room areas. Workmen also thickly dressed down the field with hay to protect the turf.

On game day, though, the new field showed the effects of the recent snow and rain and was in poor condition. Players slipped and slid in pre-game warm-ups, while the heavily bundled crowd, many arriving at the stadium for the first time, struggled to find their seats. The Northwestern backers occupied the west stands, including boxes for dignitaries such as Mayor Dever and university officials. The east stands were filled largely by Notre Dame partisans and the general public.

At 2 p.m., Notre Dame's O'Boyle kicked off to Baker, and the slog through the mud was on. The first few minutes set the tone – a Notre Dame fumble, a bad pass from center by Northwestern. Baker missed his first drop kick attempt from 40 yards, but instead of letting the ball hit the goal line, Notre Dame's Scharer fielded it and was buried at his own 3. Unable to move, ND punted, and good field position helped set up Baker for another drop kick try, which he converted from 30 yards out for a 3-0 Purple lead.

With the ball, the Irish gained a little momentum when O'Boyle charged through center to the 35 for a first down, but the drive stalled when Connell lost his footing on an end run. The first of the regulars

– Adam Walsh and Elmer Layden – entered the game. Minutes later, Walsh intercepted a Baker pass, but was called for interference. Layden's first contribution was a 35-yard punt that drove Baker back to his 30-yard line. But on the next play, the Purple star danced his way for 20 yards to midfield to the shouts from the Northwestern section. Baker picked up another five on the next snap, and Rockne brought in the rest of his regulars, the Chicago crowd issuing a mighty shout upon seeing the "four horsemen" together in the backfield. A minute later, after Rip Miller stopped Northwestern's White for no gain, Baker successfully drop-kicked from a difficult angle, increasing the margin to 6-0.

Starting from their 20, the Irish had Layden fake a kick, and he gained 11 yards. Don Miller drove off Joe Bach at left tackle and picked up eight more. On a third-down, Crowley faked a kick and went for four and a first down. Layden made a pair of nice gains through center. The Irish looked to be stopped when Stuhldreher was dropped for a 10-yard loss on a pass attempt, but Northwestern was penalized for being offside. From the Purple 25 as the second quarter began, Stuhldreher hit Miller with a pass, and the Irish halfback slipped to the turf while trying to dodge a tackler at the five. Miller was held for no gain, and Layden netted two yards in two carries, setting up fourth down and goal from the three. The Purple braced for another line buck, most likely by Layden, though the possibility of an end run by Crowley or Miller had the flanks nervous. Instead, Stuhldreher, who rarely took the snap, got the ball and followed a tremendous block by Adam Walsh into the end zone. Crowley kicked to give the Irish a 7-6 lead.

Northwestern decided to kick off, a move that backfired when Layden rumbled for 24 yards off left tackle. The teams exchanged punts, the yardage coming harder as field conditions worsened, and both teams frequently lost their footing. In a break in the action, it was reported, "old grads and Notre Dame men in all parts of the stadium rose and cheered as the Notre Dame student body sang the victory march." Their encouragement was met by a strong Northwestern defensive effort, and Layden was forced to punt. Baker and NU captain Wienecke took turns running the ball for the Purple, and picked up ground before Baker punted to the Irish 20. Again ND met an inspired defense; the purple-clad warriors, as they had a week earlier against Chicago, were truly playing "like a bunch of wildcats" and frustrating the Notre Dame attack. With its running plays stymied, the Irish went to the air. A 30-yard toss from Layden to Chuck Collins was incomplete, but Northwestern interfered, setting up the Irish at midfield in the final minutes of the half. Stuhldreher hit Miller with a pass for eight yards. With time winding down, Stuhldreher set up for another pass. This one was intercepted by White, and the teams carefully stepped through the mud to the dressing rooms, ND ahead, 7-6.

Notre Dame took the second-half kickoff determined to shake their pesky adversaries. Don Miller got free around left end for 15 yards. The drive fizzled on an incomplete pass, and Layden punted to the Northwestern 20, with Baker picking up 23 yards on the return. From there Baker and Wienecke took turns smashing the Irish line for gains, pushing Notre Dame back into its own territory. But Adam Walsh threw Wienecke for a four-yard loss, and Baker's drop kick from 30 yards split the uprights, but fell just underneath the crossbar.

The Irish again found the going rough, and Layden got off a poor punt that made it only to midfield. There, Walsh and Hanousek, in for Kizer, made a big play, dropping Baker for a four-yard loss. With little open along the line, Baker resorted to more passes, but was unable to connect and faced another punt. A penalty against Northwestern backed him up, and he boomed a 65-yarder past the Irish goal line.

Darkness was quickly descending on Grant Park, and the ball was becoming harder for the massive crowd to follow. The Notre Dame rooters let out a mighty roar as if to propel the Irish to another score as they took over the ball at their own 20. On third-and-four from the 26, Stuhldreher found an open Crowley on a 20-yard pass play. Crowley ran for three yards, then took a wide pass from Stuhldreher but was dropped for a six-yard loss. On third-and-13, the pair connected again, this time Crowley breaking tackles and taking the ball to the Northwester 24. The Purple seemed baffled by Notre Dame's array of fakes and feints.

The crowd stood and hollered as the players lined up, sensing a killing blow by the Irish. Crowley dashed for three yards, then fumbled on a reverse and lost a yard before recovering. Miller dashed through left tackle for four and on fourth down, Stuhldreher's short buck pass to Layden fell incomplete, giving Northwestern the ball on its 21. Baker dropped to punt formation, then tried to run, but Bach and Collins collared him for a short gain. On third-and-four, Hanousek broke through to drop Baker for a two-yard loss, and the Purple star punted yet again. Three Irish plays netted six yards, and Layden set up to punt as the quarter ended. ND clung to its 7-6 lead, with all players on the field competing in mud-soaked uniforms. Three straight one-sided games against Georgia Tech, Wisconsin and Nebraska seemed light years removed from the battered Grant Park turf. A perfect season was being seriously challenged in the November gloaming.

Layden, sensing the importance of the moment, extracted every ounce of energy in his right leg to drive the ball 65 yards to the Northwestern 10, where backup NU quarterback Solheim raced through an open field out to the 32. On first down, Baker sliced through the ND line for six yards, followed by Wienecke's lunge at center for two more. On third-and-two from the Northwestern 40, the Purple eschewed the run and attempted a short pass to Solheim. Timing his move perfectly, Layden stepped in front of the pass at the 45 and sprinted untouched into the end zone. In an instant, the Northwestern charge was repelled, and the Irish led, 13-6. A huge portion of the 45,000 fans stood and cheered wildly as Layden was mobbed by his teammates. Even a missed extra point didn't dim their enthusiasm.

With running becoming increasingly treacherous, Northwestern felt aerials were the way to go. On first down after ND's kickoff, Baker faded back and threw wildly downfield, Don Miller intercepting for the Irish at the Purple 40. Miller tried an end run which was sniffed out for a 10-yard loss. Stuhldreher, attempting to get the yardage back, lofted a pass but was picked off by Wienecke. NU's Baker ran once and went back to the air only to watch a roving Adam Walsh come up with the ball on Notre Dame's 44. The crowd was nearly apoplectic with the dizzying turn of possession.

Layden had to leave the game with an injury and was replaced by Chicagoan Cerney. The wet ball, muddy field and intense Purple pressure led to fumbles on his first two carries, the second one going over to Northwestern. On the next two plays, Walsh stopped Baker in his tracks, and Hanousek did the same to Wienecke. Baker, showing the range of skills and pluck that tagged him an All-American prospect, completed a pass to White for 18 yards to midfield. Baker's next pass attempt was broken up by Walsh and Crowley, and he ended up punting to the Irish end zone.

Now Notre Dame needed to keep a drive going, both to run down the clock and to get the ball out from its territory. Don Miller came through with a seven-yard gain behind Bach at left tackle. Crowley did the same, gaining a first down at the 34. Cerney made a nice run, but the Irish were penalized for holding. Crowley set up in punt formation and took off for a 22-yard run and a first down. Miller, going off tackle, lost his balance on the slippery turf but rebounded just in time and picked up seven yards. Again, though, the Irish were called for holding, and the crowd booed loudly while the referee walked off the penalty.

Notre Dame called time and huddled to discuss who would kick in Layden's absence. Not surprisingly, Crowley was chosen and went back into punt formation. But it was another fake, and the darting back lofted a perfect pass gathered in by Don Miller, who took it 50 yards to the Northwestern 25 before being shoved out of bounds. Irish rooters were besides themselves. Crowley crashed through the line, twisted through the arms of tacklers and drove down to the 17. Miller gained the needed two for a first down at the 15. Crowley made an off-tackle burst for eight yards, then drove for another two and a first-and-goal at the five. Victory was in sight.

In the dark and the mud, Miller was stopped for no gain. Crowley saw another opening at tackle, but slipped at the line. Rockne sent in Doc Connell with a play, replacing Miller. Connell gained two yards off-tackle, and it was fourth-and-goal from the three. Connell tried to hit Cerney with a pass but it sailed incomplete, giving the ball to Northwestern at its 3 with little time left.

The irrepressible Baker would not go down quietly. He tried a series of long, high passes, one of which was completed to Seidl for 15 yards. But on the others, Irish defenders had time to get under the ball and knock it away from the receiver. Finally, the gun sounded and teams shook hands, both having given the full measure of effort in difficult conditions. The Irish prevailed, 13-6, and their record stood at 8-0.

On the short train ride back to South Bend, the Irish were quietly mulling the close shave they endured when a swaying inebriate burst into their car. The conductor asked him to show his ticket, but the man scoffed. "Where are you headed?" the conductor asked, "New York, Toledo or Cleveland?"

"I don't know," replied the disoriented rider. "I guess I'm not going anywhere."

Crowley didn't miss a beat, commenting, "He must be one of the Four Horsemen."

19
Closing Out Carnegie

A SENSE OF melancholy hung over the Notre Dame football operation as it gathered itself after the Northwestern game. It wasn't so much the performance in Chicago – after all, even the best of teams have less-than-stellar days – and credit needed to be paid to the singular ferociousness shown by their hosts. No, this was a different kind of sadness, owing to the rapidly decreasing number of days the 1924 Irish team would be together. True, there would be days of practice and preparation for the elaborate trip to Pasadena, but the week-to-week rhythm of preparing for next Saturday's opponent was all but over.

This week's preparation for Carnegie Tech at Forbes Field in Pittsburgh would be gone in a moment. It was Thanksgiving week, and the Irish team, as was the case with their classmates, would leave campus Wednesday. They were scheduled to depart for Pittsburgh with arrival set for Thanksgiving in time to watch the battle between Penn State and Pittsburgh. Friday would allow a practice at the site of Saturday's game, a luxury they hadn't seen on the other trips.

WHILE THE IRISH were in their tussle with Northwestern, a

tremendous battle for the Pacific coast crown was waged at Berkeley, California. A throng of 76,000 filled the stadium with another 24,000 crowding Tight Wad Hill for a vantage that offered a clear view down onto the gridiron. Pundits described the gathering of 90,000 as the "largest sporting event in the history of the West" and said that the colorful enthusiasm of the fans surpassed any such previous contest in memory.

Stanford's star running back Ernie Nevers was sidelined with a broken ankle, causing the game between the two great rivals to be deemed a toss-up. Stanford jumped to a 6-0 halftime lead on two placekicks from Murray Cuddeback, one a sensational shot from 43 yards out. Cal mounted a furious third-quarter comeback behind Tut Imlay and appeared poised to knock Stanford from the ranks of the unbeaten. But Cuddeback, the senior halfback from Monolith, California, led a fourth-quarter Stanford surge to tie the score in what Walter Camp described as "one of the most exciting games I've seen in any part of the country." Cuddeback hauled in a pass from Ted Shipley to cut Cal's lead to 20-19 with seconds left. Sanford fans held their breath as Cuddeback lined up for the tying point. The ball was snapped, there was a perfect placement and Cuddeback booted the ball through the uprights for a 20-20 tie.

On Monday, November 24, reports began filtering out of Los Angeles that Stanford and not Southern Cal would be selected as the Pacific coast representative to face the Irish in the Tournament of Roses football classic. The losses by the Trojans on successive Saturdays, one to St. Mary's College, called by one paper "a second-rate school," seemed to seal USC's fate. Yet intense local lobbying on behalf of the Trojans kept the decision up in the air, and no official announcement was made. Rockne spent the day in Chicago, visiting friends and preparing for a speech that evening to the Chicago City club, entitled "Football as Shown in the Present Season."

Stanford made its case for being named Pacific coast champion. "The fact that California and Washington battled to a tie gives us an edge," said Paul Davis, Stanford's graduate manager. "We didn't lose a game and neither did California. But, we have one tie chalked up against us, while California has two." But with California already set to host Penn on New Year's Day, it was clear Stanford felt there was no other choice for Pasadena.

The results made it clear to the nation's top men in the sporting press. "Notre Dame should be proclaimed the national champion as it has been neither defeated nor tied," read one summation. "Notre Dame stands alone as the one eleven consistently victorious through this season." Said another: "Notre Dame is the greatest. The great power of Notre Dame is not in the flashes of its individual players but in driving of the entire eleven men as one machine."

AT 7:07 P.M. on Wednesday, November 26, a group of 33 Notre Dame gridders and their coaches pulled out of the Pennsylvania station in South Bend, bound for Pittsburgh. The venture to Pittsburgh would allow another entire region to get a look at the "four horsemen" and their teammates. With the holiday weekend, few would be coming from South Bend or the East coast, but the whole football-mad region of western Pennsylvania and eastern Ohio would be tempted to make the trip and see the imminent national champions.

One Ohio resident making the trip was William J. Stuhldreher, Harry's dad. He had never seen his son play football during Harry's high school, prep, or college years. With Saturday being the busiest day in the grocery trade, William was unable to leave the store to see a game. This time he made arrangements and joined a group of about 100 other Massillon residents who traveled to Pittsburgh for Harry's last game.

THE CARNEGIE INSTITUTE of Technology was created as the result of an amazing American success story. A self-described "working-boy" with an "intense longing" for books, Andrew Carnegie emigrated from Scotland with his family in 1848 and settled in Pittsburgh. He worked to become a self-educated entrepreneur, whose Carnegie Steel Company grew to be the world's largest producer of steel by the end of the 19th century. In 1900, Carnegie, now a philanthropist as well as industrialist, founded the institution as the Carnegie Technical Schools. His stated intention was to build a "first class technical school" in Pittsburgh for the children of local steel mill workers. By 1905, the massive buildings of the Carnegie Schools were being constructed. The first students of the School of Science and Technology began classes in unfinished buildings, still surrounded by new construction.

When the school opened, Carnegie announced, "For many years I have nursed the pleasing thought that I might be the fortunate giver of a Technical Institute to our City, fashioned upon the best models, for I know of no institution which Pittsburgh, as an industrial centre so much needs." He concluded with the words, "My heart is in the work," which would become part of the school's official seal, designed by Tiffany & Co., and adopted in 1912, the same year three different schools started classes – the School of Fine and Applied Arts, the School for Apprentices and Journeyman, and the Margaret Morrison Carnegie School for Women. The Carnegie Technical Schools changed its name to the Carnegie Institute of Technology and began offering four-year degrees.

Carnegie started played football almost from its beginning, fielding teams of varying calibers from 1906 through 1911, with a different coach each year. Dr. W. L. Marks provided some relative stability by coaching in 1912 and 1913, and the following year Wally Steffen took over the reigns. Steffen had been an all-American quarterback for Coach Stagg at the University of Chicago, following Walter Eckersall in that role. In his three varsity seasons (1906-08), the Maroons were nearly unbeatable and crushed rival Illinois by scores of 63-0 and 42-6. Steffan earned a law degree, began a practice and was named a judge in the Chicago judicial system.

Each year, Steffen spent his summer vacation preparing the Carnegie gridders for the season. Once games started in the fall, he would fulfill his judicial duties during the week and travel to wherever Carnegie was playing on Saturday. By Sunday night, he would be back in Chicago for another week on the bench.

He was a close friend and contemporary of Rockne. The two played at rival high schools in Chicago just after the turn of the century, Steffen at North Division and Rockne at Northwest Division. Steffen earned the respect of Rockne and other coaches for the way he inspired his Carnegie eleven, often outmanned against better-known schools, to perform at a high level and rack up a string of upset victories.

The Carnegie team, in honor of its founder's heritage, was known by various nicknames, including the Scotchmen, Plaid, Tartan and Skibos, the latter a castle back in Scotland. The school's famous Kiltie Band, outfitted in colorful Scottish kilted uniforms, was widely known as one of the most spirited and musically sound college bands.

CARNEGIE TECH REFLECTED Pittsburgh's power as a center of industry and technology. In 1920, the Westinghouse Company's KDKA went on the air as the first commercial radio station in the United States. Pittsburghers gobbled up sets of all kinds and were at the forefront of an innovation that, by the fall of 1924, had more than tripled nationwide in the course of one year. Pittsburgh's Heinz Company broke uncharted radio territory on October 11. A banquet in Pittsburgh honoring founder H.J. Heinz was broadcast simultaneously to 62 concurrent banquets at Heinz facilities across the United States and in Europe. A total of 10,000 employees – 3,000 at the Pittsburgh event and 7,000 at the other locations – listened via radio equipment provided by KDKA. It was the first time the leader of an international industrial company spoke to all his employees at the same time.

The broadcast also included an address by President Coolidge broadcast from the White House. KDKA broadcast both on its standard frequency and used short wave to reach repeating stations in Chicago; Springfield, Massachusetts; and Hastings, Nebraska. The short wave also relayed the broadcast to banquets in England and Scotland. At each of the 62 banquets, special receiving equipment enabled the diners to hear the talks from Washington and Pittsburgh. The next week the Electric League of Pittsburgh – an organization representing leading manufacturers of electrical appliances and lighting fixtures – opened for tours "the Electric Home" on Wilkins Avenue, featuring the latest in lighting and appliances.

IN 1924, CARNEGIE Tech was gunning for its fifth straight winning season under Coach Steffen. He worked with the team for his usual pre-season vacation and then left the day-to-day practices to assistant Bob Waddell and Coach Marks. The team's captain was one Obie Newman of Birmingham, Alabama. On a team of players majoring in Engineering and Industries, Newman was enrolled in the School of Fine Arts as a Drama major.

In the season opener, the Tartans got a look at the "Notre Dame style of play" by hosting the University of Dayton, coached by Harry Baujan, former Irish end who was a teammate of Rockne in 1913 and a starter in 1915 and 1916. Execution of the Irish plays was somewhat lacking, though, and Dayton fell, 14-3, the Flyers' only points coming on "a pretty kick from placement by Achu, their Chinese halfback." The Plaid routed outmanned Thiel, 22-0, and Toledo, 54-0, before traveling to Washington, Pennsylvania to play rival Washington & Jefferson. Despite the presence of thousands of Carnegie fans and the Kiltie band among the throng of 21,000, W&J prevailed, 10-0.

Tech threw off the disappointment of the loss, and the next Saturday, in front of 30,000 at Forbes Field, upset archrival Pittsburgh, 6-0. Steffen had the team take the unusual step of staying "in the country" the night before the game, away from the bustle of campus and fraternity parties. "Pitt was beaten," said one account, "because it was outsmarted, outfought and outgamed by the sterling crew of Steffen, which had primed itself and never gave up." The Skibos took an early 6-0 lead and then held on stand after stand deep in their own territory. In the game's final minute, Pitt again marched inside the Plaid five-yard line, only to come away empty. "The Tartans' defense of their goal line will hardly be forgotten," it was written. "It was a grand demonstration of what has been called Tech spirit, ably produced by 12 players and a coach who never heard of the word 'quit.'"

Rolling with confidence, Tech blasted Western Maryland, 27-0, and took an impressive 5-1 record heading into their battle at nemesis Penn State, coached by Hugo Bezdek. The Scotch were missing several starters due to injury and fell behind 22-0 before mounting a fourth-quarter rally. But it netted only one score, and the final of 22-7 was a bitter pill. With no game the following Saturday and the team "battered" by the Penn State game, Steffen ordered that no practices be held until Thursday.

Tech's opponent November 22 was the Quantico Marines. Similar to other service academies, Quantico was loaded with former college stars. An imbroglio developed when Penn State's Bezdek, who spent a couple of weeks before the season working with the Quantico team, invited the Devil Dogs, as they were known, to train for the Carnegie game at State College for several days. Bezdek came under heavy criticism for hosting Quantico, a Pittsburgh paper reporting that "many Skibo alumni consider his action…decidedly unethical." Rumors circulated that Bezdek would coach the Devil Dogs against Carnegie. It was also expected that "in the stands will be several thousand Marine rooters from their barracks near Washington, D.C."

The Devil Dogs were undefeated for the season, coming off a 28-0 whipping of the University of Detroit. With its manpower advantage and personal tutoring from a coach who defeated Carnegie just two weeks previous, Quantico was considered a prohibitive favorite when it came to play the Skibos at Forbes Field. On Friday, November 21, a squadron of seven fighter planes left Quantico and headed to Pittsburgh, where they were to put on an "air circus" over the city prior to the football game. Heavy fog engulfed Pittsburgh, and six of the seven planes cut short their trip or headed to other cities. The seventh circled Mayer Field near Bridgeville, west of the city, several times but could not distinguish it from the surrounding area, finally landing in a clearing atop a nearby hill. Their fellow Marines also had a difficult time finding Pittsburgh, as only a few hundred ended up making the trip.

What the spectators at Forbes saw that afternoon was another display of the indomitable Skibo spirit. The Devil Dogs came in "primed, cocky and confident" and "coached to the minute by Hugo Bezdek…who knew every Carnegie play." The Plaid went blow-for-blow with their more senior opponents and appeared headed toward a 0-0 deadlock in the final minutes. Only then did Johnny Groves, a former Maryland State star who drop-kicked that team to a win over Pennsylvania in 1922, use the same tactic from 35 yards to hand Carnegie a bitter 3-0 defeat. The Tartans wanted no talk of a "moral victory," but their doggedness still earned its share of praise. "Such fight as Carnegie exhibits," a columnist opined, "is the real spine of college football."

THE TARTANS' PREPARATION for the Irish focused on trying to stop the ND offensive attack. According to one dispatch from Pittsburgh, "Carnegie Tech has been admonished continually to guard each member of the famous quartet popularly known as the 'four horsemen.'" The correspondent also noted that "the engineers have taken much encouragement from the results of the Notre Dame-Northwestern game and the psychological situation is being capitalized by Steffen. The zest and spirit of the Tech gridders during the practice hours this week did not indicate any resignation upon the part of the players to the fate suffered at the hands of the westerners by Army, Princeton, Georgia Tech and Nebraska. The nationwide prestige of the visiting eleven has served admirably to whet the appetite of the Tech gridders for victory."

Similar to many of Notre Dame's previous opponents, the Tartans prepared to meet an Irish attack that would be likely to use the forward pass at any time. And for the first time this season, coach Steffen was able to leave his duties in Chicago and arrive in Pittsburgh two days before a game, conducting the final practice for the Skibos on Friday afternoon. Even a driving snowstorm did not prevent the Carnegie gridders from going through a dummy practice against their second-string using Notre Dame plays.

As Notre Dame worked out Friday at Forbes, various coaches and visitors milled about. "Other coaches of smaller achievements insist upon secret workouts," noted one local columnist, "Rockne's eleven probably was scouted more thoroughly than any contemporary team." The Rockmen had one handicap for the game, as an injury sidelined Layden. Bill Cerney would start with the Shock Troops and likely stay in with the first unit.

In addition to the "four horsemen," the Notre Dame line had achieved its own measure of fame. On one trip, Adam Walsh heard a knock on his door. The visitor inquired if this room was where he would find the four horsemen. Walsh replied, "Nah, we're just the seven mules." The name stuck.

A running gag among the fellows was the question of which unit was more important to the team's success. A "vote" was take and the mules won, 7-4. The following poem paid tribute to their contribution:

"The poets who sang the great battles of old
And apportioned the laurels due
To the victors, full often left untold
The praises of heroes true,
To commander or chief in each higher grade
Were allotted the honors won;
But rarely were fitting tributes paid
To the man behind the gun.

So, too, in the mimic battles fought
And won on the autumn field,
Not seldom grave Forwards seem half-forgot,
Their derring-do half-concealed.
Yet man a headliner's place in the sun
Is due to their fierce attacks;
For, like to the man behind the gun,
Are the lads before the Backs.

So, a song for Walsh and his Line that starred
The strenuous season through,
A cheer for each tackle and end and guard
Who fought for the Gold and Blue!
Here's to Kizer, and Weibel, to Hunsinger, "Rip",
To Collins and Bach, in fine!
Now, all together a big "Hip, Hip,
Hurrah!" for the Irish Line."

A CROWD ESTIMATED at between 30,000 and 40,000 made its way through the streets of the Forbes neighborhood and into the home ballpark of baseball's Pirates for the 2 p.m. kickoff. Carnegie played many of its games down the boulevard at its Tartan Field in front of crowds as thin as 6,000. But this game was big-league in all respects. Being that many college elevens had completed their schedules, the sidelines were jammed with coaches. Among the mentors in attendance

206

were Sutherland of Pittsburgh, Spears of West Virginia, Stagg of Chicago, Phelan of Purdue, Spaulding of Minnesota, and Bezdek of Penn State. Stuhldreher's prep coach Marks was there, and scouting for Leland Stanford was assistant coach Andy Kerr.

Cheers and clapping exploded as the colorful Kiltie Band marched onto the snow-swept field and delighted the crowd with its sound and spirit.

Notre Dame won the toss and chose to defend the north goal. ND's Doc Connell took the opening kickoff and returned it to the 12. Connell, starting the game with the other Shock Troops, opened with a three-yard gain around end. ND's Red Edwards booted the game's first punt, and Clem Crowe drove the Tech receiver out of bounds at the Carnegie 30. On their first play from scrimmage, the Plaid tried a double pass play but fumbled, and Doc Connell was there to recover for the Irish at the Carnegie 29. A minute later, ND's O'Boyle tried a 31-yard placekick that was blocked by Tech's Anderson. However, the ball squirted loose, and O'Boyle recovered to keep Notre Dame alive. Connell circled left end and broke free for 19 yards to the 13-yard line. The Tartans stiffened and on fourth and five, O'Boyle tried another kick and again Anderson blocked it. This time Carnegie fell on it at its own 12-yard line.

The Shock Troops, especially the seniors, relished the chance they had to contribute, and Crowe made another big play by throwing Carnegie's Bastian for a two-yard loss. Tech captain Opie Newman punted from his 12 to Red Edwards at the Tech 45. The Irish found the going tough and hurt themselves with an offside penalty, so Edwards lined up to punt from the Tech 44. Tech's Bennie Kristoff broke through a wall of interference to block the kick, scooped up the ball, and raced away from the pack 48 yards into the end zone. The Plaid had a shocking 6-0 lead. "The ball was hardly over the goal line," noted one witness near the Notre Dame bench, "before the air around Knute Rockne's head was filled with flying sweaters," as the Irish first-teamers got their orders to report. Cerney stayed in the game, as did Hanousek at right guard, but the other nine spots were now the regulars. Irish guard John Weibel looked across at the Carnegie line and saw Anderson, his old teammate from Erie's Central High, who had blocked two punts already. Weibel shook his head as if to say, "no more for you."

Three plays after the switch, Crowley completed a pass to Don Miller, which was good for 15 yards and took the ball out to the ND 36. The Irish gained eight yards on three plays before Crowley lofted a punt to Tech's 20, where Hanousek threw Carnegie's Bastian out of bounds. Collins held Bastian to a short gain and collared him again after a short pass from Beide. Newman punted to Stuhldreher, and the Irish started down the field. Crowley broke through the right side and raced 13 yards for a first down. Cerney, from the fullback spot, plowed through for another 10, then picked up four more to offset an Irish penalty. Crowley hit Stuhldreher on a 15-yard pass play for a first town at Tech's 33 as the quarter ended. Just as the Irish appeared headed for a score, Crowley was dropped for a five-yard loss and had to punt.

Notre Dame was feeling its strength on defense. With Walsh barking out the signals as usual, the Irish detected many of Carnegie's plays. Bastian tried to go wide, but ND's Hunsinger stopped him cold. Newman tested the middle only to find Walsh ready to make another stop. Newman again punted to Stuhldreher, and the Irish general ran it out to the Notre Dame 32. Crowley made eight yards around end, and Miller tried the other flank, gaining a first down near midfield. On third down, Crowley rolled out and found Miller in the open; Don corralled the pass and raced 52 yards for a score. Crowley converted, and Notre Dame led, 7-6.

Tech chose to kick off, but the Irish quickly foiled that plan by bursting out of their end as Stuhldreher hit Crowley with a pass for 27 yards to midfield. Next the Irish signal-caller hit Don Miller for another 15 yards to the Skibos' 35. Crowley followed Walsh's interference through the middle and raced for 14 more. The Irish machine was clicking as it had in earlier games, and the winded Scotchmen took a time out. It didn't help, as the Irish line was creating holes on every play. Cerney drove through one of them for a first down at the 10. On third-and-goal from the three, Cerney charged through for a touchdown and a 13-6 Notre Dame lead. The 5-foot-9 Chicagoan, as steady a reserve as a team could want, was living up to the standard set by Layden.

The Plaid kicked off again, and this time, their field-position strategy worked, when Stuhldreher fumbled and Tech recovered at

ND's 29. Newman tried a quick-strike pass, but Don Miller broke it up. Two running plays got Tech 15 yards, down to the Irish 14. On second down, the Tartans lined up with an unbalanced line, and backs stretched wide to draw out the Irish secondary. Fullback Beede took the snap from center, faked a pass to one of his backs and then, concealing the ball, turned his back to the defense. After a pause, he darted to the weak side and danced into the end zone, Notre Dame being drawn to the other side by the fake. Newman added the kick for a 13-13 tie, and the Carnegie faithful went wild with cheering as the Kiltie band played. The Tartans were tied with mighty Notre Dame as the half ended a minute later.

A sideline scribe noticed Rockne's "troubled brow" as the trick play snookered the Irish and "a mood of troubled expectancy fell upon thousands of Notre Dame shouters as the two clubs walked off the field…There were many close students of the game who seemed to sense the South Bend machine would start to hum in the last half, but fears for the worst were held by many." One half of football stood between the Fighting Irish and an undefeated nine-game schedule. They had traveled thousands of miles, and they had faced some of the nation's top teams. Now, they would have to dig into their reserve of effort, spirit and perseverance to finish what they had started.

Rockne made one personnel change to begin the second half. He split the chore of replacing Layden by putting in Bernie Livergood for Cerney. With the game in the balance, Livergood eagerly took his spot on the field. After taking the kickoff, the Tartans tried another double-pass play, but it gained nothing. Two runs netted little, and Newman punted to Stuhldreher, who returned to the Notre Dame 43. On third-and-6, Stuhldreher masterfully guided a pass to Crowley, who twisted past a horde of tacklers 35 yards to the Tech 18-yard line. Livergood's name was called, and he went for two yards and then three. Crowley drove through right guard for a first down at the 8. Livergood and Don Miller were stopped for no gain. Miller made a tough pair, and Newman buried Crowley for a 10-yard loss back to the 16.

A tied game and fourth-and-goal, but Notre Dame, as was typical all season, eschewed the placekick route. Stuhldreher barked the signals, took the snap, faked a handoff and found Livergood open over the middle. Livergood corralled the ball and raced past the safety for a touchdown. The daring call left the Tartans bewildered. Crowley's kick put Notre Dame back ahead, 20-13.

Carnegie still tried to play for field position, kicking off over the ND goal line. The Irish were only too happy to stay on offense. Now the shift, the feints, the interference were all working as they had most of the season. Livergood followed Walsh's block for a 9-yard gain. Crowley went for eight off tackle. Livergood smashed through center for a first down at the Tech 45. On a third-and-one, Livergood again delivered, advancing to the 33. Don Miller raced around end for 16 yards down to the 16. The Irish lost an apparent touchdown on an offside call, but Stuhldreher shook off the setback and ran out of pass formation for a first down to the Skibos' 9-yard line. On third-and-goal from the 4-yard line, the Tartans bunched, expecting a bolt through the line. Stuhldreher stepped back and popped a quick toss to Crowley, who darted past the safety for another score. His kick made it 27-13. The Irish were in control. In the stands, William Stuhldreher beamed. Not quite understanding the nuances of this game, he still understood his son was putting on the performance of a lifetime.

Some observers were surprised when Coach Steffen again put the ball into Notre Dame's hands. Carnegie had not run a play from scrimmage since losing yardage in the first minute of the half. This time, Joe Bach fielded Bastian's kick, and the Irish tackle made like a horseman, returning it out to the 25. On third-and-7, Stuhldreher continued his wizardry, hitting Miller for 20 yards to midfield. Livergood churned up the middle for eight yards as the third quarter ended. Irish fans were on their feet, and even the heartiest Carnegie partisans expressed amazement over the Notre Dame machine.

As the final quarter started, Steffen replaced a couple of his regulars who were drained of all energy and unable to continue. Crowley, meanwhile, playing with the joy of a 12-year-old on a Green Bay sandlot, grabbed a pass and twisted 12 yards to the 19. His number called again, he dashed for another first down to the eight-yard line. Crowley, the team leader in touchdowns and points scored, was ready to add to his totals. But Stuhldreher, the skilled leader, came up with a better plan. On four straight plays, he called the number 30 of workhorse backup

Bernie Livergood. On fourth down, Livergood plunged through center for his second touchdown of the day. Crowley's kick made it 34-13.

Now the Notre Dame regulars were primed for their final bows. One by one, Rockne sent in reserves. Adam Walsh, the warrior captain still feeling the effects of his damaged hands, was the first to leave the fray. Doc Connell came in for Don Miller, then Herb Eggert relieved Johnny Weibel. Stuhldreher stayed to guide the efforts of Connell and Livergood, who took turns smashing the ball through the weary Plaid front. With Layden out of the game, and Miller and Crowley each with one touchdown on the board, the "little general" took it over himself before Frank Reese took over at quarterback. A 13-13 halftime tie had turned into a 40-13 extravaganza.

The Notre Dame reserves poured onto the field. Tackles Bach and Rip Miller, stalwarts in every sense, gave way to McManmon and Boland. Tubby Harrington spelled Nobe Kizer at guard, and Crowe swapped places with Chuck Collins. In the closing minutes, the subs fell victim to the same fake-and-run play Beede used to close the first half, but this time it was meaningless. The final gun sounded an end to a 40-19 Irish triumph. Carnegie's Kiltie Band honored the fighting Scots, but for thousands filing out of Forbes amid the ebbing daylight, it was the play of the blue-clad visiting warriors that they would remember.

20
Leland Stanford Here We Come

MONDAY, THE FIRST of December, blew into the campus of Notre Dame blustery and cold. Don Miller shivered a bit while he made his daily stop at the Grotto. There was a hint of frost on some of the rocks that formed this quiet spot, a replica of the larger Grotto of Lourdes in France. For nearly three decades now, Notre Dame students had been praying here, lighting candles and letting the stillness soothe their spirits. On this day, Don Miller simply gave thanks. All the aspirations he brought with him to Notre Dame had been fulfilled. He had gotten an excellent education and was now barely a semester from having a law degree; he had met a "good Catholic girl" in Mae Lynch; he had stayed free from injury and had been fortunate enough to play some football for the Fighting Irish.

Long discarded was any anxiety over trying to live up to the storied achievements of his older brothers. He said a prayer of gratitude for each one of them, remembering the many ways they had supported Gerry and him – a hand-me-down suit, a little money for books or spending. Don said a special prayer for Gerry; it had to be difficult for him to play a backup role with the squad. But Gerry had held up well and wished Don nothing but success in his starring role on the team.

For a few days there would be no football, as the entire squad was given a reprieve from practice after the return trip from Pittsburgh. The exciting win over Carnegie Tech marked the end to an exhausting run – nine games in nine Saturdays, five of them requiring travels – to New York, Princeton, Madison, Chicago and Pittsburgh. It would be good to rest tired muscles, catch up on coursework, and spend more time around the fellows at Sorin Hall.

THE FOOTBALL SEASON, as viewed by most of the country, was over. But another season – the banquet circuit – was just beginning. From Pittsburgh, Coach Rockne and Harry Stuhldreher said goodbye to the rest of the team and took a train to New York City, where they were honored Monday evening at a dinner given by the Notre Dame alumni of New York. Speaker after speaker paid homage to the coach and his team. They quoted sports columnists from around the country who were proclaiming the Fighting Irish as national football champions for 1924.

"For the first time these many years," wrote Davis Walsh, sports editor of the International News Service, "we have an unchallenged national champion of collegiate football and Notre Dame is it...Notre Dame rates the national championship without a dissenting vote." And from the Associated Press: "Comparing countrywide performances, critics generally pick Knute Rockne's flashy Notre Dame eleven which blazed a conquering path through opposing teams from the east, south and middle west, as the greatest combination of the season."

Rockne would not be drawn into the discussion. "Picking or claiming championship teams is not part of a coach's or player's duty," he told the gathering. "Let the critics do that. Our job is to play football and when the schedule is completed, our work is done." The coach offered praise for his 1924 club, calling it the greatest he had ever coached. "I do not mean that it was the most brilliant team of individuals, but I never had a team in which the spirit of co-operation and team play was so fully developed. They all played together and that made them the great team they turned out to be."

As he was finishing his remarks, Rockne was asked about the

impending meeting with Stanford at the Tournament of Roses and whether he would continue his practice of starting his Shock Troops in such a big game. "They tell me Pop Warner has a great team," he replied with a wink. "Maybe the first team will not be good enough."

Three days later in Philadelphia, the Irish received an historic honor when the Veteran Athletes Association of Philadelphia voted unanimously to award its new national football championship trophy – the Bonniwell Cup – to Notre Dame. The new cup was sponsored by Judge E. C. Bonniwell, president of the association. The group, which for several years had awarded a cup to the team it judged to be Eastern champion, said it would honor Notre Dame January 24 at the Veteran Athletes Association banquet.

Back in South Bend, tickets for a banquet presented by local businessmen to honor Rockne and the team "went like hot cakes" when they were put on sale. The December 10 event was scheduled for the big dining room at Studebaker Corporation headquarters. Organizers estimated the room could seat 350 guests. Several banks in town were leading the ticket sales effort. Some tickets were also available at "cigar stores and other business places downtown which are frequented by football enthusiasts."

Meanwhile, alumni and student leaders were planning a celebration at the Notre Dame gymnasium three nights later, on December 13. Byron Kanaley, a Chicago broker and ND alum, was putting together a program that featured several prominent alumni speakers. The event, one report predicted, "will surpass anything that has ever been attempted in the way of victory celebration in the history of the school."

News also came from school officials that delighted those who frequented the gymnasium, especially basketball fans. An annex to the gym, estimated to cost nearly $50,000, was planned for the coming year. It would include a hardwood basketball floor, locker rooms with showers and modern equipment, and seating for 5,000 spectators. The News-Times speculated that "it is also very likely that the time is not far distant when Notre Dame will have a stadium of comfortable dimensions in which to accommodate the mammoth crowds that turn out to see Rockne's phenomenal football teams perform."

The paper offered several editorials proposing a new civic stadium, noting: "Notre Dame has no facilities for meeting the demand of the football fans of the nation who have shown a very real interest in men trained by Rockne. There is needed, at once, a stadium large enough to accommodate the visitors who will inevitably be drawn here next season to witness the games."

In just one season, Notre Dame had blown away all its previous attendance records. A preliminary count showed that some 265,000 fans had seen the Fighting Irish in its nine-game campaign, far exceeding the previous high of 197,000. In fact, the season total had increased nearly five-fold from that of just five years earlier. The notion of fans streaming in from out-of-town for a game other than Homecoming, as they had in setting the Cartier Field record crowd for the Nebraska game, had leaders dreaming of joining the ranks of those schools with new concrete stadiums.

All across the board, the interest in the Fighting Irish and demand for news of the "wonder team" continued to grow. In early December, as talk of Notre Dame's impending trip West intensified, many newspapers ran the unusual photo of the "four horsemen" atop the nags. Sometimes the story got mangled in translation, such as in the East Coast paper that reported the four lads had been teammates "since prep school." But many readers – finally – were able to match faces with the four names they had read so much about.

Early December was also the time of year for the nation's leading sports writers to name their all-America teams. One of the first, picked by Billy Evans, had Stuhldreher and Crowley on the first team and Adam Walsh on the second. Davis Walsh of INS loaded his team with Irish stars – Stuhldreher, Crowley and Layden comprised three-fourths of his first-team backfield, joined by Grange of Illinois. Adam Walsh made his second team, and Don Miller and Joe Bach the third. Walter Eckersall's squad included the same four men as Walsh's on his first two teams. Liberty Magazine put Stuhldreher and Layden on its first team. Walter Camp, probably the most respected expert, placed Stuhldreher on his first team, Crowley on the second and Walsh on the third.

ON MONDAY, DECEMBER 8, the Irish headed back to the practice field to begin preparations for the extravaganza at the Rose Bowl, now just a little more than three weeks distant. On some days, the cold and snow forced the Irish to practice indoors, which created quite a commotion in the Gym. While three teams of gridders ran off their shadow drills, churning up dust and dirt at intervals of approximately ten yards, track athletes limbered up along the walls, looking for the chance to safely run a sprint. Layden the track star joked with his thin-clad teammates about being AWOL. The basketball team, too, would have to wait before becoming whole; Noble Kizer and Clem Crowe were among its featured players for 1924-25. Kizer's opposite number at guard, Johnny Weibel, was re-elected captain of the swimming team, which would welcome his arrival upon the conclusion of football.

On Wednesday evening December 10, the players finished practice, cleaned up and donned suits and ties for the Studebaker banquet. When they walked with Rockne into the dining room packed with 400 people, a huge outburst of cheering and clapping arose. Local businessman Rome C. Stephenson served as toastmaster and welcomed the guests of honor: not just Rockne and his team, but two fellow coaches who had traveled from each coast to honor their friend. Army coach Major John J. McEwan traveled from West Point to attend the event, and Paul Schissler, the former Lombard coach now guiding the Oregon Aggies, made the long trek from Corvallis, Oregon. Two prominent Notre Dame leaders, Rev. Matthew Walsh and Rev. John Cavanaugh, were also at the head table. A well-known local physician, Dr. C. A. Lippincott, opened the event with a speech about the kind of man developed through football at Notre Dame.

"Rockne makes football a means to an end and not an end in itself," spoke Lippincott. "And that end is a man in all his fullness, with the proper mental, moral and physical qualities. For this reason we respect him and are gathered here tonight to pay tribute to him and his football team." Rockne was then asked to speak, and he deflected attention away from himself and toward his players. "If anyone were to ask me the reason for the success of the past season, I would say it was because each player on the team likes his fellow player and any one would give his right arm for the other. Team results rather than individual results were their aim and ambition and this united spirit carried them through to a successful close."

Rockne, in a nod to McEwan's attendance, noted the outstanding sportsmanship exhibited by Army's athletes, and said it was one reason the series between Notre Dame and Army had been such a success. He then turned his attention to his players, especially the 22 headed for graduation in June. They had made a permanent impression on the school, he said, and their places would be difficult to fill. The coach concluded his remarks by introducing each member of the first team – all except Adam Walsh, who was "away from the university receiving treatment for a football injury," reports said. When Major McEwan spoke, he echoed some of Rockne's remarks about the mutual respect between his team and Notre Dame. Army finished the season with only one loss, the October 18 game against Notre Dame, and McEwan complimented the Irish on their achievements. Frank Hering, who captained and coached Notre Dame before the turn of the century, gave a rousing speech that praised the defensive work of the Fighting Irish, especially in the Nebraska game. He also pointed out the unselfishness of the Notre Dame players, noting "it mattered not who carried the ball; the others were doing their utmost that the (ball carrier) should attain the full measure of his efforts."

Rev. Cavanaugh added levity to the affair by gleefully claiming that he had the most to do with the team's success. "Some seven years ago," he reminded the crowd, "I appointed Rockne coach."

The next evening, 75 members of the Notre Dame Villagers Club hosted Rockne at the Rotary room of the Oliver Hotel. Coach Schissler stayed over for the meeting and was joined by another good friend of Rock's, Coach W. H. Spaulding of Minnesota. Spaulding had recently agreed to a pair of games with Notre Dame, and he expressed doubt at his team's ability to keep up with the Irish. Coach Schissler, in his comments, noted that the names of Coach Rockne and Notre Dame were now known everywhere in the country, even in "the most sparsely settled districts of the west."

On Saturday, it was time for the big event at the Notre Dame gym. More than 2,000 students, alumni and fans packed the place and sent its timbers shaking with the reverberations of their chants and cheers.

A stage for the speakers was erected, and over it hung the banners of each opponent from the season. Programs cut into the shape of a cartoon football player included the order of speakers as well as the yells and songs. The stories of Notre Dame legends and traditions were told, each to long, loud applause. Rev. Hugh O'Donnell complimented the Irish players for not just their victories, but also for the way the team represented the Christian ideals of the university. A wish of success from the Western Conference was carried by Avery Brundage of the University of Illinois, the former Olympian in decathlon and pentathlon and holder of the United States' all-around title. Brundage, an athlete who had competed in numerous countries across the globe, called Notre Dame the "center of the athletic world."

Mark Foote of Chicago, from the class of 1873 and said to be the university's oldest living alumnus, paid tribute to the present athletes while expressing pride that the feats of bygone years were still being recalled. Warren Brown, sports editor of the *Chicago Herald and Examiner*, added to the tribute by noting that Notre Dame's team excelled in attracting fans to college football. Brown, in writing up the event for his paper, noted that "some of the speakers reached heights of spell-binding seldom attained outside of a political convention." Angus McDonald, from the class of 1900, was introduced as one of the school's greatest all-around athletes. Behind the scenes, McDonald was playing a key role in helping Rev. O'Hara arrange the trip west, an exercise for which McDonald had special affinity because of his role as vice president of the Southern Pacific railroad. "Notre Dame is saying good-bye to you tonight," he bid the players, "and wishing you success on the eve of your adventure into California."

The introduction of several players and Rockne brought the most thunderous ovations. Harry Stuhldreher spoke for the players, predicting that, "win or lose, Notre Dame will give Stanford a tough afternoon." Rockne, as he would to newspapermen in the coming days, painted a bleak picture of his team's chances against Stanford, but he vowed they would give their best effort. He paid tribute to his assistant coaches – Tom Lieb, Hunk Anderson, George Keogan and George Vergara – noting that it takes a team to coach a team. For nearly three hours, charged-up oratory resounded throughout the old gym.

Frank Hering was introduced as "the Rockne of the early years of Notre Dame football." In an emotional voice, he unfolded "a panorama of glorious football history" that stirred the hearts and voices of the assembled rooters. He brought to the stage four players who had helped defeat Illinois 5-0 in 1898 – John Eggeman, Angus McDonald, Thomas Cavanaugh and Charles Neizer. Hering told how these players overcame great odds, and he encouraged the 1924 Irish to carry the tradition forward in their game with Leland Stanford.

The evening concluded with Eddie Luther leading some of the loudest cheers ever heard on campus. The Glee Club performed several songs, and a takeoff written by Joseph Casasanta, to the tune of Al Jolson's current hit song "California, Here I Come," was a howling success:

"Leland Stanford, here we come
Way down here to have our fun
With horsemen and Rockmen ready to run
We'll crash you and smash you
To make the fun for everyone.
Leland Stanford, we can't wait
To make that score that you'll relate
Open up for Notre Dame
We will win this final game."

IN ALL THE hoopla of the past week, one figure was absent from each of the events. Irish captain Adam Walsh was more than 800 miles away, in Stillwater, Oklahoma, receiving treatment for a badly infected foot that had bothered him since the Northwestern game. The reports in the local press had fans scratching their heads: every preview of the big pep rally at the gymnasium had indicated that Walsh would be one of the speakers.

The answer became evident as the weekend of December 13-14 passed. Reports from Oklahoma filtered in that on Monday, December 15, Walsh was to be married to 20-year-old Miss Dorothy Fisher of Stillwater. The former St. Mary's student, the daughter of Mrs. Kate Fisher of Stillwater, naturally wanted to be wed in her hometown. Rockne pleaded ignorance of the wedding, commenting only on

Walsh's playing status. "He will play in the Pasadena game, provided
he is physically able. Of course, if he is incapacitated we will have to
use someone in Walsh's place." After the Monday morning ceremony,
Adam and his bride boarded a train that brought them back into South
Bend on Tuesday, and they registered at the LaSalle Hotel.

Walsh rejoined his teammates at practice and tested his foot.
"The foot has shown great improvement in the last two days, and if it
continues to improve there is no doubt but that I will be able to play."
Much of the work at practice revolved around mental conditioning;
heavy physical work was limited, it was said, by both the condition of
the players and by the frozen ground. Spikes squeaked on the hard
turf, and cuts lacked sharpness. Rockne longed to get on the road
to warmer locales. He had a brief reprieve with a slight warmup in
midweek, which allowed the team its first scrimmage since the Carnegie
Tech game. The warmer weather, combined with Walsh's return to the
field, added a spark of enthusiasm to the workouts. The freshmen,
under Coach Vergara, simulated the Stanford attack, using an array
of trick shifts, passes and reverse plays with some success against the
Irish regulars. Walsh's foot held up under the strain, and Joe Maxwell
returned to his spot on the second team.

On Thursday, December 18, nearly two dozen Irish seniors went
through their final practice on Cartier Field. Four years of effort, self-
sacrifice and discipline had brought them fame and adulation from
coast to coast. Now it was time to travel together one last time. Father
O'Hara, aided by Angus McDonald, had sketched out a "southern
route" which would bring the team to Chicago, Memphis, New Orleans,
Houston, El Paso, Tucson and finally Los Angeles. The players were
excited to head to new parts of the country. Several reserve players
who hailed from southern states hoped they would be included as
team hosts.

At midweek, Don Miller wrote his mother in Defiance that "the
list of who goes has not been published as yet. Gerald is prepared for
either vacation. If he doesn't go, he shall be home either Friday or
Saturday." Don described the itinerary in detail, adding, "just as soon
as the semester examinations are over (in January), I am going home
for about three of four days, but until then it will be impossible for me

to go....while I am sorry that I cannot be home during the Holidays, I am thankful for the chance to see the Pacific." His backfield mate Elmer Layden expressed similar thoughts in one of his letters: "It will be hard times not to spend Christmas at home." But he had made a trip to Davenport earlier in December, and his family had made sure that the Christmas tree was up to celebrate an early holiday with him.

Senior Ward "Doc" Connell, who played a key role as a member of the Shock Troops' backfield, had not healed sufficiently from recent injuries, which kept him off the 32-man roster headed to Pasadena. The open spot went to an underclassman, and Gerry Miller headed home to Defiance to celebrate the holidays with his family.

The official party included the players, Coach Rockne, Coach Lieb, team manager Leo Sutliffe, and Father O'Hara.

AT 10:17 ON Saturday morning, December 20, from a campus nearly deserted by students headed home for the holidays, the Fighting Irish started their journey, heading first to Chicago. Almost on cue, a winter storm featuring snow, cold and fierce winds slammed into South Bend. Rockne's support of the long trip out looked wise. At 8:15 Saturday evening the team, cheered by several hundred Notre Dame fans who had gathered, left Chicago on the Illinois Central bound for New Orleans. The first stop, at 8:50 Sunday morning, was Memphis, where a group of Notre Dame alums and Knights of Columbus met the Notre Dame party and escorted them to St. Peter's Church for Mass. The entire stop lasted an hour and a half. Hugh Magevney of Memphis, a star pitcher with the Notre Dame baseball team, accompanied the football squad as far as his hometown.

Sunday afternoon in New Orleans, the temperature dipped below freezing and for a few moments, snow flurries fell for the first time in a decade. Despite the chill, more than 600 people gathered outside the Union Station long before the approach of the Notre Dame football train, anxious to get a look at the famous team. Among the crowd were Notre Dame alumni as well as students from Holy Cross College, which like Notre Dame was operated by the Congregation of the Holy Cross. The school was founded in 1849 – just seven years after Notre Dame – when five Holy Cross priests and brothers traveled to New

Orleans from South Bend. In 1879, when Notre Dame's Main Building burned to the ground and seriously threatened the continued existence of the school, the Holy Cross school of New Orleans sold a piece of its property for $10,000 and sent the money north to help Notre Dame rebuild.

As the train pulled in on the station's outer track, cheers went up for the famous team and its coach:

"Rah rah rah rah"

"N-O-T-R-E D-A-M-E"

"Rock-ne Rock-ne Rock-ne"

"Yea Yea Yea"

Regular passengers at the station found it hard to maneuver through the huge crowd. As the Irish players stepped off the train, they were guided through the baggage room to waiting cars. Everyone wanted a glimpse.

"Say, isn't that Harry Stuhldreher, one of the Four Horsemen?"

"Isn't he simply grand," one girl remarked of Adam Walsh.

"There goes Don Miller."

"These boys are too good looking to be football players."

THE PLAYERS APPEARED small, a local reporter commented. Not like a team that has gone through a season undefeated against some of the nation's best elevens.

From the station, the squad was ferried by auto to the Roosevelt Hotel, where they were mobbed by well-wishers in the lobby. A "carnival crowd" pushed as they tried to get near the players; Stuhldreher had a large group offering congratulations. Rockne exchanged greetings with an old ND classmate, former New Orleans district attorney Tom Craven. In the banquet hall, the players devoured a turkey dinner amid some short welcoming speeches. Monday morning, they arose for 8:30 Mass at Sacred Heart Church. After a breakfast at the Roosevelt, hosted by Rev. John F. DeGroote, CSC, rector of the church, the team was taken on a boat ride through the New Orleans harbor aboard the Marie, the yacht of B.S. D'Antoni, president of the Loyola Athletic Council. After that, it was a luncheon at Holy Cross hosted by President Brother Matthew. By mid-afternoon, the Irish were on the field at

Loyola University's stadium, where some 500 fans gathered to watch the team go through its paces. Though it wasn't a full scrimmage, fans were able to see the first unit mostly on defense, practicing against the anticipated Stanford plays. After practice, it was back to the Roosevelt for a performance by a group of Loyola students, then a huge banquet put on by Notre Dame and Holy Cross alumni.

After Mass and breakfast Tuesday morning, the team returned to Loyola for another brief workout, consisting of passing and kicking, a signal practice and dummy scrimmage. Before departing for Houston on the Sunset Limited just after noon, Rockne thanked New Orleans for its gracious reception, but added that once in Houston, the social calendar would be cleared out and the players would get down to work in preparation for the big game. He also changed the team's itinerary, skipping the stopover at El Paso in order to get more quickly to Tucson, where he felt the team could establish a base of operation more conducive to working up to game readiness.

Unusual weather continued to precede the team's travels, as Houston was under a mantle of ice from a storm that dropped temperatures to 22 degrees, the city's lowest reading in years. Local trains and telegraph services were out, leaving Houston "cut off from the rest of the world," according to one report. The weather postponed a highly-anticipated football exhibition between Jim Thorpe's traveling team and the Texas Stars. The idea of acclimating the team to warm southern weather was not working out. But the traveling party pressed on, rolling over Southern Pacific lines on the Sunset Limited and pulling into Houston late Tuesday night. They were greeted by the local Knights of Columbus and taken to the Bender Hotel. A noon banquet on Wednesday, December 24, honored the team, after which a practice at the Rice Institute field elicited more pessimism from Rockne. The team looked soft and slow, he told reporters, due to too many rich meals at banquets and not enough physical exertion.

On Christmas Eve, Father O'Hara tried to lighten the mood by playing Santa Claus for the fellows, giving them each a token of the school's admiration of them. The team attended midnight Mass at Sacred Heart Church. For most of the players, it was the first Christmas away from home.

21
The Crowning Glory

WHEN KNUTE ROCKNE stepped off the train in Tucson, he looked up at a bright blue sky and broke into a wide grin, rubbing his hands together in anticipation. Finally they had encountered the mild weather he had hoped for. Minutes later, after a member of the welcoming committee gave him the schedule of receptions, dinners and banquets, his mood darkened. Rockne thought that his club was already showing the physical and psychological effects of too many feasts on the trip and that the players needed a different regimen. His hosts explained that special care was being taken to feed his players healthy food and allow them plenty of rest, and he again smiled and gave his approval.

The stop in Tucson was originally scheduled for two days, December 29 and 30, but with El Paso off the itinerary, the team would spend four days in the Arizona city. No place on the tour was more excited to be hosting the Irish. In early December, representatives of Tucson and the University of Arizona lobbied Notre Dame officials to consider taking the Southern Pacific route west and to spend some time in their area. The effort was led by several local Notre Dame alumni, including James D. Barry, a former classmate of Rockne's,

224

John B. Wright, and Jim Robbins. The university offered thorough accommodations, including use of all its athletic facilities, especially its well-maintained football field. Coach J. Fred "Pop" McHale, who had guided the school's football team since 1914, was known and respected by Rockne.

The chef at the Santa Rita hotel, Notre Dame's headquarters, was given instructions on what to prepare for the players. Each player's diet was to be strictly monitored, and even the banquets would consist of simple foods.. The players could purchase cigars for souvenirs, but they were expected to refrain from smoking them.

The team's train pulled into Tucson early Saturday morning, December 27, and by the afternoon, 1,500 local fans were watching the Irish at their first workout on the university field. A simple meal followed, and the players were in bed by 9 p.m. On Sunday, the team attended mass said by Father O'Hara at the Cathedral. Originally, there was no practice scheduled for Sunday, but Rockne decided to add one to make the best use of the good weather and available time. "We have been giving alibis for four days," the coach scolded his players. "We are going to get down to business. We've got a reputation to uphold and we are going to win from that coast gang." The players practiced blocking, tackling and running back kicks. For the final portion of the workout, the stands were cleared of onlookers so that the Irish could practice some plays they planned to use against Stanford. After the session, Rockne expressed satisfaction with the workout, saying his players were returning to form.

The local press hailed the Irish players as regular college students who happened to play football well; many had their school books along, preparing for final examinations which awaited them in mid-January back on campus.

Monday morning before breakfast, members of the squad visited San Xavier Mission. The main activity was a sight-seeing trip of the area in automobiles provided by the local Studebaker agency. The boys were well-rested and prepared for a good workout at the university. Under clear skies, with the air crisp and the field dry and fast, the Irish started to look like themselves again. The hundreds of onlookers marveled at the team's speed as it ran through rapid-fire signal drills.

One after another, the three teams of Notre Dame gridders exploded from a standstill, breaking away from the shift into an array of quick-strike moves against imaginary defenders. Rockne, now more relaxed as his players started fitting in solid workouts, spoke at a luncheon of the local Rotary club, where he expressed his thanks to the Tucson hosts and his relief at the excellent weather. In the evening, the formal banquet at the Santa Rita hotel brought out a large crowd of well-wishers led by the local alumni. Adam Walsh spoke for the players, thanking Tucson and noting that the banquet was just the right style for the team. Bishop Daniel Gercke predicted not only a victory over Stanford, but victories in life for the Irish players because of the training they received at Notre Dame. They would become known as Christian gentlemen as well as football players. The banquet ended with the Irish team and alumni singing the Victory March, much to the delight of locals who had never heard the song. The event ended promptly at 9 p.m., which allowed the Irish another good night's sleep.

On Tuesday, December 30, the final day in Tucson, Rockne addressed a regular meeting of the Pima County Bar Association. The dozen members of the Irish squad who were studying law were introduced at the meeting. In the afternoon, the Irish had their final workout at the University of Arizona before their departure at 5:30 p.m. When asked about the late departure for a game less than 48 hours away, Rockne replied, "We are not anxious to get to the scene of our game too early. There are too many people around (in Los Angeles) and we can get better practice here without the final excitement of the contest. Many people say that we are overconfident, but we are not. We recognize flatly that the Stanford game is the greatest of the season. We expect to win, if Stanford is as good as reports indicate, we will be satisfied to win by a score of 3 to 0."

The Irish received a rousing sendoff from hundreds of their new-found friends in Tucson. The high school band played the Victory March and the players were showered with confetti as they boarded the train. "While in the city," the local paper declared, "the Notre Dame party won a host of friends and supporters. Tucson…is backing Notre Dame players to win by a good margin." The new fans were excited to learn that the play-by-play returns of the game were to be announced in front of the Tucson Opera House.

The Notre Dame special had an extra car as it left Tucson. Angus McDonald, the Southern Pacific executive and former Notre Dame star athlete, added his private car to the team's train. McDonald, a member of the university's board of trustees and former president of the alumni association, was looking forward to accompanying the team to San Francisco after the Tournament of Roses, as he had come to Notre Dame in the 1890s from his hometown of Oakland.

In GLENN SCOBEY "Pop" Warner of Stanford, the Irish would face one of the most experienced, accomplished and innovative coaches in college football history. The wily veteran had seen almost everything in his 30 years as a college coach – and much he had developed himself. The spiral pass, the spiral punt, numbered plays, the dummy scrimmage, the double-wing formation, the unbalanced line were all the creative work of Warner. When he enrolled at Cornell in 1891, he was among the oldest freshmen, a fact which earned him the nickname "Pop." He starred at guard for Cornell from 1892-94, boxed as a heavyweight and earned a law degree before he started his coaching career with brief stints at Georgia and his alma mater.

His coaching genius first appeared when he came to the tiny Carlisle Indian School in Pennsylvania. There, he took boys unschooled in the sport and turned out one impressive team after another, taking on much larger schools that were far advanced in the game. At Carlisle, he coached one of the all-time greats, Jim Thorpe. His careful guidance of the talented star helped Thorpe become a name feared and respected throughout football.

In 1915, he moved on to the University of Pittsburgh, where he posted a mark of 60-12-4 in the next nine seasons. Warner was credited with developing more plays than any other man in football history. His arsenal was so deep, it was said, he could use a given play just once every few years, and coaches far and wide would wonder where this "new" play had been hiding. In 1923, he had his worst spell with the Panthers, losing four straight games. It was reported that he was coaching "with another offer signed in his pocket." Warner resigned at season's end to move west and take the reins at Stanford, where he succeeded Andy

Kerr but kept the well-liked coach as his top assistant.

In coming to Palo Alto, Warner inherited one of the great talents in the game – fullback Ernie Nevers. From his earlier days while starring for Superior Central High School in Wisconsin, Nevers had grown into an all-around player of great strength and skill.

Ernest Nevers was born on June 11, 1902 in Willow River, Minnesota, the youngest of George and Mary Nevers' seven children. The family worked in and operated hotels, dining rooms and boarding houses, and had lived in several locations in and around the western end of Lake Superior in Ontario, Wisconsin and Minnesota. While at Superior, young Ernie excelled in basketball as well as football, and nearly accepted an offer to enter the University of Wisconsin to play basketball. Instead, he moved with his family to Santa Rosa, California, where he attended high school another year before entering Stanford in 1922.

Nevers developed into an outstanding college back under Kerr in 1922 and 1923. Great things were expected when Warner took over as Stanford's coach. Warner's offense was designed to get the ball into Nevers' hands nearly every play. He was almost unstoppable as a bruising running back, accomplished as a passer and punter and ferocious on defense.

In 1924, Nevers was also frequently injured. During the regular season, he was able to play in parts of just two games. Both of his ankles were severely injured, and he had seen no action since leaving Stanford's 41-3 win over Montana on November 15, missing the monumental clash with archrival California the following week. However, by mid-December Nevers declared himself ready to play on New Year's Day. Stanford fans debated whether a not-completely-healed Nevers would be an "ace in the hole" or a detriment to the Cardinal. The latter camp had some evidence on its side. Against Utah on November 8, Nevers made some decent gains but had a hard time settling the football and he fumbled several times. If Nevers was able to play at full or nearly full strength, Stanford would have a tremendous advantage.

Another star Cardinal back, it appeared, was definitely out for the big game. Norman Cleaveland, who was also the Stanford punter, had been ruled ineligible for the California game on November 22 after it was determined he had played a few minutes in a game for St. Mary's College back in 1921. In a gesture of sportsmanship, Rockne wired Stanford president Wilbur to say that he had no objection to Cleaveland playing, as the infraction seemed minor. But the school responded that Pacific Coast Conference rules held that the same eligibility requirements apply to games against non-conference opponents as to those against league teams. Cleaveland would not play.

DECEMBER 1924 WAS an exciting time in the Bay Area of California. No other area of the country could boast that both of its major football teams were involved in New Year's Day clashes with intersectional powers. The Penn-Cal game at Berkeley was big enough that some even suggested moving it to another date so as not to conflict with the Stanford-Notre Dame battle in Pasadena. But it was determined that the move was not practical, and plans for both New Year's engagements continued.

On December 20, the area received another enormous boost to civic pride when the U.S. government approved plans for a $21-million bridge to span San Francisco Bay at the area known as the Golden Gate. The wire of approval came from Secretary of War Weeks, whose department was involved due to the strategic location of the proposed span. "The general project for construction of the Golden Gate Bridge is approved, subject to conditions which follow by letter," the message from Weeks read.

THE POSSIBLE RETURN of Nevers was not the only factor working to Stanford's advantage. Pop Warner, it turns out, had assembled a huge body of information on Notre Dame's formation and tendencies and was using it to prepare his defense.

Former Princeton all-American Franklin B. Morse, writing in a San Francisco paper, put it this way: "Never before did a coach have as much information about a team as has Warner. The intelligence section of the United States expeditionary force during the World war…was a mere amateur compared to Warner's volunteer informants." Warner had numerous photos of the Irish, some taken from the sidelines, others from grandstand roofs. All showed action immediately after the snap of the ball, as plays and blocking schemes developed. Warner consulted with coaches of Irish opponents; it was said Coach Roper of Princeton gave detailed description of Notre Dame's strategy. Some of Warner's football friends came forward to offer information. The old coach was taking all the information and devising a plan to stop "the horsemen." He also had some moving pictures of the Notre Dame system to use in his planning.

"Those fellows are a versatile lot," said Warner. "A fellow has to keep his eye peeled all the time. They have a habit of going where you least expect them. Their regular line plays are as tricky as their aerial attack." Warner described a typical Notre Dame play in which the Irish would direct all movement toward one end, and then the runner would quickly cut back through the line. "It's a smart little play, in two movements," he said. "The first, which is designed to fool the opponent as to where the play is going, is comparatively slow, so as to give the enemy plenty of time to get roped in. The second phase comes quicker'n lightnin' …they've got quite a neat little bundle of this sort of tactics."

On Saturday evening, December 27, the Stanford team of 31 players, three coaches, a trainer and a manager, boarded The Lark at Palo Alto bound for Los Angeles. The early arrival allowed the Cardinal to have several practices at Pasadena. Warner made two important lineup changes by putting Fred Solomon at quarterback and Ed Walker at a halfback spot opposite Cuddeback, the star of the Cal game. Solomon and Walker had entered that game with Cal leading, 20-6, and they helped engineer the comeback that resulted in the crucial 20-20 tie, with Walker throwing several key passes to Cuddeback and Ted Shipkey.

FOOTBALL FANS WERE now pouring into Pasadena and environs. Those still wishing to find a ticket descended on the Stanford headquarters in the hopes, against all odds, of finding one. A special train filled with Notre Dame alumni and Knights of Columbus members from the San Francisco area headed south on Monday evening. A special from Chicago carrying Notre Dame alumni and fans, organized by Edward Gould, secretary of the Chicago ND club, rolled into town Tuesday.

One report said the travelers "have plenty of money, given them by Notre Dame enthusiasts back home, to wager on the result." Stanford backers demanded 2-to-1 odds, though the "experts" were making the Irish an 8-to-5 favorite.

Stanford was expected to have the edge in color and student support. There would be a full rooting section including 1,100 Stanford students, equipped with brilliantly-colored cards and organized stunts. During the game, they would spell out "Howdy," form a clover, and show a horseshoe over the letters "ND." A 72-piece Stanford band was preparing to march in the Tournament of Roses parade and to accompany the rooting section at the game.

Notre Dame would need to rely mainly on its support within the general admission audience as well as the attending alumni. Los Angeles attorney Leo "Red" Ward, who four years earlier persuaded young Adam Walsh to make the trip East for college, was busy coordinating many aspects of support for the Irish. A local band was engaged' to play at the game, but it had no sheet music for Notre Dame tunes. Ward made several requests to Notre Dame officials for the orchestrations of the Victory March and Hike Song. The Band was unaccustomed to sharing its music beyond campus; the national attention was something new. There were delays in making and sending the arrangements.

The Irish had support from many quarters. Hundreds of alumni of various eastern and Midwest schools purchased blocks of tickets in adjoining sections and planned to cheer for Notre Dame.

BACK IN SOUTH Bend, preparations were underway for another packed house to watch the game on the grid-graph at the Palais Royale. "Direct Wires to the playing field will carry every single detail." Admission was raised to 50 cents, which was "made necessary by the added cost for telegraphic service over so great a distance." The images of Pasadena, even if only in one's mind, would help ward off the chill of a cold snap that dropped the temperature to 18-below earlier in the week.

For millions of fans across the country, the game would enter their homes via radio broadcasting, with four stations providing coverage. A direct wire from the field in Pasadena to the WGN studios in Chicago was to be relayed to WCBS in New York, resulting in "the first time in radio history that Eastern stations have broadcast direct a Pacific coast event." Two California stations, KPO in San Francisco and KHJ in Los Angeles, would also broadcast the game, KPO via a direct wire from the stadium and KHJ from its microphones at the event.

Across the Midwest, telegraph offices in countless towns and cities planned to remain open on the holiday to receive reports from Pasadena. By all accounts, the game would be the most widely followed in the history of football.

ROCKNE'S RECONNAISSANCE ON Stanford consisted of reports from two former Irish stars now coaching in the west – Slip Madigan at St. Mary's of California and Bob Matthews at Idaho. Madigan spent some time at Tucson drilling the Irish players on what to expect from the Cardinal.

This would be Rockne's first game going up against Warner as coach. As a Notre Dame player, Rockne twice met Warner-coached teams at Pittsburgh, a scoreless tie in 1911 and a 3-0 Irish win the next year.

A huge crowd greeted the Irish upon their arrival in Los Angeles, including world heavyweight champion Jack Dempsey. Fans strained to get a look at the "four horsemen," the "seven mules" and their teammates. The players were hustled into waiting autos for the ride to their headquarters at the Maryland Hotel. There, another rousing reception awaited the squad, and people jammed the lobby day and night hoping to see any of the lads in person. Chicago's Walter Eckersall, in his dispatches back to Chicago, noted that "never before in the history of football along the Pacific seaboard has so much interest been shown in a pending gridiron struggle." The game would be seen by a capacity crowd of 53,000, and "if the stadium was larger, double that number of tickets could have been sold."

Warner, knowing he had a healthy Nevers and a wealth of information on Notre Dame, set up the game in this way: "Stanford realizes that it is the under dog in this game. But Stanford is not going into the game merely hoping to keep the score down. We hope to win. We'll be trying to do that all afternoon, and the year's record of dope upsetting has been such that no one can say a new surprise will not take place here," Warner said, adding "the boys aren't afraid of Notre Dame."

ONE FINAL VERSE from Arthur Barry in the *News-Times* set the scene:

The Crowning Glory
"Was there ever such arena,
Since the age of great Athena,
As that field at Pasadena
Where our heroes fight today?
Where the country's team of Wonder
Rends the Stanford hosts asunder,
While the cheers of thousands thunder
At the magic of their play?

Far West champions "Synthetic,"
Warner's lads may be frenetic,
And their "Pop" be strategetic
As he's never been before;
But they're up against their masters,
And are courting grave disasters
From the Irish Line pilasters,
And from Rockne's Horsemen Four.

Are we ultra-optimistic?
Is this prophecy sophistic?
Not a bit —'tis realistic,
As the season's records prove:
Read tonight's inspiring story
That will tell our crowning glory,
And its terms acclamatory
All your doubting will remove."

JANUARY 1, 1925 began in customary fashion in Pasadena with the annual Tournament of Roses parade, a colorful assemblage of pageantry attracting tens of thousands of viewers to the city's streets. Throughways were clogged with traffic for hours after the last of the floats finished the route. Despite that, the 53,000 seats of the Rose Bowl stadium in the Arroyo Seco valley were filled by 1:45 p.m., a half hour before the scheduled kickoff. An estimated 10,000 cars were parked nearby. When Jack Dempsey and his date, actress Estelle Taylor, arrived, they caused a stir no different than as if he were arriving for one his prizefights.

In the hills surrounding the valley, thousands more onlookers took their spots alongside the eucalyptus trees. In the distance, the snow-capped San Gabriel mountains stood sentinel over the scene. Down below, the Rose Bowl's grass field gleamed in the brilliant sunshine. The soft breeze created perfect comfort. It was, said one observer, all the Chamber of Commerce could have hoped for. The center section of seats reserved for the Stanford students was a solid block of red – one of the many colors of cards they would use during the afternoon to form various signs. At 1:45, the Notre Dame team rushed onto the field for its pre-game workout, to the cheers of thousands. The din obliterated the sound of the public address announcer giving the score of the Cal-Penn game up at Berkeley. Great rounds of applause greeted each of Elmer Layden's punts into the bright blue sky. A few minutes later, Stanford's men appeared and began limbering up. They were missing one teammate – key substitute back Cliff Hey had suffered an appendicitis attack and was being treated at the team's hotel. Respected referee Ed Thorp, who had officiated the Army-Notre Dame game, called captains Adam Walsh and Jim Lawson to the center of the field, where Stanford won the toss.

The game began promptly at 2:15. Up until this time, Rockne had been vague about who he planned to start. The answer came when the Shock Troops ran out into kickoff formation. Harry O'Boyle, the son of a coal miner and the first in his family to attend college, was about to kick off in the most-anticipated football game in history. He started in the backfield with Scharer, Hearden and Cerney. Maxwell was at center, flanked by guards Hanousek and Glueckert. Boland and McManmon were the tackles, with Crowe and Eaton at the ends. O'Boyle's kick struck the Stanford goal post, and the Cardinal began at their own 20. On the first play, Cuddeback hit Shipkey with a pass for 7 yards. Nevers carried twice, breaking through for a first down to the 34. A Notre Dame penalty and a run by Cuddeback brought the ball to midfield. Nevers passed to Shipkey for 10 yards, and Nevers ran to the Notre Dame 27. The Cardinal eleven looked poised and confident. They delved into their trick play book for a fake double pass, but Nevers was nailed for a yard loss. Two long passes fell incomplete, and Cuddeback's 40-yard placekick attempt drifted just outside the goal post.

The Shock Troops had held, and now it was time for the regulars. The crowd roared as they saw the "four horsemen" and "seven mules" take the field. On the first play from the Irish 20, Don Miller took the snap and started around left end, as he had so many times during the season. This time, though, he lost control of the ball and Stanford's Johnston recovered on the Irish 17, sending the red-clad rooters into hysteria. Nevers plowed to the 13. The mighty fullback churned for two yards to the 11. With Walsh, Kizer and Weibel on alert, Cuddeback tried to go around end, but failed. On fourth down, Cuddeback made the 20-yard placekick for a 3-0 Cardinal lead.

Notre Dame chose to kick off, and on the runback the Irish were called for roughing, which brought the ball to the Stanford 40. Nevers gained nine yards on three runs, but the Cardinal didn't want to risk losing the ball at midfield, so Cuddeback punted, the ball going over the end line. On second-and-9, Jim Crowley touched the ball for the first time and broke loose around end, tiptoeing along the sideline for a 20-yard gain. Two plays later, Crowley took off one way, reversed field and raced through flailing defenders to the Stanford 29. Don Miller hauled in a quick-strike pass from Stuhldreher and dodged through the defense for another first down. Stanford, staggering from the rapidity of the Irish attack, called a timeout to slow the pace of the game down. But Notre Dame's forces were relentless, as Miller drove behind Joe Bach at left tackle for 10 yards and a first down at the Stanford 9-yard-line. Stuhldreher made four yards behind Walsh to the 5. Then Stanford, with the fired-up Nevers leading an aroused defense, stopped two end runs by Crowley and Miller for minus-5 yards to the nine. Notre Dame, keeping to its season-long pattern of bypassing the field goal route, tried a fourth-down pass.

The Cardinal rush was ferocious, and it forced Stuhldreher to retreat some 20 yards before he lofted a pass that landed incomplete. Stuhldreher lay crumpled on the turf. A delay to attend to the "little general" gave both teams a chance to catch their breath after the frenetic action of the last few minutes. Finally, Stuhldreher rose to his feet, and although he limped badly, he stayed in the game. His Irish mates, agitated over his injury, lined up with resolve as Stanford took possession. On first down, ND broke through to smother Cuddeback for a three-yard loss. Cuddeback, seeking to avoid further retreat, sliced a punt out of bounds at his own 32. Notre Dame again started fast on offense, as Crowley darted off tackle for 13 yards to the 19. Don Miller rushed for two yards, then Layden carried three times in a row, picking up a first down at the Stanford 7 as a pistol signaled the end of the quarter. During the break, Joe Bach had a head injury taped, which Notre Dame believed to have been caused by a brace worn by Stanford's Lawson. A delay ensued while Rockne spoke with the officials. Referee Thorp came to the Stanford bench and ordered captain Lawson to remove the steel brace he had on his knee.

With ND rooters on their feet, Crowley opened the period by taking the ball four yards to the Stanford 3. The Irish line snapped back into position briskly; Layden received the ball and charged toward the goal. A great mass of toppled bodies – some blue-clad and others red – obscured the line. Referee Thorp plunged into the melee of flailing limbs, located the pigskin and signaled a touchdown. Crowley's kick attempt was blocked, but ND was ahead, 6-3, its fans roaring their approval.

The Irish got the ball back on Cuddeback's kickoff but were held to only a one yard gain on three plays. In punt formation at his 20, Layden set a tremendous drive into the ball and it sailed 70 yards in the air, and upon landing, the ball bounced and rolled over the Stanford goal line. From its 20, the Cardinal started to move. Solomon broke loose for nine yards. Nevers drove the Irish line back another nine. A reverse by Nevers broke past midfield, then a double pass got Lawson free for 17 yards. Everything old "Pop" tried seemed to be working. He was especially fond of plays that kept Cardinal backs wide in the backfield for a pass, then upfield once they had the ball. But the Irish were spotting the pattern, and it matched what Coach Madigan of St. Mary's had told them. On a third-and-five from deep in Irish territory, Nevers faded and attempted a cross-field pass. Elmer Layden anticipated this play and perfectly timed a leap between two Cardinal targets. The ball hit his shoulder and bounced a few feet over his head. But Layden kept his eye on the ball, snared it in his arms and continued running. With his sprinter's speed, Layden dashed into an open field. Within seconds, there was only a Blue-jerseyed horseman accompanying him. Layden waltzed into the end zone to complete a 78-yard play. Frenzied Notre Dame backers jumped and hugged. Crowley made the kick and the Irish led, 13-3.

The Irish again received the kick, but this time had to punt the ball back to Cuddeback, who returned it to midfield. Ample time remained for the Cardinal to score before halftime. Nevers gained two yards on the ground before trying the aerial route. Again the Irish were opportunistic, this time with Joe Bach intercepting the ball at the ND 36. Crowley eluded a horde of red-clad defenders for a long run to Stanford's 34-yard line, but Notre Dame lost the ball on downs. Stanford, starting from its 20, made a series of good gains. A pass from Nevers to Solomon brought the ball to the ND 11 with seconds left in the half. But on the next play, Stanford's Moore fumbled and the Irish pounced on the ball as the half ended, ND leading, 13-3.

Warner's warriors felt they were getting the better of Rockne's men and that it was only a matter of time before they broke through for a touchdown. But they needed to hang onto the football; two interceptions and a fumble in one half was unacceptable.

The Cardinal forced an early break in the second half when they partially blocked a Layden punt three plays into the third quarter. Stanford retreated on a penalty, but Nevers found Ted Shipkey for a 17-yard gain to the Irish 25. On third-and-seven, Shipkey tried a pass but slipped to the turf for a four-yard loss, and another Cuddeback placekick sailed wide. Notre Dame started from its 20, went backward with a penalty and punted to midfield. In an attempt to make a tackle, Layden was knocked unconscious, and the Irish called time. Layden came around and like Stuhldreher, decided to stay in the game. Years of training and sweat to play in a game of this ferocity left Layden no other choice.

From the 50, Nevers passed to Shipkey for 17 yards to the ND 33, and the Cardinal threatened once again. But the Irish dropped Lawson for a three-yard loss around end, a Nevers pass fell incomplete and Nevers was stopped for a short gain. On fourth-and-nine, Cuddeback set up for another placekick; this one fell short and rolled harmlessly over the Irish goal line.

Notre Dame failed to get a first down on its ensuing possession and Layden lined up to punt. He kicked another perfect 50-yarder, directly into Solomon's waiting arms. But the Cardinal quarterback bobbled the ball and it bounded away from him. Solomon dove for the ball but Chuck Collins brushed him aside, and Irish end Ed Hunsinger flew past, picking up the ball and racing 20 yards into the Cardinal end zone amid an escort of blue jerseys. Another huge Stanford miscue had resulted in Notre Dame's 20-3 lead.

Back in South Bend, the crowds at the Palais Royale and the Tribune's auditorium were going berserk with the reports. And from coast-to-coast, Notre Dame rooters, Irish-Catholics and football fans in general were thinking this must be Notre Dame's day.

However, Stanford had far too much pride to lie down. The Irish took the following kickoff and again faced a fierce fight from the Cardinal defense. On third-and-five, Nevers picked off a pass by Layden at the ND 29. The muscular blond was never more determined. Nevers gained four yards over tackle, two more at right guard, then plowed for a first down to the 16. He smashed for three more, then another five. A human battering ram, Nevers drove to the Irish six yard line. Then, with the Irish line bunched, he reared back and hit Shipkey with a short pass for a touchdown. Wave after wave of ear-splitting cheers shook the two-year old stadium. Cuddeback's kick sliced Notre Dame's lead to 20-10, and the third quarter ended a minute later.

Warner's crew had ten points to make up in 15 minutes of play. The next few minutes would be critical. Stanford's Baker made the first big play, stepping in front of a Layden pass at the Irish 25. The Cardinal, now playing with the confidence of a champion, drove relentlessly. Nevers made three yards over right tackle, then three more on the left side. On fourth-and-one from the 10, the Cardinal star drove for four yards to the six.

By now the brilliant sun had dropped behind the mountains and the chill of nightfall hung over the stadium. On each play, the throngs roared. A Stanford touchdown here could cut the lead to three points. Nevers had to have the ball. He dragged Irish tacklers for four yards to the 2. Another play gained a yard. Nevers made a half-yard dash – fourth down inside the 1-yard line. Adam Walsh encouraged his mates as they bunched together on the Irish goal line. They had a pretty good idea of who was headed their way. Nevers took the snap, smacked into the ND wall and fell forward. Harry Stuhldreher ignored the piercing pain in his ankle and drove his 152-pound frame into the pile. The stack of gridders was untangled and revealed the football – less than six inches short of the goal line. Notre Dame ball. Stanford hearts sank.

Layden punted out of danger, then Crowley intercepted a Nevers pass. Layden punted again, this time driving Stanford back to its 28. From there, the Cardinal tried an array of plays, including several more passes. Chuck Collins intercepted a long throw by Nevers at the Notre Dame nine-yard line. With two minutes to play, Layden punted the Irish out of another dangerous situation. Stuhldreher, reeling with pain and utterly exhausted, finally took himself out of the game. A minute later, Layden intercepted a desperate heave by Nevers at the Notre Dame 37 and summoned the energy to outrun a beaten Stanford eleven 63 yards for a clinching touchdown. Crowley's kick made it 27-10 and Irish fans everywhere knew that the game was over. Almost all of the Shock Troops re-entered the game. The gun sounded and the battle of the ages was history.

Notre Dame had survived the knockout punches of a great opponent, made the most of its opportunities and capped its most memorable season to be truly crowned with glory.

22

Homeward Bound

THE NOTRE DAME locker room in the Rose Bowl was a mob scene after the game, with numerous well-wishers desiring to greet the victorious players. There was more urgent business, though. Three players needed immediate medical attention. Harry Stuhldreher had suffered a broken bone in his right foot and was taken to Pasadena Hospital; Joe Bach had a badly strained back; and Bill Cerney had two broken ribs. The team as a whole was terribly battered from the tremendous pounding at the hands of the larger Stanford players. That evening, as hundreds of fans swarmed the Hotel Maryland for the team's celebratory dinner-dance, many Irish players were not up for the party – an ice pack and a soft bed sounded much more enticing. Elmer Layden said his jaw was so sore he could barely eat and that Nevers and Lawson hit him harder than he had ever been hit.

Up in Berkeley, the California Bears had handled the Penn Quakers, 14-0. For about a day there was excited talk among some Cal and Notre Dame alums that there should be a "championship" game between the two victors on January 10 at the Los Angeles Coliseum. Both schools quickly shut down that kind of talk. California officials said the team

240

had already given up two weeks of vacation. Said Rockne: "The football season is over. Notre Dame came to the Pacific coast to play one game and one game it will be. I'm taking my boys back to their studies and will meet no other western eleven."

In the moments after the great battle, Warner was quoted as saying, "We spotted Notre Dame 21 points, while they actually earned but six. We completely outplayed them except for those fatal errors. Notre Dame was great, but I think I had the better team." When told of the coach's remarks, Crowley thought a minute and said: "Yeah, and next year they're going to award the American League pennant to the team that has the most men left on base."

The consensus among most observers was that in a game of mistakes, Notre Dame made far fewer of them and deserved the victory. Wrote Ed R. Hughes, who covered Stanford the entire season for the *San Francisco Chronicle*: "Stanford grads tried to make me say that the best team lost yesterday. I don't think so. Notre Dame won by taking advantage of Stanford's mistakes and that is a mighty important factor of football." Hughes went on to praise the Irish as "a modest lot of young men who are a credit to their university. Their behavior is perfect. Rockne will stand for no foolishness and the boys know it."

Walter Eckersall sent a similar dispatch to Chicago: "It is true Notre Dame got the breaks but the players were smart enough to take advantage of them. Their ability to snare the ball on Stanford's attempted forward passes was due to the happy facility of being in the neighborhood of the oval." He said Stanford also came in for its share of credit, and that "the heroes of the battle were Elmer Layden and Ernie Nevers and the supporters of both teams are loud in their praise for both warriors."

Wrote columnist Otto Floto in *The Denver Post*:

"We never beheld a team so completely exhausted as were the Rockne champions after the game. Their eyes were hollow, they breathed heavily and all were in the grip of that tired feeling which tells you a man is all in – physically. Only a superteam under the leadership and direction of a supercoach could have landed the victory at Pasadena. Notre Dame is all of the above and that's why they won. In the final quarter, the Catholic boys played on their nerve. Their fighting instinct is what kept them going."

On Friday, January 2, the Irish players, sore but satisfied, were taken on a tour of Hollywood and the motion picture studios. All day, cameras clicked as the players met movie stars. Teammates asked Adam Walsh about the big letters spelling out "Hollywood" above the city; he said the sign hadn't been there during his childhood, as it had only gone up last year. That evening, the Notre Dame Club of Los Angeles hosted a first-class dinner-dance at the Hotel Biltmore, providing the players with their first real chance to celebrate. Leo Ward put together an event that all would remember.

At 7:30 Saturday morning, the team boarded the Daylight Limited for their next stop, San Francisco, where Notre Dame alums had planned two days of celebrations. However, drama aboard the train would dampen spirits. At 9:30, Jim Crowley had just finished shaving and was walking toward his berth through the Pullman car "Onamia." He collapsed in the aisle and was carried to his bunk by Father O'Hara and teammate Charlie Glueckert. For the next half hour, they said, he appeared to be at times delirious and at others stiff and still. Before the train's noon stop at San Luis Obispo, the conductor summoned Dr. A. N. Codd, team physician for Gonzaga College, to attend to Crowley. With their teammate who was normally the life of the entourage lying quiet and pale during the afternoon, the other players mostly tried to sleep, not wanting to disturb Jim. Finally, Crowley was able to eat some toast and have a cup of tea, and his teammates' mood brightened. Upon arrival in San Francisco, he was placed in a wheelchair and taken to St. Francis Hospital. His condition was reported as exhaustion, but it was later suspected he might have had a reaction to the lobster dinner served at Friday's banquet.

With Stuhldreher on crutches and his foot in a cast and with Crowley in the hospital, the "horsemen" were not whole for the visit. In addition, Rockne had stayed behind for business in Los Angeles and rest in San Diego, and Adam Walsh was enjoying a delayed "honeymoon" visiting his family. But everyone else, led by assistant coach Tom Lieb, was ready to enjoy their time by the Bay. Some two thousand people turned out for their arrival, and a band ironically played the song titled "Hail, Hail, the Gang's All Here." That night, the team was feted at a large banquet at the Palace Hotel. Sunday morning, they received a blessing from Archbishop Edward J. Hanna during a special mass at St. Mary's Cathedral. After a sight-seeing tour, the players were taken by cars to the ranch of former Sen. James D. Phelan at Saratoga. They enjoyed the outdoor recreation and a chance to breathe some fresh air. The day concluded with a theatre party at the Columbia Theatre in the entertainment district.

The Irish left a good impression in San Francisco, with one writer commenting: "Knute Rockne's boys impressed all who met them as clean-cut, well-mannered young men. Their football record speaks for itself, and the boys don't try to help it out in any way. On the contrary, they take their honors modestly and their trips to every corner of the United States seemingly have in no way changed their outlook from that of any other collegians."

The cross-country trek back to Chicago and South Bend began as the boys said goodbye to California, loaded with a lifetime of memories. Crowley stayed behind, still hospitalized. The next stop was a brief one in Salt Lake City. The team drove through the city, listened to an organ recital given by Ed Kimball at the Mormon Tabernacle, toured around the University of Utah and enjoyed a dinner hosted by the Chamber of Commerce. The evening before the team's arrival, the first Notre Dame Club of Utah was formed, largely to organize the welcome for the team. In an editorial entitled "The Wonder Eleven," the local paper opined:

"A clean-cut, upstanding company, these Notre Dame football players – the highest type of American young manhood.... Foregathering for even a brief few hours with these healthy, clear-eyed, broad-shouldered young men, is a privilege. Contemplating them.... one feels that the future of the United States in indeed in safe and strong hands."

At noon on Wednesday, January 7, the team's stop in Cheyenne, Wyoming, was met by a delegation that included cowboys on their mounts, an old stagecoach, six-gallon hats and a military band. The stagecoach ride was the highlight, and cries of "Powder River" were frequent. The traveling party continued over the Rio Grande tracks to Denver, arriving in the late afternoon at the mammoth Union Station to a waiting crowd that included both Notre Dame alums and a group of attractive young women, part of the welcoming committee.

"Whew! What's the matter in this town – a riot?" asked Elmer Layden as he stepped off the train. One of the lasses drew closer to him, then pinned a blue-and-gold Notre Dame streamer onto his coat. It was said that, in Denver's history, the welcome it gave the Fighting Irish was equal to that it had ever given presidents or kings. Thousands strained against a traffic cordon. Leading the alumni delegation was Will McPhee, known as "Skinny Willy" when he was an honorary member of the first Notre Dame football team in 1887. The players were inundated with requests for handshakes and photographs. Next was a parade of Packard automobiles up 17th Street, through the financial district, where more crowds welcomed the honored visitors. At the University Club, the team formed a receiving line, where they met the leaders of Denver, including the governor.

Later, in a dining hall bedecked with Notre Dame's colors and with the words to the school's songs printed on placards at each table, the leaders of Denver's business and professions sat down 200 strong for a banquet "that will go down in history in Denver." Tom Lieb spoke for the team and introduced each man on the squad. He put into words what an education at Notre Dame means, and what a Notre Dame man stands for, and that "character, manliness and uprighteousness" go along with the school's football success.

The *Denver Post* summarized the team's stop with these words:

"The Notre Dame boys made a host of friends during their stay in the city. Certainly no championship team was ever more modest over their conquests. Quiet, unassuming and showing all the advantages of their country-wide travels, the championship Notre Dame team of 1924, conquerors of the east, middle west, south and far west, will be remembered in Denver in every sense of the word."

A FINAL STOP on the trip completed a circle for the 22 Notre Dame seniors that began with two difficult defeats in 1922 and 1923, and one very memorable victory in November of 1924. On Friday, January 9, the Irish pulled into Lincoln, Nebraska. There, they were honored at a dinner attended only by members of the Nebraska and Notre Dame teams, Nebraska's university officials, a limited number of faculty members and a few newspapermen. To be hosted by an opposing team – especially one with whom such fierce battles had been fought – reminded everyone that sportsmanship was the highest calling for those privileged to play college football.

"Notre Dame played its best game against Nebraska," noted Coach Lieb. "The team was pointed for that game and gave all it had."

After the dinner, the Irish were the guests of Gov. Adam McMullen at his inaugural reception. Back on the train, they rolled into Chicago, a three-week odyssey concluded. For the entire season, the team logged approximately 15,000 miles on trains. They had become the first football squad to play in front of sold-out stadiums in New York, Chicago and Los Angeles all in the same year.

Once back in South Bend, Father O'Hara smiled as he recalled how the events of the past eight months had unfolded. The ugliness with the Klan in May had opened an opportunity to promote Notre Dame and a Catholic ideal to people across the country. And the men who achieved the task were the Fighting Irish football players. Not only had they gone unbeaten and brought national attention to the school as never before, they had proven themselves to be upstanding citizens, model Christians, gentlemen and above all . . . Loyal Sons.

Epilogue

IN RETROSPECT, THE 1924 football season can be seen as the arrival of Notre Dame on the national stage. The Fighting Irish, the first football team of any kind to play games in New York City, Chicago and the Los Angeles area in the same season, emerged as a significant force in the sport. But in a larger sense, it marked the arrival of Notre Dame itself as a national presence, a national treasure. The team connected with countless waves of new supporters—those new to the U.S., Catholics, veterans, city and country folk, those getting used to the five-day work week and the freedom to enjoy weekend entertainment such as college football.

It paved the way toward decades of advancement for the University in the public's mind and heart. The Fighting Irish were known to play by the rules, support one another in a spirit of teamwork, and show sportsmanship along with achievement. All were attributes that spoke well of the mission of Notre Dame. It resonated with an increasing wave of people who were coming on board as "subway alumni."

So much of what makes Notre Dame a major force in U.S. higher education today can be traced back to the Rockne era. And 1924 especially was a breakthrough year in numerous ways. The Alumni Association and the Monogram Club galvanized connection and support from former students and former student-athletes as never before. Radio brought Notre Dame games into the homes of millions from coast to coast, foreshadowing the eventual exclusive television contract with NBC. The national press found a willing subject in Coach Rockne, and the Irish became the most written and talked about team in the nation. Games were straining the capacity of Cartier Field, as plans for Notre Dame Stadium percolated. And the big home contests against powers Georgia Tech and Nebraska created the template for the tradition of every home game being a huge event for the University and the South Bend business community and citizenry.

Plus, the success of Notre Dame football at stadia far and wide helped fill the coffers that built the residence halls, dining facilities and classroom buildings that form the heart of today's University. It all happened in 1924 and has led to a century of advancement and achievement.

From a strictly football standpoint, 1924 laid the groundwork for a tradition of phenomenal success. A "century of champions," including another 10 consensus national championships. Seven Heisman Trophy winners. More than 150 All-Americans. A record number of NFL draft picks. Honorees in both the College and Pro Football Halls of Fame.

Together, the individuals associated with the 1924 Fighting Irish left their mark not just on athletics, but in medicine, law, politics, business, the military and communities across the nation. Every one of them carried the spirit of Rockne, centered around achievement with honor, into their varied pursuits. Here is what happened in the ensuing years.

WITH THE LENGTH of the Rose Bowl return trip, the Notre Dame players arrived back on campus in early January 1925 with little time to spare before the start of the second semester.

But the celebrations weren't quite finished. In February, Rockne made a trip to Green Bay, Wis., where he joined "300 good citizens and true" at the Beaumont Hotel to honor hometown hero Jim Crowley. The toastmaster was the ever-present Bobby Lynch, former Notre Dame baseball captain and prominent Green Bay businessman and politician, who was "witty beyond even his usual capacity."

Lynch introduced Rockne as "a man of sterling character, judgment, and vision. The coach of the Notre Dame football team has brought a new spirit into football. When this man came from obscurity to the wonderful institution he now represents, he rose by merit of sheer ability, force of character and cleanliness of vision, to become the most respected, the most talked-of athletic director in the entire world."

Rockne demurred that "only about one percent of this is true," and turned the attention toward Crowley. "If Jimmy had been merely a brilliant football player, and nothing else, I wouldn't have come here. But I am glad to be here, and to help do honor to him, because I know him to be a clean-minded, modest, unselfish boy—always trying to do a good turn for some other fellow."

Supporting his players was more than just banquet talk for Rockne. He had gained their trust due to his unwavering investment in their future. To a man, Rockne had studied his players, understood them and how far they had grown into productive adults. He also had clear ideas of what their futures could hold. Largely, it wasn't about playing football. Rockne actively dissuaded his Notre Dame players from pursuing what then passed for professional football. It was a risky enterprise, he believed, with uncertain paychecks and danger of serious, lasting injury.

Much better, Rockne felt, would be for his men to continue in the game by serving as coach or athletic director at an appropriate college or university, prep school, or high school. Rockne's Notre Dame office became a de facto athletic employment agency. Schools constantly sought his advice in their hiring, and he obliged by suggesting which player or players to interview. Often, he guided the player with such advice as, "They're offering $2,500, but I think you can get $3,000."

For all the records and accomplishments of The Four Horsemen and The Seven Mules, there remains one amazing statistic: each was coaching college football in the fall of 1925. Their performance as players and as students of the game, along with the respect Rockne commanded, made them highly sought-after additions to coaching staffs across the country. Even before the 1924 season concluded, rumors swirled as to which schools were approaching which Notre Dame players.

The lineup for the fall of 1925:

Harry Stuhldreher, head coach, Villanova
Adam Walsh, head coach, Santa Clara
Elmer Layden, head coach, Columbia (IA)
Jim Crowley, backfield coach, Georgia
Don Miller, backfield coach, Georgia Tech
Joe Bach, line coach, Syracuse
Chuck Collins, assistant coach, Chattanooga
Ed Hunsinger, assistant coach, Villanova
Noble Kizer, line coach, Purdue
Rip Miller, line coach, Indiana
John Weibel, assistant coach, Vanderbilt

Nearly all 22 seniors from the '24 team graduated with their
class in the spring of 1925. Several completed Notre Dame's course
of law; others commerce, engineering, or science. They were well
prepared to make their way into the larger world. Here is a closer
look at what the members of the 1924 Fighting Irish accomplished:

The Four Horsemen

For decades after 1924, the Four Horsemen held sway in
popular American culture. It was said that during World War II, a
common security question at U.S. military checkpoints was, "What
college did the Four Horsemen play for?" The four were in regular
demand as guest speakers at athletic banquets coast to coast, and
on the occasions when three or four of them gathered, there were
special moments of celebration and frivolity.

Field general **Harry Stuhldreher**, who probably learned
more football from Rockne than anybody, broke quickly into the
coaching game. At Villanova, he took over a program that was 2-5-
1 in 1924, including losses to Dickinson, Lehigh, and Muhlenberg.
Stuhldreher engineered an immediate turnaround as the 1925
Wildcats went 6-2-1, including a 20-0 shutout of Rutgers. In 11
years on the job, he had just one losing season, and finished 65-25-
9 overall. The 7-2-1 1929 season was typical. It included wins over

Duke, North Carolina State, and Temple, and a tie with Boston College at Fenway Park.

In 1935, Stuhldreher traveled to Detroit with a 5-0 Villanova team. There he took on another former Notre Dame star quarterback, Gus Dorais, who coached the Titans. Detroit eked out a 19-15 win, but a week later, Villanova won the second half of this most unusual "doubleheader," scoring their first ever victory over Detroit in front of 10,000 raucous fans at Villanova Stadium. Nova's only other loss that season was at Penn State.

Stuhldreher felt the itch to coach at a larger school and in 1936 accepted an offer at Wisconsin, which had dropped to the bottom of the Big 10 in 1935 with a 1-7 overall mark. Within two years, Stuhldreher had the Badgers on the winning side of the ledger, at 4-3-1. By far the best of his 13 seasons in Madison came in 1942, when he guided the Badgers to an 8-1-1 record, a No. 3 AP ranking, and the Helms Athletic Foundation's national championship. Highlights included a 7-7 tie with Notre Dame, in Frank Leahy's second season leading the Irish, and victories over then No. 1 Ohio State and No. 10 Minnesota.

Stuhldreher finished with a career coaching record of 110-87-15 and was elected to the College Football Hall of Fame in 1958.

Elmer Layden, like Stuhldreher, spent no time as an assistant coach. He quickly made a name as a winning head coach in the Catholic college world. He started at Columbia College in Dubuque, Iowa (today's Loras University), going 8-5-2 in two seasons before taking over at Duquesne in Pittsburgh. Over the ensuing seven seasons, he brought the Dukes to a level of respectability in a city where the Pitt Panthers and Carnegie Tech Tartans dominated as big-time programs. Layden gradually replaced the Slippery Rocks on his schedule with opponents such as West Virginia. In 1931, he led the Dukes to a scoreless tie with Carnegie before 50,000 depression-era fans at Pitt Stadium in a charity game played for the local Welfare Fund.

Layden's finest season at Duquesne was his final one, in 1933. The Dukes reeled off eight straight victories, including a 19-7 trouncing of West Virginia, before suffering their only loss of the year, 7-0 to Pitt before 60,000. After a 9-1 regular season, they were invited to the second-ever Festival of Palms Bowl (precursor to the Orange Bowl) on Jan. 1, 1934, in Miami, where they trounced the unbeaten Miami Hurricanes, 33-7. Layden had clearly proven himself as an outstanding coach. With his alma mater parting ways with Hunk Anderson, Layden beat out a host of other quality candidates to become head coach of the Fighting Irish for the 1934 season.

In South Bend, Layden inherited a far different program than he had played for a decade earlier. Gone were the early-season games with Lombard and Wabash, Coe College, and Beloit. Every game was against big-time opponents, from every section of the country. Each came gunning to knock off the program that the late Knute Rockne had brought to preeminence—including in Layden's first game, a hard-fought 7-6 home loss to the Texas Longhorns. The Irish finished 6-3 in 1934.

Things fell into place in 1935, with Notre Dame bringing a 5-0 record to Columbus, Ohio, for their first-ever meeting with mighty Ohio State, also unbeaten. The Irish, trailing 13-0 in the fourth quarter before 81,018 at Ohio Stadium, pulled off one of the greatest comebacks in history to record an 18-13 victory. But a 14-7 home loss to Northwestern and a 6-6 tie with Army at Yankee Stadium kept the Irish from national championship consideration. Layden's closest call came in 1938, when he led the Irish to eight straight victories and a No. 1 national ranking before a season-ending, 13-0 loss at Southern Cal before 97,146 at the LA Coliseum.

In his seven seasons leading the Irish, Layden posted a mark of 47-13-3, with four teams finishing in the Top 15, three in the Top 10. It was a pressure-packed environment that took its toll on any coach's health. The National Football League, meanwhile, had advanced to the point where it felt it needed a full-time commissioner. Notre Dame grad Arch Ward, sports editor of the *Chicago Tribune*, declined the job, but he suggested the NFL hire Layden, which it did in February 1941.

Layden led the league through the tumultuous war years, which included teams merging, folding, or leaving for the new All-American Football Conference. He left his post in 1946 and became a successful Chicago businessman. Layden was inducted into the College Football Hall of Fame in 1951.

"Sleepy Jim" Crowley dabbled as an NFL player in 1925 for the Green Bay Packers and Providence Steam Rollers, but his real job was as assistant coach with the Georgia Bulldogs. He served in Athens until obtaining his first head coaching job, at Michigan State College in East Lansing, Michigan, in 1929. Crowley led Michigan State to its first winning season in five years, at 5-3. In the second game of his second season, on Oct. 4, 1930, before 50,000 at Michigan Stadium, Crowley's team tied mighty Michigan, 0-0, the only blemish that season for the eventual 8-0-1 Big 10 champions.

Again in 1931, Michigan State played the Wolverines to a scoreless tie. In four seasons, Crowley posted a 22-8-3 record. By 1933, numerous colleges sought his services. The bright lights of New York City beckoned, and nine years after helping the Irish defeat Army at the Polo Grounds, Crowley became head coach at Fordham University. Over the next nine seasons, he led the Rams to unprecedented heights—a 56-13-7 record, six consecutive finishes in the AP Top 20 (in the first six years it existed) and a pair of bowl-game appearances.

Crowley assembled his coaching staff at Fordham by hiring four former Notre Dame players: his '24 teammate Ed Hunsinger, along with Frank Leahy, Glen Carberry, and Earl Walsh. They had a daunting schedule in 1933, with three straight games at the Polo Grounds against West Virginia, Boston College, and Alabama. They blanked the Mountaineers, 20-0, and blitzed BC, 32-6. Then came the Crimson Tide, coached by former Notre Dame quarterback Frank Thomas and featuring All-American Dixie Howell in the backfield and a pair of sophomore ends named Paul "Bear" Bryant and Don Hutson. Before 60,000 fans, Fordham blocked a Howell punt into the end for a safety and a 2-0 victory, the only loss in Alabama's 7-1-1 season.

In 1936, Crowley had the Rams at 5-0-1 and under serious consideration for a Rose Bowl berth, before a 7-7 tie against the Georgia Bulldogs dropped Fordham to No. 8 in the rankings. The next season was their finest, at 7-0-1, with successive wins over TCU,

North Carolina, and Purdue, and a scoreless tie against eventual national champions Pittsburgh, who would defeat Notre Dame, 21-6, later that year. The Rams, who allowed just 16 points all season, were No. 3 in the final AP rankings.

A most unusual series during Crowley's tenure was the annual battle with St. Mary's College of California and their colorful coach, Edward "Slip" Madigan, former Notre Dame lineman under Rockne. Madigan had the Gaels playing a big-time schedule and regularly scoring victories over the likes of Stanford and California. After an initial meeting in 1933 at Kezar Stadium in San Francisco, St. Mary's made the long train trek to New York City to meet Fordham every year from 1934-41. The team was accompanied by numerous hearty-partying fans in what was called "the world's longest bar." The games were nearly always entertaining, tight affairs—like the 1936 battle, when No. 12 Fordham defeated 16th-ranked St. Mary's, 7-6, in front of 50,000 at the Polo Grounds.

Fordham's forte was defense, and its front line coached by Leahy. It earned the title of the "Seven Blocks of Granite" and included Alex Wojciechowicz, a future inductee in both the College and Pro Halls of Fame, and a youngster from Brooklyn, N.Y., named Vincent T. Lombardi. The latter would eventually reach the heights of coaching success in Crowley's hometown of Green Bay, Wis.

Crowley's last two teams each went to bowl games. The Rams lost, 13–12, to Texas A&M in the 1941 Cotton Bowl Classic and defeated Missouri, 2–0, in the 1942 Sugar Bowl, played just 25 days after the surprise attack on Pearl Harbor launched the U.S. into World War II. Crowley left Fordham to serve in the U.S. Navy in the South Pacific during the war. He also coached the North Carolina Pre-Flight School team to an 8-2-1 mark in 1942. In late 1944, he became the first commissioner of the new All-America Football Conference. With Layden heading the NFL, half of the Four Horsemen now guided pro football. Crowley also briefly coached the AAFC's Chicago Rockets before pursuing business interests. He was inducted into the College Football Hall of Fame in 1966.

Of the Four Horsemen, halfback **Don Miller** had the briefest of coaching careers—for good reason, as he joined "the family business" of law and politics in Ohio. The five Miller brothers from Defiance, Ohio, who all played football at Notre Dame, received their law degrees and made an impact in their home state. Ray Miller, who was a backup end behind Rockne in 1911-12, was elected mayor of Cleveland in 1932 and served as the chairman of the Cuyahoga County Democratic Party for more than 20 years.

Don Miller initially stayed in football as an assistant coach at Georgia Tech from 1925-28, helping the 1928 Golden Tornado to national championship recognition after a 10-0 season and 8-7 victory over California in the 1929 Rose Bowl. From there, Miller became an assistant at Ohio State from 1929 until 1932, when he left football to practice law full-time. In 1942, he began 10 years as U.S. attorney for the northern Ohio district, and later was named a federal judge. He served with great distinction and was honored with numerous civic awards.

Miller was voted into the College Football Hall of Fame in 1970.

The Seven Mules

In addition to Coach Rockne and the Four Horsemen, two of the Seven Mules—center and 1924 team captain **Adam Walsh** and right tackle Edgar "Rip" Miller—made the College Football Hall of Fame.

Walsh, whose toughness and leadership were heralded far and wide, joined Horsemen Stuhldreher and Layden as a head coach immediately after finishing at Notre Dame. He took the reins at the University of Santa Clara (today's Santa Clara University) in the fall of 1925. Against schedules that included Stanford, Cal, and USC, Walsh led the Broncos to winning records in three of his four seasons. Walsh had the distinction of serving as line coach at both Yale and Harvard, and in a brief pro coaching career, led the 1945 Cleveland Rams to the NFL championship.

But Walsh left his most lasting impact at Bowdoin College in Brunswick, Maine. He was head coach of the Polar Bears from 1935-42 and again from 1947-58. He won or tied 11 times for the Maine Intercollegiate Athletic Association title. Walsh always kept a portrait of Rockne in his office. Whenever he faced a difficult decision, Walsh said, he "would ask Rock what he would do in the situation. He never failed me."

After retiring from coaching, Walsh served two terms as a Democrat in the Maine House of Representatives. He was appointed the U.S. Marshal for Maine under Presidents Kennedy and Johnson.

Rip Miller started his coaching career as an assistant to Bill Ingram at Indiana in 1925. The following year, Ingram was named head coach at the U.S. Naval Academy in Annapolis, where Miller joined him, starting a nearly five-decade association with the academy. Miller succeeded Ingram as head coach of the Midshipmen in 1931. His final victory in a three-year stint was a 7-0 win over Hunk Anderson's Irish at Baltimore in November of 1933. Miller then returned to his role as line coach for Navy from 1934-47 and served as assistant athletic director from 1948-74. His long service to Navy was honored with the naming of Rip Miller Field in 1995. And his name adorns the Rip Miller Trophy, which honors the traditions of both Notre Dame and Navy football at their annual meeting.

Left end **Chuck Collins** started coaching as an assistant at the University of Chattanooga in 1925; he became head coach at the University of North Carolina the following year. In eight seasons leading the Tar Heels, he posted a record of 38-31-9. His best season was 1929, when the 9-1 Heels scored lopsided victories over Wake Forest, Maryland, North Carolina State, South Carolina, and Duke, while losing only to Georgia. The team outscored the opposition, 346-59.

Right guard **Noble Kizer** remained in his home state of Indiana, landing as line coach for Purdue under former Irish quarterback and Boilermaker head coach James Phelan. After five seasons (1925-29) of guiding the Boilermakers line, Kizer became head coach in 1930. In seven seasons Kizer guided Purdue to Big 10 championships in 1931 and 1932 and a .750 winning percentage. Among his many honors, Kizer was selected by a nationwide vote of football fans as the first coach of the College All-Star team in its annual meeting with the professional football champions in 1934. As Purdue athletic director, he traveled the state extensively, helping high schools to start football programs and encouraging the overall advancement of the sport. His career was cut short by illness, and he died at age 40 in 1940.

Left tackle **Joe Bach** began his long coaching career as an assistant at Syracuse in 1925, before moving to Duquesne in 1929 to assist Layden. When Layden took over as Irish head coach in 1934, Bach succeeded him for one season before a two-year stint as head coach of the NFL's Pittsburgh Pirates. Bach guided the Niagara Purple Eagles for five seasons (1937-41), winning four conference titles, then coached at Fort Knox in 1942. He spent several more seasons as an NFL assistant before guiding the Steelers in 1952-53. He remained in the Steelers family as a scout for years. On Oct. 24, 1966, an athletic banquet in Pittsburgh's Hotel Roosevelt honored Bach with induction into the Hall of Fame of a local coaches' group. Only a few minutes after the conclusion of the event, Bach collapsed and died of a massive heart attack.

Like Rockne, left guard **John Weibel** was an outstanding student in the sciences. He followed a path to Nashville, where he entered medical school at Vanderbilt and was eagerly welcomed to the school's football coaching staff, as he "comes to the Commodores bearing the enthusiastic commendation of Knute Rockne." As an assistant and scout for long-time head coach Dan McGugin, Weibel helped Vandy continue its string of highly successful seasons, going 6-3 in 1925 and 8-1 in 1926, with wins over Texas, Tennessee, Georgia, and Georgia Tech. In 1927, Weibel joined the staff of former Irish teammate Elmer Layden at Duquesne. Weibel returned to Vanderbilt the next year to complete his course in medicine. In early 1931, just weeks before Rockne's death, Weibel was nearing completion of his medical internship at Pittsburgh's Mercy Hospital. He was stricken with appendicitis and died of peritonitis. He was just 26.

Right end **Ed Hunsinger** had a brief foray in the fledgling NFL before joining former Irish teammates in the coaching ranks. He served as an assistant to Stuhldreher at Villanova from 1926-32 and to Crowley at Fordham in 1933-34. Hunsinger had a stint as head coach of Niagara University in 1935-36 before leaving football.

He served in the U.S. Navy during World War II, then went to work as a construction engineer in Philadelphia, where he died in 1960 at age 59.

The Shock Troops

Joe Boland, a sophomore left tackle for the 1924 champs, went on to become the voice of Notre Dame football. After his playing days, he served as head coach at the College (now University) of St. Thomas in Minnesota from 1929-32. He then became Notre Dame line coach under Layden from 1934-40. He began calling Irish games on the radio, and single-handedly built the Irish Football Network. He was a popular South Bend sportscaster until his death in 1960 at age 55.

Bill Cerney, sometimes called the "Fifth Horseman" as fullback behind Layden, helped Chuck Collins install the Rockne system as backfield coach at the University of North Carolina. He later returned to Notre Dame and served a variety of roles on the coaching staff from 1935-41, including freshman coach and head of scouting.

Ward "Doc" Connell took what he learned in Rockne's backfield and returned to his home state of Wisconsin, where he coached the backs for the University of Wisconsin. In 1927, he suited up to play one more time, joining the NFL's Milwaukee Badgers, organized by former Notre Dame star John Mohardt and including ex-Irish end Roger Kiley, for a game against the Duluth Eskimos and its captain, 1925 Rose Bowl standout Ernie Nevers of Stanford.

Left end **Clem Crowe**, captain of the Irish in 1925, was also an All-American basketball player at Notre Dame who went on to a distinguished career coaching football and basketball. He started at St. Vincent College in Latrobe, Penn., then coached both sports at Xavier University from 1932-43. He served as assistant football and head basketball coach at Notre Dame in 1944-45. He briefly coached in the NFL, before a nearly decade-long head coaching stint in the Canadian Football League. He led the Ottawa Rough Riders to the 1951 Gray Cup.

Wilbur Eaton, right end for the Irish, coached the Notre

Dame freshman in 1925, before he took assistant roles at Carroll College in Helena, Mont., Howard College (today's Samford University) in Alabama, St. Thomas in Minnesota, and finally as an assistant to former Irish star Marchy Schwartz at Creighton. He entered the University of Nebraska Medical School in 1933 and practiced medicine in Iowa until he died of a heart attack at age 43.

Left guard **Charlie Glueckert** earned a law degree from Notre Dame and became a prominent South Bend attorney. He served for 37 years as a Democratic precinct committeeman.

Dick Hanousek came to Notre Dame as a star back from St. Thomas in Minnesota. He switched to the line and became a member of the Shock Troops. After graduation, he returned to the Twin Cities as an assistant coach at St. Thomas. He later entered business, making occasional headlines as an outstanding amateur golfer.

Center **Joe Maxwell** played 38 games in the NFL for the Frankford Yellow Jackets from 1927-29. He then coached at St. Louis University, where he also earned a law degree. He worked for Philco Ford Co. as an attorney and as labor relations director from 1946-69.

After graduating from Notre Dame, right tackle **John McManmon** remained to help coach the Irish freshmen. He then returned to the Boston area and was an assistant coach at both Boston College and Boston University. Always a proud and active alumnus, he was honored with the Alumni Association "Man of the Year" Award in 1981.

Halfback **Harry O'Boyle** was a member of the Green Bay Packers for three seasons, primarily as a blocking back. For two seasons, he was head coach at St. Anselm College in New Hampshire.

Backup quarterback **Eddie Scharer** resembled Stuhldreher at just 5-foot-8, 145 pounds. Despite his size, Scharer had some success in the NFL, leading the league in touchdown passes with the Detroit Panthers in 1926. The next season, he was a second-team All-Pro with the Pottsville Maroons.

Reserves

Halfback **Bernie Coughlin** came from a family of newspaper publishers in Waseca, Minn., and returned to that state after graduating from Notre Dame. Ordained a priest of the Archdiocese of St. Paul and Minneapolis, he served for decades as a teacher, athletic administrator, and dean of students at the College (now University) of St. Thomas in St. Paul.

Center **Joe Harmon** went into coaching in 1925, helping to mold what became the football powerhouse at St. Xavier High School in Cincinnati. He led St. X to a 34-11-3 record in six seasons. He later returned to his hometown of Indianapolis, where he coached Cathedral High School to the 1940 city championship. He served as athletic director at Bishop Chatard High School from 1964-74.

Guard **Vince Harrington** served his home state of Iowa and the United States in several ways. He spent four years as a state senator before he was elected a U.S. Congressman in 1936. He resigned in September 1942 to serve full time with the Army Air Force. He was a commander on a troop carrier in the European theatre and died of a heart attack in Rutlandshire, England, in November 1943.

Halfback **Tom "Red" Hearden** captained the 1926 Irish to a 9-1 record, falling just short of another national championship. He then embarked on an overwhelmingly successful coaching career. He went 26-3-3 in four seasons at St. Catherine's High School in Racine, Wis., before he guided his alma mater Green Bay East to an astonishing 51-3-1 mark from 1936-42. After service in the U.S. Navy, he coached St. Norbert College to a 40-14 record and two league championships from 1946-52. He was a Green Bay Packers assistant in 1954-55 and again in 1957. Health problems kept him out of consideration for the Packers' head coaching position—the team eventually turned to Vince Lombardi.

Bernie Livergood, the fullback who was always at the ready to make good, as he did in the 1924 victory at Carnegie Tech, settled into life as an insurance agent in Decatur, Ill. His athletic pursuits consisted of regularly competing for amateur golf titles in the area.

After graduating from Notre Dame with a fine arts degree, end **Joe Rigali** joined his family's business, the Daprato Statuary Company (today's Daprato Rigali Studios), an industry leader in church interior design and renovation.

John Roach enlisted in the U.S. Army after the attack on Pearl Harbor and served in the Pacific Theater on Gen. Douglas MacArthur's staff. When U.S. troops liberated the Philippines, Roach was made the Military Provost Marshal of Manila. After the war, he served as the Adjutant General of Wisconsin's Red Arrow National Guard Division and headed up the Wisconsin Veterans Administration.

In 1925, tackle **John Wallace** took over the presidency of the Notre Dame Monogram Club from Layden. Wallace went on to a long career as a judge in his hometown of Calumet City, Ill., and Chicago. He was active with the Notre Dame Club of Chicago and a popular speaker at athletic functions around Chicago.

As FOR THE coaching staff, **Coach Rockne** would go on to win two more national championships with undefeated teams in 1929 and 1930 before his death in an airline accident in eastern Kansas on March 31, 1931. During the 1929 season, when Notre Dame Stadium was being built and the Fighting Irish played the entire schedule away from South Bend, Rockne missed several games due to severe phlebitis and **Tom Lieb** filled in as acting head coach, playing a vital role in leading the team. Lieb went on to a stellar career as coach and athletic director at Loyola University in Los Angeles, head football coach at the University of Florida, and assistant at Alabama.

Hunk Anderson took over as Notre Dame head coach after Rockne's death and led the Irish from 1931-33. He became head coach at North Carolina State, assisted at Michigan and for the Detroit Lions, and led the Chicago Bears in 1942-45, capturing the NFL championship in 1943.

Trainer **Verly Smith** expanded his clientele from the athletes at Notre Dame to the businessmen of South Bend, operating a successful downtown gymnasium and later a "health farm" near Culver, Ind. He staged numerous amateur boxing cards that drew large crowds and became a popular figure around town.

George Strickler, the student publicity aide responsible for the iconic publicity photo of The Four Horsemen, had a long, productive career as sports editor of the *Chicago Tribune*. He created the College All-Star Game, long played at Soldier Field, and served as publicity director of the National Football League, first president of the Professional Football Writers Association, and a founding director of the Pro Football Hall of Fame.

Rev. John O'Hara, C.S.C. served as the 13th president of the University of Notre Dame from 1934-39, the bishop of Buffalo, N.Y., and as the Archbishop of Philadelphia from 1951 until his death in 1960. In 1958, he was elevated to become John Cardinal O'Hara.

As PRESIDENT OF Notre Dame's class of 1925, Don Miller had a hand in creating the class pledge. It could have served as the football team's motto as well, reading in part:

"Oh! Notre Dame! You have developed our minds. You have endowed us with knowledge. You have developed us physically and inculcated the principles of fair play. You have sent us from home to contest for your honor and name. You taught us to fight unflinchingly hard; never to quit in defeat, but always to be fair, honorable and merciful.

"These principles are inculcated. Our minds and hearts are steady. Your ideals shall always govern."

Love thee, Notre Dame.

Notes From The Families

Our dads both came to the University of Notre Dame from middle-class upbringings in Catholic families in Ohio, sons of a machine shop foreman and a grocer. They learned early in life the value of work, the importance of family and faith in God.

Both of our fathers followed older brothers to Notre Dame. Their mothers were delighted they made the choice to continue the family tradition of attending this outstanding Catholic university. And once there, they found a new family in the students, faculty and administrators. Whether it was the fellows in their residence halls, their teammates on the football team, their favorite professor, Father John O'Hara or Coach Knute Rockne, relationships were formed that would last a lifetime.

They enjoyed the sense of camaraderie the University encouraged and participated in all the important daily rituals of life at this place, whether that was joking around in a residence hall, visiting the Grotto or preparing for football practice. Without perhaps even realizing it, they understood the fleeting nature of their youth and the importance of making every minute count. Their experience at Notre Dame helped them live life to the fullest. They seized opportunities and enjoyed the moment.

As football players, they came to Notre Dame with some experience as good high school athletes, but could not have envisioned in their wildest dreams what was to take place in the next four years. In those days, athletes did not arrive at college as full-blown stars like today. You simply showed up, took your place on the freshman team and did your best to work your way up the ladder. At a place like Notre Dame, just making the varsity as a sophomore was quite an accomplishment. The idea of being a starter in the backfield of a national power, like four young sophomores were late in the 1922 season, was almost too much to believe. And to go on to the kind of fame they did in 1923 and especially 1924, as recounted in this volume, must have seemed like a dream.

Yet from all accounts, it appears our fathers and their teammates humbly accepted the football fame that came their way and the spotlight it shone on them. The publicity wasn't something they sought, and they seemed a little embarrassed by it. Football was not an end in itself, and they had little aspiration for pro ball, such as it was at the time. Playing football at Notre Dame was simply something they enjoyed – a chance to continue pursuing an activity they loved. And what made it enjoyable was the time spent with their buddies on the team. Many of their jokes and pranks are lost to history, and perhaps just as well. For it was in those private moments that they drew closer to one another and formed the fighting spirit that they brought to the football field.

The last line of the Notre Dame Victory March says, "while her loyal sons are marching, onward to victory." We'd like to think our dads, and all the 1924 team, embodied the image that line describes.

Don Miller Jr.
Harry Stuhldreher Jr.
July 2008

THE FORMATION OUR dads received at the University of Notre Dame molded them and prepared them for everything that followed in their lives. Like many others, they came in as freshmen far from home and unsure about college life. And, due in no small part to the role of Coach Knute Rockne, they left college as men, ready to offer their contributions to the world.

Rockne acted like a father to them, knowing exactly when to offer an encouraging word, a reprimand, a joke. He modeled courage, perseverance, an infectious spirit of teamwork and a sense of humor. Yes, knowledge of football technique was important, but much more so were hard work, discipline, self-sacrifice, and dedication to team effort. Rock's sense of loyalty, tradition, spirit and unselfish service were handed down to the fellows he coached, who were all the richer for it.

It took plenty of courage to play football in those days of relatively flimsy equipment. Little protection was offered much of the body, and injuries were common. Injury treatment was primitive compared to today.

But these guys loved the game; they relished the nature of competition. They accepted the challenge of putting their best up against the best of a quality opponent. Notre Dame never shied away from playing the top teams from around the country. In 1924 alone, they met the best of the East (Army, Princeton), South (Georgia Tech), Midlands (Nebraska) and Far West (Stanford). The Fighting Irish defeated all of them and had a perfect season, the kind of year most teams can only dream about.

Our dads both went on to significant careers in football. One of them (Elmer Layden) guided the Fighting Irish to a record of 47-13-3 from 1934 through 1940, then was hired as the first commissioner of the National Football League. The other (Jim Crowley) achieved success as head coach at Michigan State and Fordham, going on to become the commissioner of the new All America Football Conference, a rival pro league which gave us several NFL franchises.

Throughout their careers as coaches, commissioners and businessmen, they enjoyed meeting folks who remembered their exploits on the field – the great games and great teams. But most of all, they enjoyed the reunions with their fellow players. The Four Horsemen developed a bond that lasted as long as they lived. They shared plenty of laughs and memories in those get-togethers. As the years went by, stories got stretched and facts were embellished.

But one theme always prevailed: those were the best years of their lives.

Patrick Crowley
Elmer Layden Jr.
July 2008

Appendices

Appendix A

1924 Notre Dame Fighting Irish

No.	Name	Pos.	Ht.	Wt.	Yr.	City, School
17	Joe Bach	LT	5-11	186	Sr.	Chisholm, Minnesota, Chisholm HS/ Carleton College
62	Joe Boland	LT	6-0	215	Soph.	Philadelphia, Pa. Roman Catholic HS
23	Bill Cerney	FB	5-9	165	Sr.	Chicago, Illinois St. Ignatius HS
27	Chuck Collins	LE	6-0	177	Sr.	Oak Park, Illinois St. Ignatius HS
9	Ward Connell	RH	5-10	168	Sr.	Beloit, Wisconsin Notre Dame Prep
43	Bernie Coughlin	HB	5-10	147	Soph.	Waseca, Minnesota Waseca HS
5	Clem Crowe	LE	5-9	169	Jr.	Lafayette, Indiana Jefferson HS
18	Jim Crowley	LH	5-11	162	Sr.	Green Bay, Wisconsin East HS
21	Wilbur Eaton	RE	5-8	165	Jr.	Omaha, Nebraska Creighton Prep
25	Gene Edwards	QB	6-1	160	Soph.	Weston, W. Va. Kiski School
67	Herb Eggert	T	5-9	170	Soph.	Chicago, Illinois St. Mels HS
49	Oswald Geniesse	HB	5-10	175	Sr.	Green Bay, Wisconsin East HS
67	Charles Glueckert	LG	5-11	185	Sr.	South Bend, Indiana Central HS
2	Dick Hanousek	RG	5-10	177	Jr.	Antigo, Wisconsin St. Thomas (Minn.)
20	Joe Harmon	C	5-9	165	Sr.	Indianapolis Indiana Cathedral HS
6	Vince Harrington	LG	5-8	175	Sr.	Sioux City, Iowa Trinity College Acad.
19	Tom Hearden	FB	5-9	156	Soph.	Green Bay, Wisconsin East HS
47	Max Houser	LH	6-1	170	Jr.	Mt. Vernon, Wash. Staunton Military
12	Ed Hunsinger	RE	5-11	172	Sr.	Chillicothe, Ohio St. Mary's HS

No.	Name	Pos.	Ht.	Wt.	Yr.	City, School
11	Noble Kizer	RG	5-8	165	Sr.	Plymouth, Indiana Plymouth HS
30	Bernie Livergood	FB	5-10	175	Sr.	Stonington, Illinois Stonington HS
5	Elmer Layden	FB	6-0	162	Sr.	Davenport, Iowa Davenport HS
8	Joe Maxwell	C	6-1	180	Soph.	Philadelphia, Pa. Roman Catholic HS
7	John McManmon	RT	6-2	202	Soph.	Dracut, Massachusetts Lowell HS
51	John McMullan	LT	6-0	204	Jr.	Chicago, Illinois DePaul Academy
16	Don Miller	RH	5-11	160	Sr.	Defiance, Ohio Defiance HS
14	Edgar (Rip) Miller	RT	5-11	180	Sr.	Canton, Ohio McKinley HS
65	Gerry Miller	HB	5-11	180	Sr.	Defiance, Ohio Defiance HS
24	Harry O'Boyle	LH	5-9	160	Soph.	Des Moines, Iowa East HS
31	Frank Reese	QB	5-10	152	Sr.	Robinson, Illinois Township HS
57	Joe Rigali	LE	5-9	147	Jr.	Oak Park, Illinois Lane Tech
5	John Roach	FB	6-0	139	Soph.	Appleton, Wisconsin Appleton HS
33	Eddie Scharer	QB	5-8	145	Jr.	Toledo, Ohio Scott HS
32	Harry Stuhldreher	QB	5-7	151	Sr.	Massillon, Ohio Washington HS Kiski School
46	John Wallace	RT	6-0	178	Soph.	Calumet City, Illinois Emeron HS
4	Adam Walsh (C.)	C	6-0	187	Sr.	Hollywood, Calif. Hollywood HS
3	John Weibel	LG	5-9	165	Sr.	Erie, Pennsylvania Central HS Head C

Coach: Knute Rockne
Assistant Coach: Tom Lieb
Assistant Coach: Hartley Anderson
Freshman Coach: George Keogan
Asst. Fresh. Coach: George Vergara
Trainer: Verly Smith
Manager: Leo Sutliffe

Appendix B

1924 Results

Oct. 4	Lombard	Cartier Field	W	40-0
Oct. 11	Wabash	Cartier Field	W	34-0
Oct. 18	Army	New York (Polo Grounds)	W	13-7
Oct. 25	Princeton	Princeton, N.J.	W	12-0
Nov. 1	Georgia Tech	Cartier Field	W	34-3
Nov. 8	Wisconsin	Madison, Wis.	W	38-3
Nov. 15	Nebraska	Cartier Field	W	34-6
Nov. 22	Northwestern	Chicago (Grant Park)	W	13-6
Nov. 29	Carnegie Tech	Pittsburgh, Pa. (Forbes Field)	W	40-19
Jan. 1, 1925	Stanford	Pasadena, Calif. (Rose Bowl)	W	27-10

Total Points For: 285
Total Points Against: 54

Appendix C

1924 Game Summaries

Saturday, October 4, 1924
Notre Dame 40, Lombard 0
Cartier Field
Attendance: 8,000

Lombard	0	0	0	0	-- 0
Notre Dame	0	14	14	12	-- 40

ND – Miller, 24, run (Layden kick)
ND – Miller, 15, run (Crowley kick)
ND – Crowley, 13, run (Layden kick)
ND – Connell, 57, run (Crowley kick)
ND – Cerney, 2, run (kick failed)
ND – O'Boyle, 55, run (kick failed)

Saturday, October 11, 1924
Notre Dame 34, Wabash 0
Cartier Field
Attendance: 10,000

Wabash	0	0	0	0	-- 0
Notre Dame	7	7	0	20	-- 34

ND – Cerney, 1, run (O'Boyle kick)
ND – Layden, 1, run (Stuhldreher kick)
ND – Crowley, 44, run (Layden kick)
ND – O'Boyle, 1, run (Reese kick)
ND – Reese 45, punt return (extra point nullified, ND offsides)

Notre Dame 13, Army 7
Polo Grounds, New York
Attendance: 55,000

Notre Dame	0	6	7	0	-- 13
Army	0	0	0	7	-- 7

ND – Layden, 1, run (kick failed)
ND – Crowley, 20, run (Crowley kick)
Army – Harding, 15, run (Garbisch kick)

Officials -- Thorp, De LaSalle, referee; Costello, Georgetown, umpire; Eckersall, Chicago, head linesman; and Tyler, Princeton, field judge. Time of periods: 15 minutes.

Notre Dame 12, Princeton 0
Palmer Stadium, Princeton, New Jersey
Attendance: 40,000

Notre Dame	0	6	0	6	-- 12
Princeton	0	0	0	0	-- 0

ND – Crowley, 12, run (kick blocked)
Fourth Quarter
ND—Crowley, 10, run (kick blocked)

Statistics	ND	Princeton
First downs earned	18	4
Rushing Yards	326	89
Passes (Att.-Comp.-Int.)	10-4-1	2-2-0
Passing Yards	48	8
Total Yards	374	97
Punt Return Yards	35	28
Kickoff Return Yards	57	18
Yards Penalized	65	72
Fumbles-Lost	4-1	3-3
Punts (ave.)	41	42

Officials -- Referee, V. A. Schwartz, Brown; Umpire, Lt. H. M. Nelly; Linesman, Col. Mumma; Field judge, F. P. Gillender. Time of periods – 15 minutes.

Notre Dame 34, Georgia Tech 3
Cartier Field
Attendance: 22,000

| Georgia Tech | 3 | 0 | 0 | 0 | -- | 3 |
| Notre Dame | 0 | 21 | 0 | 13 | -- | 34 |

Tech – FG, Williams, 30 yards
ND – Miller, 7, pass from Crowley (Crowley kick)
ND – Layden, 1, run (Crowley, kick)
ND – Roach, 5, run (Reese kick)
ND – Roach, 4, pass from Scharer (Roach kick)
ND – Livergood, 1, run (kick failed)

Saturday November 8, 1924
Notre Dame 38, Wisconsin 3
Camp Randall Stadium, Madison, Wisconsin
Attendance: 28,425

| Notre Dame | 3 | 14 | 14 | 7 | -- | 38 |
| Wisconsin | 3 | 0 | 0 | 0 | -- | 3 |

ND – FG, O'Boyle, 17 yards
Wis. – FG, Harmon, 11 yards
ND – Miller, 22, run (Crowley, kick)
ND – Crowley, 29, pass from Stuhldreher (Crowley kick)
ND – Layden, 3, run (Crowley kick)
ND – Crowley, 8, run (Layden kick)
ND – Roach, 13, run (Reese kick)

Officials – Birch, Earlham, referee; Magledoon, Michigan, umpire; Kearns, DePauw, head linesman; and Haynes, Yale, field judge.

Saturday November 15, 1924
Notre Dame 34, Nebraska 6
Cartier Field
Attendance: 22, 000

Nebraska	6	0	0	0	-- 6
Notre Dame	0	14	14	6	-- 34

Neb. – Myers, 1, run (kick failed)
ND – Stuhldreher, 1, run (Crowley kick)
ND – Miller, 10, run (Crowley, kick)
ND – Miller, 18, run (Crowley kick)
ND – Crowley, 75, pass from Layden (Crowley kick)
ND – Layden, 3, run (kick failed)

Statistics	Nebraska	ND
First downs earned	3	24
Rushing Yards	56	465
Passes (Att.-Comp.)	7-1	11-8
Passing Yards	20	101
Total Yards	76	566
Punt Returns-Yards	1-2	3-17

Notre Dame 13, Northwestern 6
Grant Park Stadium, Chicago
Attendance: 45,000

Notre Dame	0	7	0	6	-- 13
Northwestern	6	0	0	0	-- 6

Nor – FG, Baker, 30 yards
Nor. – FG, Baker, 35 yards
ND – Stuhldreher, 1, run (Crowley, kick)
ND – Layden, 45, intercepted pass (kick failed)

Saturday November 29, 1924
Notre Dame 40, Carnegie Tech 19
Forbes Field, Pittsburgh
Attendance: 38, 000

Notre Dame	0	13	14	13	-- 40
Carnegie Tech	6	7	0	6	-- 19

Tech – Kristof, 40, run with blocked punt (kick blocked)
ND – Miller, 52, pass from Crowley (Crowley kick)
ND – Cerney, 3, run (kick blocked)
Tech – Beide, 14, run (Neuman kick)
ND – Livergood, 16, pass from Stuhldreher (Crowley kick)
ND -- Crowley, 5, pass from Stuhldreher (Crowley, kick
ND – Livergood, 1, run (Crowley kick)
ND – Stuhldreher, 3, run (kick wide)
Tech – Beide, 15, run (kick wide)

Notre Dame 27, Stanford 10
Rose Bowl, Pasadena, California
Attendance: 53,000

| Notre Dame | 0 | 13 | 7 | 7 | -- 27 |
| Stanford | 3 | 0 | 7 | 0 | -- 10 |

Stan – FG, Cuddeback, 18 yards
ND – Layden, 3, run (kick blocked)
ND – Layden, 78, intercepted pass (Crowley kick)
ND – Hunsinger, 20, run with fumbled punt
     (Crowley kick)
Stan – T. Shipley, 6, pass from Walker (Cuddeback
     kick)
ND – Layden,63, intercepted pass (Crowley kick)

Appendix D

1924 Statistics

Scoring

	TD	C	FG	Pts
Jim Crowley	9	20	0	74
Elmer Layden	9	4	0	58
Don Miller	7	0	0	42
Harry Stuhldreher	3	1	0	19
John Roach	3	1	0	19
Bill Cerney	3	0	0	18
Bernie Livergood	3	0	0	18
Harry O'Boyle	2	1	1	16
Frank Reese	1	3	0	9
Doc Connell	1	0	0	6
Ed Hunsinger	1	0	0	6
Totals	42	30	1	285

Rushing

	Att.	Yds.	TD
Don Miller	107	763	5
Jim Crowley	131	739	6
Elmer Layden	111	423	5

Passing	Att.	Comp.	Yds.	TD
Harry Stuhldreher	33	25	471	4
Jim Crowley	26	14	236	2

Receiving	No.	Yds.	TD
Don Miller	16	297	2
Jim Crowley	12	265	3

Punt returns	No.	Yds.
Harry Stuhldreher	22	194

(Note: Scoring statistics are for all 10 games; others do not include Rose Bowl)

Appendix E

Grantland Rice
In the New York Herald Tribune

POLO GROUNDS, New York, October 18 -- Outlined against a blue-gray October sky the Four Horsemen rode again.

In dramatic lore they are known as famine pestilence, destruction and death. These are only aliases. Their real names are Stuhldreher, Miller, Crowley and Layden. They formed the crest of the South Bend cyclone before which another fighting Army team was swept over the precipice at the Polo Grounds this afternoon as 55,000 spectators peered down upon the bewildering panorama spread out upon the green plain below.

A cyclone can't be snared. It may be surrounded but somewhere it breaks through to keep on going. When the cyclone starts from South Bend where the candle lights still gleam through the Indiana sycamores those in the way must take to the storm cellars at top speed. The cyclone struck again as Notre Dame beat the Army 13 to 7 with a set of backfield stars that ripped and rushed through a strong Army defense with more speed and power than the warring Cadets could meet.

Notre Dame won its eighth game in eleven starts through the driving power of one of the greatest backfields that ever churned up the turf of any gridiron in any football age. Brilliant backfields may come and go but Stuhldreher, Miller, Crowley and Layden, covered by a fast and charging line, Notre Dame can take its place in front of the field.

Coach McEwan sent one of his finest teams into action, an aggressive organization that fought to the last play around the first rim of darkness, but when Rockne rushed his four horsemen to the track they rode down everything in sight.

It was in that 1400 gray clad cadets pleaded for the Army

line to hold. The Army line was giving all it had but when a tank tears in with the speed of a motorcycle, what chance had flesh and blood to hold? The Army had its share of stars in action, such stars as Garbisch, Farwick, Wilson, Wood, Elinger and many others, but they were up against four whirlwind backs who picked up top speed from the first step as they swept through scant openings to slip on by the secondary defense. The Army had great backs in Wilson and Wood, but the Army had no such quartet who seemed to carry the mixed blood of the tiger and the antelope.

Rockne's light and tottering line was just about as tottering as the Rock of Gibraltar. It was something more than a match for the Army's great set of forwards who had earned their fame before, yet it was not until the second period that the first big thrill of the afternoon set the great crowd into a cheering whirl. and brought about the wild flutter of flags that are thrown to the wind in exciting moments. At the game's start, Rockne sent in almost entirely the second string cast. The Army got the jump

and began to play most of the football. It was the Army attack that made three first downs before Notre Dame had caught its stride.

The South Bend cyclone opened like a zephyr and then, in the wake of a sudden cheer, out rushed Stuhldreher, Miller, Crowley and Layden, the four star backs who helped best the Army a year ago. Things were to be a trifle different now. After a short opening flurry in the second period the cloud in the west at this point was no larger than a football. There was no sign of a tornado starting, but it happened to be at just this spot that Stuhldreher decided to put on his attack and begin the long and dusky hike.

On the first play the fleet Crowley peeled off 15 yards and the cloud from the west was now beginning to show signs of lightning and thunder. The fleet, powerful Layden got six yards more and then Don Miller added 10. A forward pass from Stuhldreher to Crowley added 12 yards and a moment later Don Miller ran 20 yards around the Army's right wing. He was on his way to glory when Wilson, hurtling across the right of way, nailed him on the 10 yard line and threw him out of bounds.

Crowley, Miller and Layden -- Miller, Layden and Crowley -- one or the other, ripping and crashing through as the Army defense threw everything it had in the way to stop this wild charge that had now come 70 yards. Crowley and Layden added five yards more and then on a split play Layden went 10 yards across the line as if he had just been fired from the black mouth of a Howitzer.

Speed Beat West Point

It was speed that beat the Army, speed plus interference. And when a back such as Harry Wilson finds few chances to get started you figure upon the defensive strength that is barricading the road. Wilson is one of the hardest backs in the game to suppress, but he found few chances yesterday to show his broken field ability. You can't run through a broken field until you get there.

One strong feature of the Army play was its head long battle against heavy odds. Even when Notre Dame had scored two touchdowns and was well on its way to a third, the army fought on with fine spirit, until the touchdown chance came at last, and when this chance came in the fourth quarter coach McEwan had the play ready for the final march across the line.

The Army has a better team than it had last year. So has Notre Dame. We doubt that any team in the country could have beaten Rockne's yesterday afternoon, east or west. It was a great football team brilliantly directed, a team of speed, power and team play. The Army has no cause for gloom over its showing. It played first class football against more speed than it could match.

Those who have tackled a cyclone can understand.

Bibliography

Armstrong, James E. *Onward to Victory: A Chronicle of the Alumni of the University of Notre Dame.* Notre Dame, Ind.: University of Notre Dame Press, 1974.

Beach, Jim, and Daniel Moore. *Army vs. Notre Dame: The Big Game, 1913 - 1947.* New York: Random House, 1948.

Burns, Robert E. *Being Catholic, Being American: The Notre Dame Story, 1842 - 1934.* Notre Dame, Ind.: University of Notre Dame Press, 1999.

Danzig, Allison. *Oh, How They Played the Game: The Early Days of Football and the Heroes Who Made it Great.* New York: Macmillan, 1971.

Fountain, Charles. *Sportswriter : The Life and Times of Grantland Rice.* New York: Oxford University Press, 1993.

Francis, David W., and Diane D. Francis. *Cedar Point : The Queen of American Watering Places.* Fairview Park, Ohio: Amusement Park Books, Inc., 1995.

Grant, Chet. *Before Rockne at Notre Dame.* South Bend, Ind.: Icarus Press, 1978.

Gullickson, Denis, and Carl Hanson. *Before They Were the Packers: Green Bay's Town Team Days.* Black Earth, Wis.: Trails Books, 2004.

Gullifor, Paul F. *The Fighting Irish on the Air: The History of Notre Dame Football Broadcasting.* South Bend, Ind.: Diamond Communications, Inc., 2001.

Harper, William A. *How You Played the Game: The Life of Grantland Rice.* Columbia, Mo.: University of Missouri Press, 1999.

Holtzman, Jerome (Editor). *No Cheering in the Press Box*. New York, NY: Holt, Rinehart and Winston, 1973.

Hope, Arthur J., CSC. *The Story of Notre Dame*. Notre Dame, Ind.: University of Notre Dame Press, 1999.

Kaye, Ivan N. *Good Clean Violence: A History of College Football*. Philadelphia: J. B. Lippincott Co., 1973.

Langford, Jeremy, and Jim Langford. *The Spirit of Notre Dame : Legends, Traditions, and Inspiration from One of America's Most Beloved Universities*. New York: Doubleday, 2005.

Layden, Elmer, and Ed Snyder. *It Was A Different Game: The Elmer Layden Story*. Englewood Cliffs, N.J.: Prentice-Hall, Inc., 1969.

MacCambridge, Michael (Editor). *ESPN College Football Encyclopedia: The Complete History of the Game*. New York: ESPN Books/ Hyperion, 2005.

McCallum, John D., and Paul Castner. *We Remember Rockne*. Huntington, Ind.: Our Sunday Visitor, Inc., 1975.

Oriard, Michael. *King Football : Sport and Spectacle in the Golden Age of Radio and Newsreels, Movies and Magazines, the Weekly and the Daily Press*. Chapel Hill, N.C.: University of North Carolina Press, 2001.

Rice, Grantland. *The Tumult and the Shouting: My Life in Sport*. New York: A. S. Barnes & Co., 1954.

Samuelson, Rube. *The Rose Bowl Game*. New York: Doubleday, 1951.

Smith, Red. *Strawberries in the Wintertime: The Sporting World of Red Smith*. New York: Crown, 1974.

Sperber, Murray. *Shake Down the Thunder: The Creation of Notre Dame Football*. New York: Henry Holt & Co., 1993.

The Sporting News. *Saturday Shrines: College Football's Most Hallowed Grounds*. St. Louis, Mo.: The Sporting News, 2005.

Steele, Michael R. *Knute Rockne : A Portrait of a Notre Dame Legend*. Champaign, Ill.: Sports, Inc., 1998.

Steele, Michael R. *Knute Rockne: A Bio-Bibliography*. Westport, Conn.: Greenwood Press, 1983.

Stuhldreher, Harry A. *Knute Rockne: Man Builder*. New York: Grosset & Dunlap, 1931.

Wallace, Francis. *The Notre Dame Story*. New York: Rinehart & Co., 1949.

Watterson, John Sayle. *College Football : History, Spectacle, Controversy*. Baltimore, Md.: Johns Hopkins University Press, 2000.

Whittingham, Richard. *Rites of Autumn : The Story of College Football*. New York: Free Press, 2001.

Young, Eugene J. *With Rockne at Notre Dame*. New York: G. P. Putnam Sons, 1951.

Sources

Research material for LOYAL SONS included hundreds of articles from the newspapers and periodicals named below, as well as dozens of interviews with family members of the 1924 Fighting Irish. Many of the books listed in the Bibliography were also helpful.

Newspapers
Atlanta Journal
Canton Repository
The Chicago Tribune
Chicago Evening American
The Daily Princetonian
Defiance Crescent-News
The Denver Post
Detroit Free Press
Green Bay Press-Gazette
The Houston Chronicle
Los Angeles Times
Massillon Independent
The Commercial Appeal,
    Memphis
The Times-Picayune,
    New Orleans
The New York Times
New York Herald
New York Tribune
The World-Herald, Omaha
The Philadelphia Inquirer
Pittsburgh Post
Pittsburgh Gazette-Times
San Francisco Chronicle
South Bend News-Times
The South Bend Tribune

Tucson Daily Citizen
Wyoming State Tribune

Periodicals
Colliers
Notre Dame Alumnus
Notre Dame Daily
Notre Dame Scholastic
The Dome

About The Author

JIM LEFEBVRE IS an award-winning journalist, author, and speaker, and one of the leading college football historians in America.

His books *Loyal Sons: The Story of the Four Horsemen and Notre Dame Football's 1924 Champions* and *Coach For A Nation: The Life and Times of Knute Rockne* have both been honored for excellence by the *Independent Publisher* Book Awards.

Jim was born and raised in the football hotbed of Green Bay, Wisconsin, following the fortunes of the famous Packers as a youngster. He attended the same Catholic grade school that Green Bay football star Jim Crowley had a half-century earlier, so it was fitting that he took an interest in the Notre Dame "Four Horseman" halfback.

Jim cut his teeth as a young sportswriter for a number of Wisconsin newspapers, and also served as editor of the nation's leading trade publication for athletic administrators. He worked in corporate communications before turning his attention to researching and writing about the Rockne era of Notre Dame football history.

He is the co-founder and executive director of the Knute Rockne Memorial Society, which honors the life and legacy of Coach Rockne by presenting the Knute Rockne *Spirit of Sports* Awards each year. He also writes the *Irish Echoes* historical column in each issue of *Blue & Gold Illustrated*, America's foremost authority on Notre Dame football.

Jim has made speaking presentations on Rockne and Notre Dame football history at locations on campus—Notre Dame Stadium, Purcell Pavilion, the Morris Inn and others—as well as to Notre Dame clubs and other groups from coast to coast. Along the way, he has befriended dozens of families of the 1924 Notre Dame team members.

Jim and his wife Joanne are proud parents of two Notre Dame alums, daughters Dr. Kerry (B.A., 2007) and Elizabeth (B.A., 2009), who were both four-year members of the Band of the Fighting Irish. They live in a suburb of Minneapolis, Minnesota.

Index

287